Taking
Charge of
Diabetes

READER'S DIGEST

Published by
The Reader's Digest Association, Limited
London • New York • Sydney • Montreal

Taking
Charge of
Diabetes

The definitive guide to
living well with diabetes

CONTENTS

1 Take charge today 8

You can look at diabetes in two ways • Do you have diabetes? • Dealing with the diagnosis • What can you expect • What's the game plan? • Where to get support • Start to take charge now

2 Understanding diabetes 30

What exactly is diabetes? • Typecasting: a key to understanding • Type 1: an insulin no-show • Type 2: a system breakdown • Gestational diabetes: a disappearing act • Testing one, two, three • 'Almost' diabetes: impaired glucose tolerance • When diabetes becomes an emergency • The agenda for action

3 Monitoring and measuring 58

Tests: the key to success • Worth the effort • Setting blood sugar goals • Testing your blood sugar • Four essential testing tools • Seven steps to reliable results • Advances in testing technology • Highs and lows: why they happen and how to fix them • Getting the whole story • Four more important tests

4 Healthy eating for diabetes 86

Healthy eating for diabetes • What's on the menu? • Carbohydrates • Fatty foods • Protein • The importance of fruit and vegetables • Milk and dairy foods • What is the Glycaemic Index? • Making weight loss work • Calorie counting and willpower • Fluids

5 Exercise as medicine 112

Powerful treatment • Tailor-made training • The aerobic prescription • Putting the muscle on blood sugar • Good ways to get going • Taking the first steps • An all-you-need routine •

Drugs and surgery 136

Treatment options • When do you need medical help? • Medication marriages • Insulin: who needs it? • The ins and outs of insulin therapy • Calling the shots • Injection alternatives

Preventing complications 164

Looking ahead • Cutting cardiovascular risks • Caring for your kidneys • Be wise with your eyes • Nipping nerve damage in the bud • Sidestepping foot problems

Alternative therapies 188

Dugs and alternative therapies • What is alternative medicine? • The natural medicine cabinet • Exploring other therapies

Living well with diabetes 208

Focus on quality of life • The feelings factor • Coping with your emotions • Putting stress in its place • Battling 'diabetes burnout' • How to think about diabetes • Sex and diabetes • Planning for when you're ill • Travelling with diabetes

Breakthroughs of the future 230

The pace of innovation • Building on the present • The future of insulin delivery • The disease frontier • Working on weight loss • Controlling complications • Eye protection • Head-to-toe help • Patching up the pancreas • Islet cell transplants

Recipes 248
Index 280

Consultant Dr Vince Forte
Project Editor Lisa Thomas
Art Editor Heather Dunleavy
Editor Liz Clasen
Researchers Alison Baker
Proofreader Ron Pankhurst
Indexer Hilary Bird

Reader's Digest would like to thank Diabetes UK for their help in preparing this book.

Reader's Digest, London
Editorial Director Julian Browne
Art Director Anne-Marie Bulat
Managing Editor Alastair Holmes
Head of Book Development Sarah Bloxham
Picture Resource Manager Sarah Stewart-Richardson

Senior Production Controller Deborah Trott
Production Editor Rachel Weaver
Pre-press Accounts Manager Penelope Grose
Origination Colour Systems Limited, London
Printing and binding Cayfosa Quebecor, Barcelona, Spain

Reader's Digest USA
Editor-in-Chief Neil Wertheimer
Senior Editor Marianne Wait
Senior Designer Judith Carmel
Recipe Editor Nancy Shuker
Production Technology Manager Douglas A. Croll
Manufacturing Manager John L. Cassidy
Contributors
Writer Richard Laliberte
Designer Andrew Ploski
Copy Editor Gina Grant
Indexer Nanette Bendyna
Medical Consultant
Carol J. Levy, M.D., C.D.E.
Assistant Professor of Medicine New York-Presbyterian Hospital
Weill Medical College Division of Endocrinology

ABOUT THIS BOOK

Diabetes is a bit like an uninvited house guest. You didn't want it in the first place, and it won't go away. Worse still, it demands daily attention. But, while you can't send diabetes away, you can minimize the impact it has on your health and your quality of life.

Unlike most diseases, diabetes is patient-centered – meaning that you, not your doctor, are calling the shots (and perhaps even *giving* yourself shots) every day. Your doctor and your dietitian will help you to formulate a game plan for keeping your blood sugar under control, but it's up to you to make healthy food choices, monitor your glucose levels, and put together an exercise regime that you'll really stick with. That's the bad news (because yes, it will take a bit of effort on your part); it's also very good news because it means you're in control. And *Taking Charge of Diabetes* will show you how to take the reins.

Each chapter is packed with information that will help you manage your condition, whether you have type 1 diabetes, type 2 diabetes, or impaired glucose tolerance (sometimes called pre-diabetes). If you're at risk for developing diabetes but aren't sure you have it, you'll learn how to find out – a critical first step that millions of people haven't taken. If you have the disease, you'll discover a host of practical strategies for everything from meal planning to weight loss to battling diabetes burnout. You'll also find a comprehensive guide to the latest drug and insulin options and learn how to fine-tune your regimen for the best possible blood-sugar control.

Living with a chronic condition can be downright frustrating at times. That's why we've included inspiring profiles of people just like you who successfully faced the various challenges of diabetes and are living better, happier lives as a result. Finally, because food is a large part of the blood-sugar solution, we've put together a collection of nearly 50 satisfying recipes that will make eating to manage diabetes a pleasure.

The overall message is one of hope. Doctors have made huge strides in their ability to predict, diagnose, and treat diabetes with a wide variety of therapeutic options. And now we know just how powerful diet and exercise can be in keeping the condition, and related complications, in check. Best of all, if you take to heart the lifestyle advice that will help you control your blood sugar, chances are you'll feel better than you've ever felt before.

Take charge today

If you have diabetes and aren't taking measures to stop it in its tracks, there's no time to waste. Diabetes is a serious disease, but it's well within your power to control both high blood sugar and the complications that it can cause. If you're at risk for diabetes or are uncertain whether you have it, get the tests you need. Then, if you are diagnosed, start to take charge. Lifestyle changes such as adopting a healthy diet and losing weight, plus taking medication or insulin if necessary, will make you feel better physically and mentally, now and in the future.

ONE

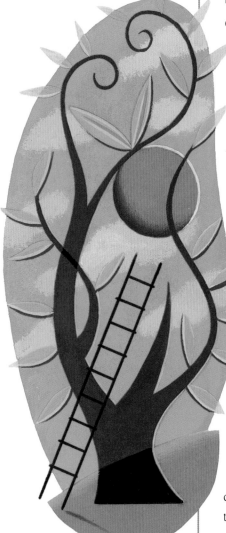

You can look at diabetes in two ways.

One is the big picture which, frankly, is not encouraging. Diabetes ranks fifth in the top causes of death in the UK and is becoming increasingly common. The other is the small-scale picture, the scale of one – you. Here, the news is much brighter. More than ever before, diabetes is a disease that you can control and even conquer. And the tools available to help you are getting better all the time.

On the large scale, you can't ignore the fact that if you have diabetes, you have got plenty of company. Across the country (and throughout the world) rates of diabetes have grown to epidemic proportions. In the UK alone, 1.8 million people are known to have diabetes – an increase of 400,000 (almost 30 per cent) since 1996. According to the charity Diabetes UK, the figure is set to rise to 3 million by 2010 – although some doctors predict that it could be closer to double that level, affecting one in ten of us. The rates among children, who in the past rarely developed the most prevalent form of diabetes (Type 2), are also climbing in the UK.

The silver lining in this cloud of gloom and doom is the fact that few serious diseases allow you to fight back as much as diabetes does. If you take the right steps to keep the condition under your control, you can live a full and active life. In fact, some people who successfully gain control of their diabetes say that because of action they took, they now feel healthier overall than they have done in years.

Your take-charge tool kit

If there is an upside to the diabetes epidemic, it's this. Chronic diseases that threaten growing numbers of people also capture the interest of researchers. As a result, the past decade has seen significant advances in the way doctors understand, prevent and treat diabetes. Look at how new findings have improved three key components of diabetes treatment.

Blood-sugar control Complications of diabetes, such as cardiovascular problems, poor vision, kidney disease and nerve damage, were once thought to be inevitable no matter how hard you tried to manage erratic swings in blood sugar – the core problem of diabetes. But that thinking is no longer acceptable. Several major studies from around the world have shown that if you bring blood sugar into a normal range with drugs, insulin, diet, exercise, or some combination of these, you can reduce your risk of complications by between one-third and three-quarters. If you're diagnosed before you develop complications, it is possible to sidestep diabetes-related health problems completely, sometimes with lifestyle changes alone. Meanwhile, technology for monitoring your own blood sugar continues to improve and is now both convenient and relatively pain-free.

Lifestyle Diet and exercise are powerful tools for lowering blood sugar – so powerful, in fact, that they free many people with diabetes from medication and insulin. And using these 'power' tools is easier than ever before. Recent research into how foods affect blood sugar has shown that your diet need not be as restrictive as experts once believed. It can include virtually any food you like, as long as you watch your calorie intake. On the exercise side, research shows that your workouts don't have to be as vigorous as once thought. Even short bouts of activity throughout the day add up to significant benefits to your health.

Drugs Earlier generations of diabetes medications have been bolstered by a growing roster of newer drugs that tackle the disease in a variety of ways. In many cases, you can combine these drugs to take advantage of the different ways in which they work. The fact that there are also several varieties of insulin (which regulates the body's use of blood sugar) gives you more flexibility in finding a regimen that matches your lifestyle.

Do you have diabetes?

If you don't know the answer to this question but feel that you have cause to wonder, that's probably reason enough to see a doctor. In its early stages, when it is easiest to control, diabetes can be sneaky and silent, slowly causing damage throughout your body without obvious symptoms. But if you are alert to subtle signs, you can catch the disease at the outset and get a head start on beating it.

It's human nature not to look for problems if they haven't already found you – which explains why an estimated 1 million people in the UK are thought to be living with diabetes but without knowing it as the condition has not yet been diagnosed.

?

DID YOU KNOW

Researchers have been toying with the idea that starting insulin therapy before the onset of diabetes can help to prevent it in people at risk of developing Type 1 diabetes, although it is unclear whether this would actually work. In mid 2002, a disappointing study published in the *New England Journal of Medicine* found that pre-disease injections made no difference. Researchers still hold out hope that some day an insulin pill, which would work in a different way, may prevent the disease.

People with Type 2 diabetes, which often produces only mild symptoms, may have had the condition for between 9 and 12 years before it is diagnosed, by which time as many as half of them will have already developed some degree of complications.

How can you recognize when diabetes is at your door? There are three fundamental ways.

Work out your risk factors The first thing to look at is whether you have a greater than average likelihood of developing diabetes. Among the most important factors to evaluate are:

▶ **Family history** If anyone in your immediate family – a parent, sibling or grandparent – has had diabetes, you have a greater chance of developing the disease yourself. The extent of the risk depends on the type of diabetes and how closely related you are to the person who has it (the risk is highest among identical twins).

▶ **Ethnic group** The most common type of diabetes is most prevalent in those of Asian and Afro-Caribbean origin in the UK. Some 20 per cent of South Asians and 17 per cent of the Afro-Caribbean community has Type 2 diabetes, compared with 3 per cent of the general population.

▶ **Weight** Being overweight, particularly if you store fat around the waist, significantly raises your risk of developing Type 2 diabetes. The rising incidence of this type of diabetes in the UK is directly linked to the rise in obesity.

▶ **Age** Type 1 is almost always diagnosed before the age of 40. Type 2 generally affects people over the age of 40, although it is becoming more common in younger people.

Keep a sharp eye out for symptoms While the early signs of diabetes can be subtle, they are not impossible to detect. The longer diabetes progresses, the more likely symptoms are to become obvious and troublesome. The hallmarks of diabetes are:

▶ Excessive thirst
▶ Increased appetite
▶ Frequent urination
▶ Fatigue
▶ Blurred vision
▶ Frequent infections
▶ Tingling in your hands and feet
▶ Sexual dysfunction

Get tested Tests for diabetes are simple. They involve nothing more painful than a finger prick to draw a drop of your blood (although some tests require that you prepare by fasting ahead of time).

It is advisable to see a doctor for a full evaluation if you want to confirm your diagnosis. If your results fall short of a diagnosis but your background suggests that you are at risk, schedule a return visit to the doctor or practice specialist diabetic nurse for a urinalysis or fasting blood glucose at least once a year to make sure that nothing has changed.

Dealing with the diagnosis

Hearing that you have a chronic disease is never easy. One day it seems that you have a clean bill of health (although you may suspect something is wrong), and the next you have a problem for the rest of your life. But don't despair. You have probably had diabetes for some time and, now that you know it, you have taken a major step towards being healthier.

Still, it can be tough to be optimistic initially. You might feel as if your body has betrayed you or that it is out of control. Some people assume that the worst they have heard about diabetes (accurate or not) lies just around the corner, and they jump to panicky conclusions such as 'I'll go blind!' or 'I can never eat dessert again!' Others are nonchalant, reasoning that they've managed to get by up to now with diabetes, so 'worrying about it won't get me anywhere'.

You're probably somewhere in the middle of the spectrum between panic and denial. You may even be relieved finally to know why you have been feeling so lousy. All of these emotions are normal. In fact, you can anticipate moving through several emotional stages after being diagnosed. Typically, an I-can't-believe-it phase gives way to feelings of anger and the realization that there is a long road ahead, which can sometimes lead to depression. To deal with the dismay a diagnosis can produce:

➲ **View your emotions as progress** The next time you snap at a family member or find yourself in a fog and staring out of the window, play the moment out as a mental movie – an emotional scene in an unfolding story that continues to move

Hall of fame

If you need proof that diabetes doesn't have to put a damper on dynamic living, take a look at some of the people who have made major contributions in their field while waging a blood-sugar battle on the side:

Jack Benny, TV funnyman

James Cagney, actor

Paul Cézanne, painter

Thomas Edison, inventor

Ella Fitzgerald, singer

Jerry Garcia, rock musician

Dizzy Gillespie, jazz innovator

Jackie Gleason, comedy great

Mikhail Gorbachev, statesman

Ernest Hemingway, author

B.B. King, blues immortal

Billie Jean King, tennis champion

John Prescott, politician

Steve Redgrave, Olympic gold medallist oarsman

H.G. Wells, science fiction pioneer

Mae West, sex symbol

!

CAUTION

Type I diabetes puts
you at increased risk
for thyroid disease,
another autoimmune
condition. Make sure
that your doctor checks
your thyroid function
on a regular basis.

progressively towards something better. When you accept your feelings as a natural, important part of an ongoing process, it is an indication that you're actually working through them and going ahead with the rest of your life.

➲ **Talk to someone** Sharing emotions with a loved one, joining a support group or attending a class about diabetes in which you can meet others with the disease can help to put your feelings in perspective and make you feel less alone.

➲ **Think short-term** You may feel overwhelmed by all the changes you have to make in your life, the new self-care skills you have to learn, and the sheer volume of medical information you need to absorb. Rest assured that eventually it will all seem second nature. For now, focus on immediate goals ('Today I'll meet my dietitian') that will help you along the road.

➲ **Forge ahead** Don't let your diabetes diagnosis paralyse you. The sooner you take action, the sooner you will feel you have regained control of your life – and will start to feel better.

What you can expect

When you are diagnosed with diabetes, your doctor will need to cover a lot of ground in a short time. In fact, he or she will want to know virtually everything about you: your eating patterns, weight history, blood pressure, any other medications you're taking, whether you smoke or drink and if so, how much, how satisfying you find sex, how many children you have had, any family history of heart disease, and any treatment you have received for other problems, including endocrine and eating disorders. If you're a woman, you will even be asked about your children's development. All of this information has a bearing on your condition and the management programme you will eventually follow.

Your doctor will also want to carry out a thorough physical examination, including a cardiac workup that may involve an electrocardiogram (which records the heart's electrical activity) and a careful look at your mouth, feet, eyes, abdomen, skin and thyroid gland. You'll have a battery of tests, including a blood-lipid test for cholesterol (among other things) and at least two blood-sugar tests – one that shows what your blood sugar is now, the other what it has averaged for the past two to three months.

It may seem like a lot to begin with, but this initial assessment is arguably the most important phase of your overall care.

Your assessment may also include questions that determine how much you know about your disease and how motivated you are to do something about it – for example whether you are likely to be prepared to lose weight or increase the exercise you take. Eventually, you will move on to the next phases, in which you're in charge from one day to the next and your doctor is a resource for follow-up assessments and treatment of any complications.

Will you need insulin?

Taking insulin generally involves needles and injections, and dealing with the fear of needles is the single biggest challenge for many people with diabetes to overcome.

Whether you will actually have to confront the business end of a syringe depends on which type of diabetes you have. All people with Type 1 diabetes need insulin (and often find injections to be less daunting than they had imagined), but not everybody with Type 2 needs it. If you have Type 2 diabetes, your requirement for insulin will depend on a number of factors, including:

▶ **How much insulin your body makes** If you have Type 1 diabetes, your body does not make any insulin. If you have Type 2, your body's insulin-making ability is only partially impaired; the extent of the impairment differs from one person to the next.

▶ **How well your body uses the insulin available to it** If your cells have trouble using the insulin that is naturally available, you may need prescribed insulin to supplement this.

▶ **Your blood-sugar levels** How high above normal your blood-sugar levels tend to be will help to guide your doctor in deciding whether insulin is necessary.

INTERESTING STATISTICS

- Number of diabetics in the UK . . . .1.8 million

- Approximate percentage of the population this represents 3

- Estimated number of people who have diabetes but don't know it . . . . 1 million

- Increased risk of heart disease in people with diabetes . . . . 3 times

- Increased risk of stroke in people with diabetes . . . . 2–3 times

- Importance of diabetes as a cause of cases of blindness in people of working age . . . . Number 1 cause

- Importance of diabetes as a cause of kidney failure . . . . Number 1 cause

- Importance of diabetes as a cause of 'nontraumatic' lower-limb amputations . . . . Number 1 cause

- Percentage by which these risks can be lowered with diet and exercise alone in people with impaired glucose tolerance 58

- Percentage by which effectively controlled Type 2 diabetes reduces the risk of heart disease, stroke, kidney disease and eye disease, respectively 44, 46, 33, 33

- Percentage by which effectively controlled Type 1 diabetes reduces the risk of new eye disease, worsening of existing eye disease, early kidney disease, more serious kidney problems and nerve damage, respectively 76, 54, 54, 39, 60

▶ **How effective other forms of treatment have been** As a general rule, with Type 2 diabetes insulin is the last resort treatment, and is used only after lifestyle changes and oral medications have failed to bring your blood-sugar levels under control. An estimated 325,000 (one in four) of those people in the UK diagnosed with Type 2 diabetes do have to inject insulin.

Where do you stand?

Your doctor looks at several variables when deciding how to treat your diabetes, but will pay particular attention to your blood-sugar readings. If your blood sugar is sky-high in your initial assessment, you may go straight to drug and insulin therapy until the levels are brought down. If you have Type 2 diabetes, once your blood sugar has stabilized and you begin to make lifestyle changes, you may be able to go off insulin and other medications.

One of the numbers your doctor will focus on is your fasting blood-glucose level, a key test of blood sugar. While other tests also need to be considered and each case must be managed individually, you can roughly anticipate your options depending on your fasting blood-glucose levels (in the UK numbers are expressed as millimoles per litre (mmol/l)). As a general guideline:

▶ If fasting blood glucose is between 6.1 and 6.9mmol/l, you have impaired glucose tolerance, a condition in which raise blood-sugar levels significantly raise the risk of developing diabetes. You will be advised to adopt a healthier diet and to take more exercise, but you're unlikely to get a prescription for drugs or insulin.

▶ If fasting blood glucose is 7–7.8mmol/l you have full-blown diabetes, but you'll probably still be able to control

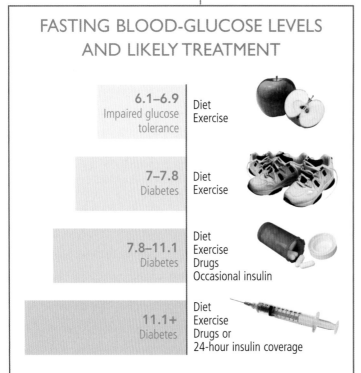

FASTING BLOOD-GLUCOSE LEVELS AND LIKELY TREATMENT

Level	Treatment
6.1–6.9 Impaired glucose tolerance	Diet Exercise
7–7.8 Diabetes	Diet Exercise
7.8–11.1 Diabetes	Diet Exercise Drugs Occasional insulin
11.1+ Diabetes	Diet Exercise Drugs or 24-hour insulin coverage

your blood sugar with diet and exercise, depending on your condition and results from other tests.

▶ Once fasting blood glucose is between 7.8 and 11.1mmol/l you are likely to need drugs in addition to diet and exercise. You may also need occasional doses of insulin for better control at certain times of the day (after meals, for example) when blood sugar tends to be higher.

▶ When fasting blood glucose goes above 11.1mmol/l, you may need drugs or 24-hour insulin coverage – possibly both – along with lifestyle changes.

What's the game plan?

Once you have diabetes, you have got it for life, and no operation, therapy or drug can cure it (at least, not yet). The good news is that controlling it can almost be like a cure in that lowering high blood sugar can stop diabetes in its tracks and reduce your risk of developing the health problems that go along with it.

Bringing diabetes under control is an important task – and there's no one better qualified to do it than you. Taking charge of diabetes doesn't have to be a full-time job, but you have to be mindful of it throughout your entire day, whether you're eating, gardening or getting ready for bed. You will have a team of other people to help you, but the doctors, nurses and specialists are not your primary care givers: you are. And your success ultimately depends on managing a treatment plan that puts you squarely in charge. These are the key steps you need to take to control your diabetes.

Start damage control immediately

Think about what happens when you spill honey. It gets on your fingers, sticks to everything you touch and generally gums up your whole kitchen worktop. Now imagine a honey spill taking place inside your bloodstream – which is essentially what high blood sugar is. What happens? Cells, proteins and fats become stickier, slowing circulation, holding back tissue repair, and encouraging material to adhere to your artery walls and cause clots. In short, excess blood sugar gums up your entire body.

You wouldn't dream of leaving honey on your kitchen worktop. Likewise, you should clean up blood sugar as quickly and thoroughly as possible because the 'stickiness' only gets worse. Doing so can make you feel better almost immediately. And even if you have no symptoms of diabetes, taking this action will start to reduce your risk of such problems as these:

▶ Damage to delicate blood vessels at the back of the eye (the retina), which can lead to vision problems.

▶ Ruined capillaries in the kidneys that filter waste from your body via the bloodstream.

▶ Impaired nerve function due to reduced nourishment from damaged blood vessels.

▶ Damage to artery walls that makes them more likely to snag blood clots and plaque that can cause heart attack, stroke and high blood pressure.

These complications wreak all kinds of havoc, including impaired healing, infections, lack of sensation that can lead to injury (especially in the feet), loss of vision, swollen ankles, fatigue, sexual dysfunction – the list can be long. Fortunately, the following steps will help you to clean up the excess blood sugar and halt this parade of problems.

Know the problems and the solutions

That's the guiding rule in business, sports and politics, and it's just as important when you are fighting for your quality of life –

Take-charge tips

Although there may seem to be a wealth of details to deal with in the first days of a diagnosis, the steps you should take boil down to a handful of key objectives:

➲ Learn how to test your own blood sugar using lancet devices, test strips and a blood-glucose meter.

➲ Use the results to determine your average blood-sugar levels and how they tend to fluctuate throughout the day.

➲ Learn more from your doctor or a diabetes nurse about how to stabilize your blood sugar with diet and exercise.

➲ Read everything you can about diabetes – a step you are already taking.

➲ Have an eye test about a month after your diagnosis. Because high blood sugar can temporarily cause blurry vision, a complete visual exam to screen for more permanent damage will be more useful after a few weeks, when your blood sugar has been brought under better control.

if not for your life itself. The power to tame diabetes is within your grasp, but to use it, you need some know-how. Without a doubt, that means grappling with a mass of information – about your particular type of diabetes, medications, insulin varieties, blood-sugar tests, meal planning and exercise, to name a few. But there are plenty of people to help you with this – including specialists whose sole purpose is to impart knowledge and dispel any confusion.

Keep tabs on blood sugar

The problem with diabetes is that you are not aware of your blood sugar unless it is extremely high or low – two situations that you definitely want to avoid. How can you tell what's going on with the blood inside your body? There is only one way: you remove a small sample of blood from your body and do a little analysis. You don't need to go to a doctor for this. Handy, easy-to-use, and relatively painless lancets, test strips and blood-glucose meters allow you to check your own blood sugar anywhere, at any time. Some people take readings four or more times a day, depending on their needs.

The blood-sugar readings that you – not your doctor – gather every day are the means by which you gain control over your disease. They provide data that will be a critical component of your care by allowing you to see how your blood sugar varies throughout the day and how much it swings in response to food, exercise, stress or anything else that may affect it. They will help guide everything from which drugs you take (if you need them) and when you administer insulin to what you eat for breakfast.

Lose excess body baggage

Nothing signals more clearly that you are at risk for Type 2 diabetes than being overweight (which accounts for nine out of ten cases of the disease). Excess baggage – especially in the gut – makes you more likely to develop insulin resistance, a condition in which cells don't use glucose (a form of sugar from food) as well as they should, causing glucose to accumulate in the blood. Having a spare tyre also increases the body's demand for insulin, which the pancreas (the maker of insulin) may have trouble meeting – again resulting in high blood sugar. Being overweight increases the risk of raised blood pressure, high cholesterol and heart disease. One recent Boston University study found that obese people with Type 2 diabetes had an alarming 99 to 100 per cent chance of developing heart disease by age 85.

Losing weight may be the single most important thing you can do to control Type 2 diabetes. There's no need for anything extreme; a slow and steady drop in weight keeps pounds off better than crash diets – which you're unlikely to stick to anyway. And rest assured: you don't have to slim down to supermodel size to make a difference. Losing as little as 4.5kg (10lb) can give you a significant edge over diabetes if you manage to maintain the lower weight.

Deconstruct your diet

When it comes to food, it may surprise you to learn that the main issue is not the amount of sugar or other carbohydrates you eat but how many calories you derive from all types of food. A dietitian will demonstrate how you can eat ample amounts of appetizing foods (including all of your favourites – within limits, of course) and yet still keep down the calories so that you lose weight. If you have Type 1 diabetes, you will need to balance your carbohydrate intake with your insulin injections to prevent blood sugar levels from soaring too high or dropping too low.

Whatever your diabetes type, you should put five food strategies into action straight away.

(1) Work out a meal plan that will hold the reins on your blood sugar (see Chapter 4 for details).

(2) Aim to include more – not fewer – carbohydrates in your diet; they supply the greatest amount of energy with the lowest number of calories.

(3) Fill up on fibre. It slows digestion and so controls the rise of blood sugar after a meal, keeps your appetite

under control by making you feel full; and scours damaging fats from your blood.

(4) Reduce your intake of saturated fat from foods such as chips and fry-ups, but allow yourself healthier monounsaturated fats in foods such as oily fish and olive oil.

(5) Eat a variety of fresh fruits and vegetables, such as apricots, spinach and tomatoes to provide vitamin C and magnesium, in which people with diabetes are sometimes deficient.

Get physical

Exercise gobbles up glucose, and this immediately brings down your blood sugar. Regular exercise also enables your cells to use glucose more efficiently, even when you're not active. That can make you less dependent on insulin or medication. In addition, exercise helps you to lose weight, lowers your cholesterol and blood pressure, and makes your heart and lungs more powerful – all of which reduce your risk of complications from diabetes.

If you hate exercise, don't worry. Your workout plan need be no more involved than making sure you pump up your heart rate and breathe a little harder several times a week, preferably for 20 minutes or more at a time. Classic aerobic exercises such as walking, running and cycling are ideal, but ordinary chores, such as washing your car, mowing the lawn and cleaning your house, can do the trick, too, if undertaken vigorously.

Beat back related risks

Eating a healthy diet, taking more exercise, and losing weight are the most important things you can do to prevent complications from diabetes – but they're not the only steps you can take.

➲ **Ask about aspirin** Studies show that taking low-dose aspirin every day can reduce your risk of a heart attack by as much as 60 per cent. Check with your doctor to see if aspirin therapy might be right for you.

➲ **Give up smoking** About one-third of people in the UK with diabetes smoke. Besides damaging your lungs and increasing your risk of cancer, smoking narrows arteries, which raises your risk of heart attack and stroke and reduces circulation to your

WHEN DIABETES STRIKES YOUR CHILD

Treating diabetes in a child can be more challenging than dealing with the disease yourself. Depending on their age and temperament, children vary in their ability – or desire – to understand what's happening to them, take care of themselves and follow your instructions. But you can put your child on the road to responsible self-care with either Type 1 (the most common type in children) or Type 2 diabetes if you bear these principles in mind.

TODDLERS AND PRE-SCHOOLERS

Learn to recognize how hypoglycaemia and hyperglycaemia affect your child's behaviour, since your child simply doesn't have the words to tell you how he or she feels. Expect some battles over insulin injections and blood-sugar tests around toilet-training time, as your child starts to be more assertive, but persevere to get them done. Don't worry too much if blood sugar ranges between 7.8mmol/l and 11.1mmol/l (higher than what is recommended for adults). Children need more blood sugar for normal development. Forget trying to control when your child eats. Instead, accept irregular eating patterns and compensate by using shorter-acting insulin when your child does have a snack.

PRIMARY SCHOOL CHILDREN

As your child develops physically and mentally, he or she will be better able to understand why treatment is necessary and become more willing to cooperate with its demands. Explain to your child how caring for the condition now will protect his health in the future, but don't discuss the details of complications, which could frighten a child. Tighter blood-sugar control now becomes more important, especially at night, when there's a higher risk of hypo glycaemia. Make sure that your child has a snack at bedtime and doesn't skip meals. Encourage participation in school and social activities to build friendships, promote self-esteem and make him or her feel less different from other children. At about the age of eight, your child can start taking on some of the responsibility for injections and blood tests – maybe with the daytime help of teachers or classmates, who benefit from the opportunity to learn about diabetes from your child.

PRE-TEENS AND ADOLESCENTS

Control – over a number of things – now starts falling into your child's hands. Studies show that tight blood-sugar monitoring as early as age 13 can prevent complications in adulthood, so encourage your child to take charge – but don't expect the thought of future consequences to be strongly motivating. Now is not the time to let go of the reins completely. Worries about what others think might cause your child to leave out important steps in the care routine. Make an issue of it, expect an argument – but be confident that using you as an excuse ('My parents make me do it') can help your child to do the right thing. Gradually hand over responsibility as your child is able to cope with it. By the time your child is choosing a college or looking for work, responsibility should pass to him.

legs so that wounds take longer to heal (especially on the feet). It also raises blood pressure and increases the risk of kidney and nerve damage.

⟳ **Reduce the pressure** High blood pressure contributes to cardiovascular disease and kidney damage. If you eat plenty of fruits and vegetables, you are already helping to lower blood pressure. You can bring it down further by reducing your intake of sodium (common or table salt) – widely found in packaged foods – and eating more potassium, found in foods such as potatoes, yogurt, avocados and bananas. Consider cutting back on caffeine, too: a single cup of coffee can raise your blood pressure for about two hours.

Get on a schedule

It won't be long before dealing with diabetes seems normal. Once you have become accustomed to the changes in your diet and exercise habits and learned to handle medications, day-to-day life may start to seem routine again. But you will need to see your doctor regularly to make sure that everything is going according to plan. Once a year, you should have a complete physical examination, including an eye exam, a cholesterol test and a urine test to detect signs of kidney damage. In addition, every three to six months you should book in for a haemoglobin A1c test, which shows your long-term average blood sugar.

Where to get support

You're in charge of managing your diabetes from day to day (and hour to hour) because you're the one who is always there – to lace up your walking shoes, pour a bowl of bran cereal, take your medication, or prick your finger. But you're hardly in this alone. In fact, one of your most important jobs as the manager of your care is to know who is there to help you – and what their role should be.

Your first stop is your primary-care physician, who probably diagnosed your diabetes. Your family doctor is a general practitioner, not a diabetes specialist, but just because you have a specific disease doesn't mean you will be bidding your regular doctor good-bye. In fact, GPs can readily refer you to a range of specialists when you need them. So your primary-care physician will be your first line of help, but you will also receive care and get advice from a wide range of experts, including the following.

Diabetologist

This is a doctor who specializes in the management of diabetes, often with special experience in endocrinology, the study of hormones and metabolism. A diabetologist will know more than your general practitioner about how to match your treatment to your blood sugar, eating and exercise patterns and is more likely to be aware of the latest drugs and research. Talk to your GP about whether you need to be referred to a diabetologist. If you and your GP are finding it difficult to control your blood sugar then this would be a good idea and it is certainly worth suggesting if your GP has not already mentioned this option. A diabetologist would be primarily concerned with controlling your diabetes but would be very aware and interested in related and relevant health problems such as high blood pressure and obesity. These are increasingly seen as being of great importance in diabetes and not easily separable from it as health problems.

Diabetes nurse

A specialist nurse will help you to learn all the ins and outs of dealing with diabetes. In the UK this is usually a trained nurse or nurse practitioner with a special interest in diabetes who will head a primary care diabetes clinic. There are also specialist nurses in hospital diabetes clinics who work in close conjunction with the primary care team. They liaise between a GP surgery and the hospital diabetes clinic and help to keep the care as smooth as possible for those whose diabetes is particularly difficult to control and those with complications.

A diabetes nurse will be able to show you how to prepare and administer insulin and perform blood and urine tests, explain how to balance your eating and exercise with your blood-sugar readings, and tell you more about how diabetes affects your body. The nurse may even offer classes on diabetes, at which you can pick up more background information and meet other patients.

In the UK there is no specific single qualification in diabetes nursing. A diabetes nurse might have a diploma in diabetes or some kind of further education or training in diabetes, depending on the university or college. Also, according to the Royal College of Nursing, having passed an exam at some stage is no true indicator of a nurse's expertise in diabetes. It is more important that nurses further their education in their specialist field with continuous professional development so that they keep up to date. This is particularly true in the field of diabetes, which is constantly changing.

Dietitian

Controlling calories, assessing carbohydrates, finding hidden fats, sorting out sugars – your dietitian can help you with all of this. Meal planning (which involves everything just mentioned and more) is key to your care whether your main goal is to lose weight or to fine-tune your glucose intake. A state registered dietitian – with the letters SRD after the name – will carefully match your food to your drug or insulin use, your exercise habits and your daily schedule. If anything about your treatment changes – or you become bored with your meal plan – your dietitian can help you to adjust. Most of your contact with a dietitian will be at the beginning of your care, when you establish your meal plan. Further dietary advice will always be available from a specialist community diabetic nurse, either hospital or GP-based.

WHERE TO GET MORE INFORMATION

DIABETES UK
10 Parkway
London
NW1 7AA
Tel: 020 7424 1000
Careline: 0845 120 2960 (Mon–Fri 9am–5pm)
www.diabetes.org.uk

JUVENILE DIABETES RESEARCH FOUNDATION
19 Angel Gate
City Road
London
EC1V 2PT
Tel: 020 7713 2030
www.jdrf.oug.uk

INTERNATIONAL DIABETES FEDERATION
Avenue Emile De Mot
B-1000 Brussels
Belgium
Tel: 32 2 538 5511
www.idf.org

USEFUL WEBSITES
Diabetes Insight
www.diabetes-insight.info

Diabetes.co.uk
www.diabetes.co.uk

NHS Direct Online
www.nhsdirect.nhs.uk

FINDING THE RIGHT DOCTOR

There is a choice of doctors available at most GP's surgeries, and one may even specialize in diabetes care. You may feel that your present GP is right for you, otherwise you should:

■ **Ask around** Start by getting recommendations from friends, other diabetes patients, and the doctors and nurses you already see. Ask what they know about any doctor they suggest: Does he/she listen? Does he/she work well with other people?

■ **Schedule a visit** Book an initial appointment. You should keep your medical details to a minimum at this session and focus on asking questions. Find out what tests you would have to undergo, and how often you would come back for follow-ups.

Most GP practices have diabetes clinics in-house; a few patients will be managed by a hospital diabetes clinic with which your doctor will have strong links.

■ **Qualifications** Anyone who works for the NHS or Primary Care Trust will be appropriately qualified. If you want to reassure yourself about qualifications, ask the practice manager, check the practice leaflet, or check with your local hospital trust. Strict controls govern the clinical performance of GPs and set standards they are expected to meet.

■ **Ask about experience** Even endocrinologists don't treat only diabetes, so ask how much your doctor works with people who have diabetes, particularly those with your type and at your age.

■ **Talk philosophy** Does the doctor prefer sticking to well-established therapies or trying out new approaches? Neither way is necessarily better, but the doctor will probably have an opinion on the merits of one approach over another. Ask yourself whether you agree with the doctor's philosophy.

Opthalmologist

Because diabetes is a leading cause of eye disorders and even blindness, you constantly need to guard against vision problems. The only person qualified to diagnose and treat eye damage from diabetes is an ophthalmologist – a medical doctor who specializes in the eyes. Don't rely on check-ups by an optometrist, who is qualified to do vision screening and prescribe spectacles or contact lenses but is not an expert on eye diseases and cannot do surgery to correct them. Annual retinal screening is routinely offered on the NHS. Plan to visit your ophthalmologist at least once a year, but don't wait for your annual eye examination if you notice changes in your vision or feel pain or pressure in your eyes – possible signs of damage that require immediate attention. Ideally, the ophthalmologist you see should be someone who specializes in diseases of the retina. This is particularly important if you have already developed eye complications.

Chiropodists and podiatrists

High blood sugar makes you prone to foot problems, partly because it hinders circulation: blood has difficulty travelling all the way from the heart to the feet and back. Small sores and calluses, common in people with diabetes, quickly become worse if you don't look after them with the help of a chiropodist or podiatrist – a medical doctor who specializes in foot care. Your GP should check your feet when you go for an examination (and you should check them every day). But a chiropodist or podiatrist is the best person to treat sores, calluses, corns, bunions and other infections and can give practical advice on how you can keep your feet healthy. Your GP or endocrinologist should refer you to a chiropodist or podiatrist who has a number of patients with diabetes.

Dentist

Bacteria thrive on sugar, and if you have diabetes, high blood sugar makes you prone to the destructive effects of gingivitis – infection of the gums – even if you faithfully brush your teeth every day. There is no reason to change your dentist; you just need to make sure that you actually go for a check-up and a cleaning session every six months – as everyone should but rarely does. However, you should tell your dentist and hygienist that you have diabetes, and ask how you can improve your brushing and flossing techniques.

Pharmacist

You may know your pharmacist only as someone who stands behind a counter and puts medicines in bottles. But the special training that pharmacists receive about how drugs affect the body and how medicines interact with each other can make them an invaluable source of information.

It may be worth using a stand-alone pharmacy, with one full-time pharmacist rather than a chain. Keep going back to the same person, so that they can keep an up-to-date record of all your medications. There are now repeat dispensing schemes whereby patients on stable doses of long-term

WHAT THE STUDIES SHOW

How well your doctor relates to you through words and body language has an impact on your health. According to a recent review of 14 studies, doctors whose patients have the best outcomes are upbeat, supportive and reassuring; share information openly; are friendly; and have a good sense of humour. They also tend to face their patients, lean forwards, and nod when talking – and they don't cross their arms.

medication only request such medication once yearly from their GP: the pharmacist does the rest.

Whenever you start a new drug – including over-the-counter remedies – or make a change in your prescriptions, your pharmacist can give you pointers on how your body may react. He or she should also be able to supply you with a print-out of all the drugs you are taking (with their dosage and side effects) to take when you see members of your medical team.

In the UK, anyone with diabetes is entitled to free prescription drugs for life, whether or not the drugs are for diabetes.

Exercise specialists

Your GP can approve an exercise plan, but he or she can't be your coach. If you are out of shape and haven't exercised for years (or if you just want a trainer's individual attention), you might want to design your fitness programme with the help of a personal trainer. Many gyms now offer such a service to their members. A personal trainer can custom-design a programme that is safe for you, help you to set realistic goals, and give you advice on how to improve your technique.

Counsellors

Whether you need help handling the emotional aspects of diabetes is your decision, but you should realize that it is not strictly a mental-health issue. People who are angry, depressed or anxious are more likely to neglect their care, so emotional support can, in effect, help to stabilize your blood sugar as well as your mind and mood.

You have three basic types of mental-health experts from which to choose. A psychiatrist is a medical doctor who has received advanced training in psychological disorders and can write prescriptions for drugs, such as anti-anxiety medications or antidepressants. A psychologist does not normally have a medical degree (but may have a degree in psychology or a related subject) and may not prescribe drugs, but can help you to recognize and overcome destructive or self-defeating ways of thinking. If you need a psychologist, look for one with chartered status from the British Psychological Society. There are also other counsellors who can help you to deal with negative feelings associated with your illness. The availability of counselling is very limited on the NHS. Private counselling and charitable trusts are more available but you will have to pay something towards your treatment. It is essential that you check the professional accreditation of anyone you consider using: all counsellors should also be undergoing their own supervision counselling themselves. If not, you should not go near them.

Start to take charge now

You know exactly what kind of opponent you're up against, you understand the tools at your disposal, you have formulated a battle plan and know the people who can help you to put it into action. So what will it take to win the fight? The same things it takes to succeed in just about any other worthy struggle: patience, strength, determination, good communication skills, the ability to cooperate with your team, and confidence that you will prevail. Last but not least, a sense of humour always helps.

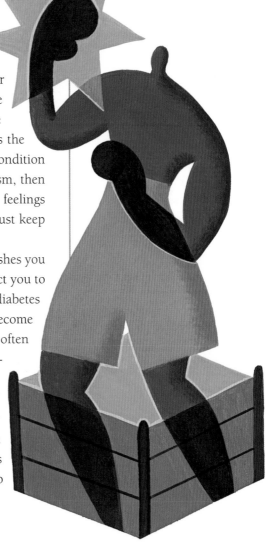

A confident attitude may be the most important quality of all. It is easy to feel (especially just after your diagnosis) that diabetes has already won the battle. It has stolen your health and made you feel like a 'diseased' or 'damaged' person – a statistic. So what's the use of fighting when you know your essential condition won't change? If you give in to pessimism and defeatism, then diabetes really has won after all. Acknowledge these feelings when you have them, but don't allow them to linger. Just keep moving forwards.

Diabetes is like the classic playground bully who pushes you down and then turns his back because he doesn't expect you to get up and fight back. Standing up for yourself when diabetes lets down its guard means you have refused to become a victim of the disease. And you'll find that diabetes often backs down in the face of diet, exercise and drugs – although you should never turn your back on it.

If you're willing to fight, you will find plenty of weaknesses in diabetes that you can exploit. Remember that you have a team of heath professionals backing you up who know how to handle the cruellest tricks diabetes can pull. Roll up your sleeves, make a fist and prepare to knock diabetes off its feet.

Understanding diabetes

You can't see it, you usually can't feel it, so what exactly is diabetes? It's a complex disease to be sure, one that affects your entire body, and it can seem difficult to get your mind around. But learning about the basics braces you for battle with your condition. In fact, education is a cornerstone of care. The more you know about diabetes, the better you'll be able to use all the tools at your disposal to keep your blood sugar in check and avoid complications that can compromise your quality of life.

TWO

2

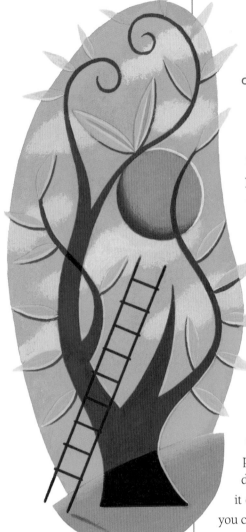

What exactly is diabetes?

Unlike, say, high blood pressure, the term diabetes does not convey a clear picture. Even doctors sometimes have a difficult time when it comes to describing diabetes. Is it an endocrine disorder, a blood-related disease, a metabolic problem? In fact, it's all three of these – and more.

If you don't understand what diabetes is all about, you are not alone. But it is worth finding out, because whenever you're faced with an important mission (and managing diabetes certainly qualifies), taking effective action means gathering good intelligence first.

Aside from being complex, diabetes is often the subject of misconceptions. For example, many people think it comes from eating too much sugar, but that is not really the case. It is also widely assumed that having diabetes means constantly jabbing syringes full of insulin into your body, but while many people benefit from treatments involving injections, thousands of others control their disease by making relatively simple lifestyle changes.

And then there's the idea that people with the condition are defined by the term diabetic. This may seem like a small point, but it is worth making. You are not your disease, and your life is not about diabetes, even if managing it demands your attention. Rather, diabetes is a condition that you can control day by day, so that you can celebrate, take part in, and enjoy the truly important aspects of your life which really define who you are.

A hidden fuel spill

Imagine that the nation's intricate system of lanes, roads and motorways is your body and that the millions of cars humming along this system are your cells. Every car needs regular replenishment with fuel and, fortunately, petrol is widely available. When everything is working normally, cars and petrol come together, fuel tanks open, petrol is dispensed, and the cars go about their business, brimming with the energy they need.

Now suppose something goes fundamentally wrong. The petrol flows out of the pump, but there is no one around to open the cars' fuel tanks. The petrol spills all over the forecourt, floods the roads, rushes down the gutters and pollutes the entire system. That is the nature of diabetes.

In the real-life disease, the source of energy (that is, the 'petrol') is a substance called glucose, and the car driver or petrol-station attendant who opens the fuel tank is equivalent to a hormone called insulin.

Why glucose matters

Glucose, also known as blood sugar, is the major source of energy powering your brain, muscles and tissues – all your body's functions. In fact, glucose is one of nature's great dynamos, providing an almost universal energy source for living things. Scientists know down to the molecule how glucose is made and what it does, but, interestingly, they have never been able to create it in a lab. Only plants can make glucose through the magic mix of sunlight, water and other elements, and pass this energy along to other creatures through the food chain.

When you eat, your body breaks down the food into smaller, simpler components that move through the small intestine and into the bloodstream. Once in the blood, these nutrients are carried to cells throughout the body.

Different foods break down into different types of nutrients. Protein breaks down into amino acids, which are often used to build or repair tissue. Fat breaks down into fatty acids, which are mostly stored as energy reserves. Carbohydrates (from foods ranging from bread and pasta to fruits and vegetables) mainly break down into glucose, which is used almost immediately for energy. In order to feel at your best, you need enough glucose powering your cells at all times.

With diabetes, however, glucose in the blood doesn't make it into cells. The cells are deprived of energy, which explains why fatigue is one of the hallmarks of diabetes. And since the glucose cannot enter cells, it builds up in the blood. High blood sugar wreaks havoc with the body. In the short term, for example, the excess glucose essentially soaks up water from the bloodstream, creating a paradoxical condition in which you need to urinate more often while feeling parched with thirst. Too much glucose

DID YOU KNOW

The term diabetes comes from the Greek word for 'siphon', based on the observation that people with the condition seemed to lose fluid in urine as quickly as they could slake their thirst. The second term in the disease's full name, diabetes mellitus, also comes from Greek and means 'sweet' – a reference to sugar in urine that is typical with diabetes. It is said that in ancient times, the sweetness of urine was judged by tasting it – reason to be thankful that blood tests can detect diabetes mellitus today.

can also hinder the immune system's infection-fighting white blood cells, making you more vulnerable to illness. Over the longer term, persistently high blood sugar can lead to serious complications, such as damaged nerves, kidneys, eyes, blood vessels, liver and heart.

A wild blood-sugar ride

Blood sugar fluctuates normally throughout the day, rising after you eat a meal. In people who do not have diabetes, these fluctuations stay within a range (measured in units of millimoles per litre of blood) of about 3.9 to 7.8mmol/l. When you have diabetes, though, the patterns become more erratic.

▶ Blood-sugar levels spike to mountainous heights (rather than gentle hills) after meals.

▶ Levels drop more slowly as the body metabolizes the food you have eaten.

▶ Blood-sugar levels are, on average, higher than what is considered to be normal and healthy.

▶ The less you control your diabetes, the more likely your blood sugar is to swing wildly between highs and lows or simply to stay high all the time.

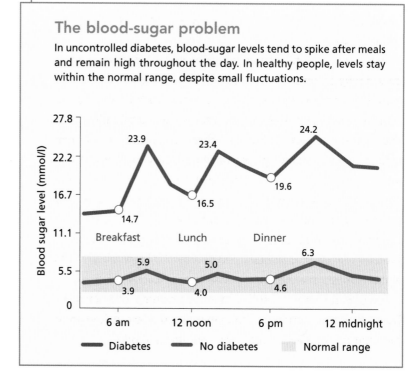

The blood-sugar problem

In uncontrolled diabetes, blood-sugar levels tend to spike after meals and remain high throughout the day. In healthy people, levels stay within the normal range, despite small fluctuations.

Insulin's inside job

Glucose may inflict the damage done by diabetes, but it is not really to blame. The real trouble-maker is the hormone insulin, manufactured by the pancreas. Insulin's job is to 'unlock' cells so that glucose can enter. As glucose leaves the bloodstream and enters cells, blood-sugar levels fall. When that happens, insulin levels also plummet so that blood sugar does not drop too low – a condition called hypoglycaemia.

When you have diabetes, the delicate dance of glucose and insulin is thrown out of step, either because the pancreas has trouble manufacturing insulin in the first place or because the body's cells have difficulty allowing insulin to do its job. The term that describes the latter condition is insulin resistance – a critical breakdown in the body's ability to use insulin properly. Insulin resistance is the underlying cause of the vast majority of diabetes cases.

Scientists are still struggling to understand exactly what goes wrong to cause insulin resistance. (In one recent medical textbook containing a diagram of how insulin may work at the cellular level, many steps in the process are simply illustrated with question marks.) But the sheer complexity of normal insulin function allows plenty of opportunity for things to go awry. It is possible, for example, that insulin resistance occurs when problems develop in the normal chain of chemical reactions that must occur to permit glucose to be transported through cell membranes. Or perhaps an intricate system of proteins in cells, sometimes called the metabolic switch, loses its ability to sense the presence of insulin and react accordingly.

Even if the biology still remains something of a mystery, however, it is important to remember that the factors known to raise the risk of diabetes are fairly well understood.

INSULIN OPPOSITES

Insulin is not the only hormone that can affect blood-sugar levels. A number of others, sometimes called insulin antagonists, or counterregulatory hormones, have the opposite effect of insulin. These include:

■ **Glucagon** Produced in the pancreas along with insulin, it blocks insulin's ability to lower blood sugar by causing the liver to release stored glucose when the body requires it.

■ **Epinephrine** Also called adrenaline, this so-called stress hormone is released when the body perceives danger. Epinephrine raises blood sugar in order to make more energy available to muscles.

■ **Hydrocortisone** Another stress hormone, also called cortisol, it can also raise blood-sugar levels.

■ **Growth hormone** Produced by the pituitary gland in the brain, it makes cells less sensitive to insulin.

Typecasting: a key to understanding

Diabetes was long assumed to be one disease. But it has become clear that it actually takes several forms which, while fundamentally similar, differ in many important ways. The two main forms are known as Type I and Type 2 (other types are far less common). Both occur when glucose cannot enter cells. As a result, they share many symptoms, including the following:

Feeling tired When body cells are unable to get the glucose they need and are deprived of energy, you can suffer from both physical and mental fatigue. The brain, in fact, is a glutton for glucose, using far more glucose for its weight than do other types of tissue. Mental fatigue can make you fuzzy-headed and emotionally brittle, while physical fatigue can make your muscles feel weak.

Frequent urination When the body is awash with blood sugar, the kidneys, which recirculate nutrients and filter out waste products, are among the first to react. When overwhelmed by glucose, they attempt to flush the excess out of your system by boosting production of urine, especially after blood-sugar levels reach or exceed about 10mmol/l.

Unquenchable thirst Each time that urine is excreted, you lose fluid. To urge you to replace it, the body triggers a persistent thirst.

Snack attacks The irony of diabetes is that although your body is overflowing with nutritional energy, your cells are starving. Deprived of sustenance, they tell the body's appetite system to send a call for more food – which only creates more glucose that can't be properly used.

Blurry vision Diabetes can degrade your eyesight in two seemingly contradictory ways. In one, lack of body fluid due to loss of urine can dry out the eyes, constricting the lens and distorting vision. In the other, excess blood sugar can cause the lens to swell, which also creates distortion. Both of these effects are temporary, although diabetes can cause other complications that may eventually result in serious visual impairment and, in severe cases, blindness.

More frequent infections Having too much glucose in your bloodstream makes your body's immune-system cells less effective at attacking viruses and bacteria that cause infection.

To make matters worse, some of these invaders actually feed on glucose, making it easier for them to multiply and become an even bigger threat to the immune system. This can result in frequent upper respiratory tract illnesses such as colds and flu, as well as urinary tract infections, gum disease and, in women, vaginal yeast infections.

Tingling hands and feet High blood sugar can damage nerves, a condition that may first become noticeable in the touch-sensitive extremities as a tingling or burning sensation. Damage caused by excess blood sugar can also affect nerves in the digestive tract, provoking nausea, diarrhoea or constipation.

A pancreas primer

The pancreas is a fist-size organ that resembles an overgrown tadpole. It lies just behind and below the stomach. In its 'tail', cells known as beta cells (which are clustered in clumps called the islets of Langerhans), produce insulin and release it when needed. Other cells, called acinar cells, secrete enzymes that help to break down proteins, carbohydrates and fats. Normally, the pancreas acts as a kind of glucose meter, closely monitoring levels in the blood and releasing insulin in spurts to mirror glucose levels. It also helps to regulate a process in which the liver stores glucose as glycogen and then releases it back into the blood-stream to raise glucose levels when they fall too low. Certain diabetes drugs work to improve the function of the pancreas.

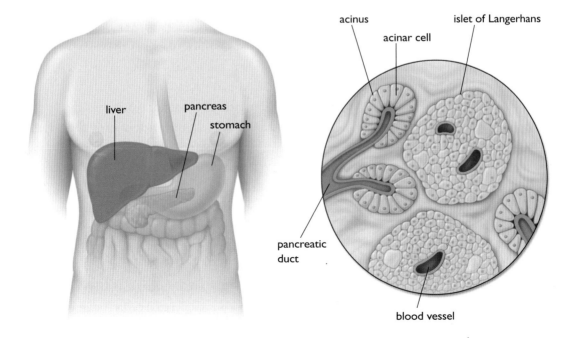

liver

pancreas

stomach

pancreatic duct

acinus

acinar cell

islet of Langerhans

blood vessel

Type I: an insulin no-show

So how do the two main types of diabetes differ? First, Type I is much rarer, accounting for only 13 per cent of all diagnosed cases of diabetes. With Type I diabetes, the body's immune system destroys special cells in the pancreas that manufacture insulin. These cells, called beta cells, are the only places in the body where insulin is produced. Without them, the body lacks the insulin it needs to move glucose out of circulation and control high blood sugar. Other major characteristics of Type I are:

Needles are necessary Because the body cannot produce insulin, Type 1 patients need an outside supply of the hormone, self-administered by daily injections. That is why Type 1 is sometimes called insulin dependent diabetes mellitus, or IDDM. This term is used less frequently today, however, because people with Type 2 diabetes also sometimes need to take insulin. But the fact that injections are an inevitable part of daily life for all Type 1 diabetes patients remains one of the key characteristics of this form of the disease.

It strikes early Type 1 diabetes often sets in during childhood. About half of all cases in the UK develop before the age of 15, and 90 per cent have been diagnosed by the age of 30.

Diabetes at a glance

	TYPE 1	TYPE 2	GESTATIONAL
Characteristics	Sudden onset; pronounced thirst and hunger; frequent urination; fatigue; nausea and vomiting; weight loss	Slow, difficult-to-detect onset; pronounced thirst; frequent urination; fatigue; slow wound healing; tingling hands or feet; frequent infections; weight loss	Pronounced thirst; frequent urination; fatigue and other symptoms similar to those of Type 2
Age at onset	Usually 20 or younger	Usually 40 or older, although rates are escalating among younger people	Child-bearing years
Physical condition	Usually lean or normal weight	Usually overweight	Pregnant
Cause	The immune system destroys the cells in the pancreas that produce insulin	Lack of exercise, poor diet and resulting obesity; genetics	Hormones produced by the placenta hinder the function of insulin
Mainstay of treatment	Insulin injections	Lifestyle changes, possibly augmented by insulin and drugs	Lifestyle changes, possibly augmented by insulin injections

It is very unusual for Type 1 diabetes to occur in anyone over 40. Because it is widely seen as a disease of the young (although you continue to have it all your life), Type 1 is sometimes called juvenile-onset diabetes. This term, too, has fallen out of favour, both because adults can get Type 1 diabetes and because the prevalence of Type 2 diabetes in children is increasing.

It strikes fast The onset of Type 1 diabetes is rapid compared with Type 2, which can take years to develop. If you (or your child) have Type 1, such classic symptoms as fatigue, excessive thirst and frequent urination will probably become worse over a period of just weeks or months.

There is a 'honeymoon' period In the first several months after Type 1 is diagnosed and treatment begins, 20 per cent of patients seem to improve as the pancreas temporarily begins to increase insulin production once again. This period of remission may last up to a year, during which blood-sugar levels become more stable and insulin injections may not even be necessary. While all honeymoons must come to an end, researchers see this period as a potential window of opportunity. One day it may allow yet-to-be-perfected therapies to preserve beta cell function before it is too late.

Blood sugar jumps wildly With Type 1, the pancreas loses its ability to monitor and control blood sugar. As a result, blood-sugar levels tend to spike and crash with greater volatility than in people who have Type 2 diabetes, since their pancreatic function is generally less severely impaired. With Type 1, the job of the pancreas essentially falls to you. You control your blood-sugar level with the timing and dosage of your insulin injections. This makes monitoring your blood sugar critically important (see Chapter 3).

What causes Type 1?

Type 1 diabetes seems to appear out of nowhere and, as far as anyone knows, is not easily preventable – something that is definitely not true of Type 2. So why does Type 1 occur? There are many theories, but as yet, no definite answers.

Researchers don't know yet. But clues can be found in the nature of the disease. Type 1 diabetes is thought to involve a misguided attack by the immune system on the body's own tissue – specifically, the beta cells of the pancreas. This

?
DID YOU KNOW

The discovery of insulin, a major breakthrough in understanding and treating diabetes, came in the 1920s, following the earlier discovery that when beta cells of the pancreas were missing, people developed diabetes. Building on this observation, a team of doctors led by researchers Frederick Banting and John MacLeod extracted insulin from beta cells and injected it into diabetes patients. When the patients improved, the researchers knew they had made a major discovery – one that brought Banting and MacLeod the Nobel prize for medicine. Another 50 years passed, however, before researchers fully understood the distinction between Type 1 and Type 2 diabetes.

type of attack is known as an autoimmune response. Other autoimmune diseases include lupus, multiple sclerosis, rheumatoid arthritis and Grave's disease.

Scientists are studying the different players involved in helping the body distinguish its own cells from foreign cells. Eventually they may be able to develop new therapies to prevent and treat Type 1 diabetes. Meanwhile, the question still lingers as to why an autoimmune attack occurs in the first place. There appear to be a number of factors at work in Type 1.

Genetics Having a family history of Type 1 diabetes may be the single most important risk factor in determining who will develop the disease. Even so, the genetic connection is fairly weak, and of those who inherit the genes for Type 1 diabetes only a small proportion actually develop the condition. Between 12 and 15 per cent of young people with Type 1 diabetes have a family history of the disease. If a mother has the condition, the risk of her children developing it is 2 to 3 per cent; whereas, for reasons not fully understood, if a father has the condition, the risk of transmission to his children rises to 8 or 9 per cent.

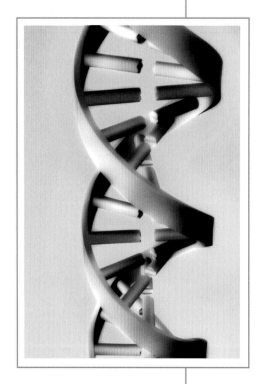

Among identical twins, there is only a 40 per cent chance that if one twin develops the condition, the other twin will too.

Even though genetics does not completely predict the condition, scientists are working towards a better understanding of the genes involved with Type 1 diabetes, and they may one day be able to develop genetic therapies for people who are most at risk.

Viruses Could Type 1 be caused by an infection? It is possible. One reason researchers think so is that the onset of the disease appears to follow a seasonal pattern, with the fewest new cases in summer and the most in winter – when many viral illnesses are more common. A number of viruses have been implicated as suspects, in particular Coxsackie virus (a family of viruses which cause different illnesses, including the mild childhood illness of hand, foot and mouth disease), mumps and rubella. Some studies have found that a high percentage of people newly diagnosed with Type 1 have Coxsackie virus antibodies in their blood, suggesting that the body has been fighting this viral infection. In laboratory tests, a cousin of the Coxsackie virus has been shown to produce Type 1-like symptoms in animals.

Some researchers question whether the virus idea has any merit, but a number of theories explain how it might work. One hypothesis is that the immune system may have trouble telling the difference between certain viruses and the insulin-producing beta cells in the pancreas. After fighting off the virus, according to this premise, the immune system continues the battle by attacking the pancreas. Other theories suggest that viruses may change the beta cells in ways that make them appear foreign to the immune system. Or they may destroy proteins in the pancreas that manufacture insulin.

Cow's milk This idea is mostly speculation and far from proven, but some research has suggested a link between feeding children cow's milk before three or four months of age and the risk of developing Type 1 diabetes. People with Type 1 sometimes have higher levels of antibodies that bind to both a protein found in milk and a protein sometimes found on beta cells, but the significance of this is not clear. Other studies have failed to find any connection between cow's milk and Type 1 diabetes. Still, the concern offers additional reason not to wean a baby from breast milk or formula before 12 months of age, as recommended by the Department of Health.

Free radicals These unstable molecules are formed as a by-product of natural bodily functions (such as breathing) that involve the use of oxygen. Free radicals have a single, unpaired electron instead of the usual pair, making them unstable. As they circulate around the body, they try to latch on to other molecules, inflicting damage on healthy cells in the process. Normally, enzymes in the body neutralize free radicals and keep this damage to a minimum. But toxins, such as air pollution and tobacco smoke, can boost their numbers to levels which the body cannot adequately handle. Studies suggest that the insulin-producing cells of the pancreas may be especially vulnerable to free-radical damage because they are less well guarded by protective enzymes than other parts of the body are.

WHAT THE STUDIES SHOW

Type 1 diabetes occurs when T-cells in the immune system, which normally protect against infection, instead start to attack the insulin-producing islet cells of the pancreas. In a joint study, researchers from King's College London and the University of Bristol compared the T-cell immune reactions of those with and without diabetes, using novel technology. The study showed that T-cells from diabetes patients made a factor called interferon, known to cause inflammation; and those from 'control' subjects made interleukin-10, known to have natural immune suppressive qualities. Researchers concluded that interleukin-10 could be part of a natural protection against diseases such as diabetes; the next step is to find ways of promoting the natural production of interleukin-10.

Type 2: a system breakdown

Compared with Type 1, Type 2 is far more common, accounting for more than 85 per cent of all cases of diabetes. It is also much more complex. High blood sugar is still the basic problem. But with Type 2, the pancreas does not completely shut off insulin production. Instead, the body's use of insulin becomes impaired in a variety of ways.

▶ The beta cells of the pancreas are able to produce plenty of insulin, but they take their time releasing it in response to the surge of glucose that follows a meal. By the time the pancreas puts out the large amount of insulin the body is waiting for, blood glucose levels have already built up.

▶ The number of beta cells is lower than normal, so the pancreas has difficulty keeping up with the demand for insulin.

▶ There is plenty of glucose and insulin, but cells do not allow insulin to do its job – a condition known as

insulin resistance. The problem can arise from a number of causes: a lack of proteins called insulin receptors on cells (think of insulin as a key and the receptor as a lock), a mismatch of insulin and receptors (the keys don't fit the locks), or flaws in the chemistry that allows insulin to pass into cells. Whatever the cause may be, the result is the same: glucose is unable to travel where it needs to go and instead it accumulates in the bloodstream.

▶ Excess body weight boosts the need for insulin and the pancreas can't keep up with demand.

Often, Type 2 diabetes results from a combination of these factors, which tend to be interrelated. For example, obesity both creates more demand for insulin and promotes insulin resistance.

The major symptoms of Type 2 mirror those of Type 1, but Type 2 is different in other ways:

It takes time Unlike Type 1, Type 2 develops slowly over time, and symptoms do not show up straight away. When you finally notice that something is wrong, you may already have had diabetes for many years. That can make Type 2 diabetes seem rather vague – if it appears so gradually, when does it actually begin? And once you are diagnosed, do you really, truly have it? Doctors readily admit that it is sometimes difficult to say exactly when any given case of diabetes actually started – especially after the fact. However, exact criteria based on blood-sugar levels clearly indicate when you have diabetes and when you don't. Once you have the condition, you can control it to a remarkable degree, but it never goes away. There is no such thing as 'a touch' of diabetes.

Adults suffer most Type 2 diabetes is sometimes called adult-onset diabetes because it generally strikes after the age of 40 and is more likely to develop as you get older. This is partly because insulin resistance increases with age. In the UK, one person in 20 aged over 65 has diabetes, and the figure rises to one person in five of those aged over 85. But, as with other terms for diabetes, 'adult onset' is becoming a misnomer because of the increasing prevalence of Type 2 in children.

Blood sugar is more stable Because the pancreas still produces and releases at least some insulin when it is needed, glucose levels in the blood don't tend to swing as wildly as they do with Type 1 – even though, on average, unmanaged blood-sugar levels with Type 2 are still too high.

What causes Type 2?

The causes of Type 2 diabetes have much more to do with lifestyle issues, particularly obesity. But weight doesn't tell the whole story. In fact, it is unlikely that Type 2 develops because of any single cause. Instead, a number of factors appear to come together, potentially even magnifying each other, with unhealthy results. The following are some of the factors that may come into play:

Genetics Again, patterns in twins indicate how strong the genetic link is – and it is much stronger with Type 2 than with Type 1. In the case of Type 2, if one identical twin has diabetes, the chances of the other developing it are as high as 90 per cent. If one parent has Type 2, the children have a 15 per cent chance of developing it, too. (If both parents have it, the risk to children is 75 per cent.) This makes Type 2 a serious concern for ethnic groups that seem predisposed to it – and it is more prevalent among people of South Asian and African Caribbean descent.

? DID YOU KNOW

Although the reasons are not understood, the incidence of Type 1 diabetes appears to be rising steadily, despite the fact that, unlike Type 2 diabetes, the disease is not clearly related to lifestyle. Researchers point to a virtual epidemic of Type 1 diabetes, with rates as much as five times higher today in the Western world than 40 years ago. The incidence of Type 1 in the UK has doubled every 20 years since 1945. Still, rates of Type 2 diabetes are rising faster than rates of Type 1.

Inactivity Physical activity improves the body's use of insulin. This happens for a variety of reasons. Muscle, for example, uses glucose more efficiently than other types of tissue, and exercise builds muscle. Unfortunately, the opposite is also true. Lack of physical activity makes cells more prone to insulin resistance. It also contributes to weight gain.

Poor diet How much you eat matters. But what you eat is equally important. And the fat-laden foods that are so common in the British diet are more likely to pack on pounds than comparable amounts of other, leaner foods.

Age Type 2 diabetes becomes more common with age, partly because cells in older bodies tend to be more insulin resistant. But also people tend to become more sedentary with age. Their metabolism slows down, yet they often eat just as much – sometimes more – than they did when they took more exercise. All of those elements are a prescription for an increased risk of diabetes.

Obesity: the big difference

Type 1 diabetes doesn't 'look' like anything – there is nothing to distinguish a person who has it from anybody else. That is usually not true of people with Type 2 diabetes, who are overweight or obese in 80 to 90 per cent of cases. Being overweight is the single most important contributor to Type 2 diabetes. It is no coincidence that the soaring incidence of diabetes in recent years has been matched by obesity rates, which almost trebled in England between 1980 and 1998. Of course, having put on a few extra pounds doesn't automatically mean you will get diabetes, but the risk of developing Type 2 diabetes increases by up to ten times in people with a Body Mass Index of more than 30.

The potbelly peril Research studies have made it clear that fat accumulated around your belly – what scientists call visceral adipose tissue and the rest of us call a spare tyre – contributes to diabetes more than fat located on the hips, thighs or other parts of the body. According to scientists at Birmingham University, waist measurements can predict the risks of Type 2 diabetes and heart disease more accurately than weight. Men with waists of more than 102cm (40in) and women with waists of more than 89cm (35in) have a far higher risk of developing Type 2 diabetes and heart disease because fat cells around the waistline are highly active, producing and pumping out proteins and hormones. In excess, they cause damage to the way insulin is used, and also by raising blood pressure and increasing the amount of cholesterol in the bloodstream.

Other 'diabesity' dangers Diabetes is not the only chronic disease linked to abdominal fat. A spare tyre is also a critical risk factor for heart disease and a raft of associated conditions such as high blood pressure and raised levels of cholesterol and triglycerides. In fact, obesity, insulin resistance and risk factors for heart disease appear together so often that some researchers now think of them as different expressions of a single disorder called syndrome X, or metabolic syndrome.

It is not clear precisely how the components of metabolic syndrome affect one another, but in 1999 the World Health Organization for the first time defined how to diagnose it (see 'Do you have metabolic syndrome?' below). In the UK some 25 per cent of the population show clear signs of metabolic syndrome. What does this mean to you? If diabetes goes hand in hand with heart disease, taking charge of your blood sugar can help to protect you against both.

Do your genes make you fat? Like diabetes itself, obesity seems to run in families. Scientists believe that genes play a role in how well hormones, enzymes and other chemicals are able to control appetite by, say, signalling the brain to stop eating or establishing how heavy the body thinks it ought to be. Does that mean you are a victim of genetic fate and unable to do anything about your weight? Absolutely not. Genes may contribute to weight, but they don't tell the whole story. Some of the ethnic groups in which obesity and diabetes rates are highest, such as people of South Asian and African Caribbean descent, are not historically heavy people. Only

?

DID YOU KNOW

There are 250 million obese people worldwide. Britain now has the fastest growing rate of obesity in the developed world: the numbers of obese adults increased from 14 to 22 per cent of the population in the past 10 years. One in four children in Britain are either overweight or obese, as are about half of all women and about two-thirds of all men.

DO YOU HAVE METABOLIC SYNDROME?

According to the World Health Organization, you suffer from metabolic syndrome – and have a higher risk of both diabetes and heart disease – when you have diabetes or impaired glucose tolerance or insulin resistance plus two of the following:

■ **Triglycerides:** more than 1.7mmol/l and/or HDL cholesterol: less than 0.9 (men), less than 1.0 (women)

■ **Hypertension:** blood pressure more than 140/0mmHg and/or medication

■ **Obesity:** Body Mass Index (BMI) more than 30kg/m^2

■ **Microalbuminuria:** the presence of microscopic amounts of the protein albumin in the urine.

Size matters

The Body Mass Index

Research has shown that you are at risk for Type 2 diabetes if you are overweight and that your risk increases substantially if you are obese. The Body Mass Index is generally regarded as a better indicator than weight as to whether people are overweight or obese.

To calculate your BMI:

1 Measure your height in metres and multiply that number by itself.

2 Measure your weight in kilogrammes.

3 Divide your weight by the number you got in step 1. This number is your Body Mass Index.

■ A BMI of more than 25kg/m² indicates that you are over-weight.

■ A BMI of more than 30kg/m² indicates that you are obese.

Though a good general indicator, the Body Mass Index does not differentiate between muscle and fat. So muscular individuals may find that they have a high BMI even though their levels of fat are actually very low.

when they took up a high-fat, high-calorie diet and became more sedentary did they 'adopt' obesity and diabetes, too.

You hold the key If weight is such an important contributor to diabetes risk, that is actually good news because it is almost entirely within your control. You can manage your weight through diet and exercise – and you can control Type 2 diabetes the same way. That may sound a formidable challenge, but it's an opportunity that Type 1 patients don't have: to change the course of their disease simply by making changes in the way they live.

Gestational diabetes: a disappearing act

At first, gestational diabetes sounds innocuous. In the UK it affects fewer than one in 20 pregnant women during the second half of gestation (usually in the third trimester) as hormones guiding foetal development in the placenta interfere with the normal insulin function. The basic symptoms mirror those of other forms of diabetes, but once the baby arrives, gestational diabetes mellitus – or GDM – usually goes away and blood glucose levels return to normal.

But don't be lulled into thinking that gestational diabetes is strictly temporary or is not worth taking seriously. GDM increases the risk of miscarriage (although it makes a child no more likely to have birth defects or diabetes) and, because it often causes the baby to grow large before birth, can contribute to complications at delivery. (Having given birth in the past to a baby weighing 4kg (9lb) or more suggests you are at risk for GDM.) Just as important, most women who develop GDM do so because their pancreas is already weak (they are often over-weight), so they have a higher risk of developing Type 2 diabetes in later life – about two in five women with gestational diabetes will go on to have diabetes.

Protecting your pregnancy

GDM is not considered a severe form of diabetes, but it does require treatment, which is why obstetricians routinely test for it. In fact, blood-sugar goals with GDM are fairly tight – you are aiming for the normal glucose levels found in a healthy woman who is not pregnant. Generally speaking, this is not difficult to achieve, because the pancreas still produces insulin

A WARNING FOR THE FUTURE?

Type 2 diabetes is known as adult-onset diabetes because it starts in adulthood – that is, until recently. The past decade has seen an alarming increase in Type 2 cases in children in the USA. Before the 1990s, Type 2 accounted for less than 4 per cent of US childhood diabetes cases. Now it accounts for about 45 per cent, according to the American Diabetes Association (ADA).

The few studies that have been done in the UK to date suggest that the number of British children with Type 2 diabetes is still extremely limited. But we need to be aware of the factors that have led to the increased incidence of juvenile Type 2 in the USA and act now to prevent it becoming a problem on the same scale here.

Why is this happening in the USA? A dramatic rise in juvenile obesity seems to be a starting point. Today about 25 per cent of American children are overweight – twice the number in the 1970s. In an attempt to clarify the diabetes risk to heavy children, researchers writing in The New England Journal of Medicine in March 2002 reported that, of 167 obese children and adolescents they studied, about a quarter were already glucose intolerant – the first step down the path to diabetes.

'This is all very new, and we're still not exactly sure how to treat Type 2 diabetes in children', says Sonia Caprio, MD, director of Yale's Paediatric Obesity/Type 2 Diabetes Clinic. Doctors remain unsure whether they should prescribe medication to treat children who have Type 2 diabetes or to prevent it in those who are glucose intolerant. Studies in adults suggest that drugs can greatly reduce risks, but the side effects of drug treatment in children are unknown.

Less controversial are the benefits of addressing lifestyle issues that contribute to the obesity epidemic. 'More food is available to American children at any time of day than has ever been the case before', says Dr Caprio. High-calorie snacks and soft drinks are available from vending machines in schools. Supersize portions are another problem. 'Kids are used to immense servings in restaurants', she says. 'They don't even think about it.'

On top of that, American children are far less physically active than they were in the past. Because of distance and safety issues, they seldom walk to school, and only 25 per cent of high schools still have daily gym classes. Back at home, children spend increasing amounts of time on sedentary activities, such as watching TV, using computers, or playing video games.

To counter these trends, some US schools have decided to screen children for obesity and notify parents of the associated health risks. The ADA recommends diabetes testing for overweight children with at least two other risk factors – for example family history, high blood pressure, or membership of an at-risk ethnic group. But parents have to be the real focus of diabetes education and the instigators of change. 'Parents need to learn more about proper nutrition and go outside to play more themselves – like most of our parents did 30 years ago.'

and glucose levels remain fairly stable. Your doctor may recommend that you:

▶ Ease insulin demand on the pancreas by spreading your total daily calorie intake over smaller, more frequent meals. Of course, you still need enough calories to maintain a healthy weight.

▶ Lower blood-glucose levels with light exercise such as walking or swimming.

▶ Make use of insulin injections if you have difficulty controlling blood sugar through diet and exercise alone.

Testing one, two, three

The most important thing to know about diabetes is whether or not you have it. This may sound strange. But diabetes can take even the smartest of us by surprise. And people with early signs of the disease need to monitor their condition closely because symptoms alone will not tell you if you have developed full-blown diabetes.

There is currently no national screening programme for diabetes in Britain. The government's plan in its National Service Framework for Diabetes is to have a national programme in place by 2013, and the National Screening Committee is due to provide advice and guidelines for it during 2005. In the meantime, some screening is being carried out in certain areas, but it is very patchy.

Diabetes UK believes that testing is the only way to address the fact that, of the estimated 2.9 million people in the UK who have diabetes, 1 million don't know it. Many more who are at risk of diabetes and could stop the disease before it starts are not taking preventive measures because they don't know that they are in danger. Screening of people with a possible vulnerability to diabetes and early identification of people with Type 2 diabetes would help to reduce the impact of diabetes both on individuals and on National Health Service resources.

Testing for diabetes is a relatively easy and painless procedure. There are three tests that doctors use in order to measure blood glucose in slightly different ways. Any one of them will provide you with the information you need.

Fasting plasma glucose test

If you make an appointment to see your doctor today, this is the test that he will probably schedule for you. Scheduling is necessary, because accurate results depend on you preparing for the test in advance. The test will be done either at your GP surgery, if it offers blood-taking or at the local pathology lab.

How it works First, you must fast for at least eight hours before the test, consuming nothing but water. That way, when blood is drawn, your gastrointestinal system has long since digested all food. As a result, your blood-sugar levels will be at their lowest ebb, providing the bottom measure of what is typical for you. If you are healthy, your reading will be 6.1mmol/l or lower. If the reading is 7mmol/l or higher, you have diabetes. If your reading only just crosses the line into a bad-news diagnosis, your doctor may want to repeat the test on a different day, in order to be sure – although if your numbers are well above 7mmol/l this may not be necessary.

Why it is used The fasting plasma glucose (or FPG) test is the preferred diagnostic tool because it is easy for both patients and doctors, it is relatively cheap, and it generally delivers consistent results – a nearly perfect balance of what you want in a test.

➲ **Take the test in the morning, not the afternoon** When researchers at the US National Institute of Diabetes and Digestive and Kidney Diseases (NIDDK) compared more than 6,000 morning test results with a similar number of afternoon results, the average readings differed by as much as 5mg/dl (equivalent to 0.28mmol/l). The researchers concluded that up to half the cases of diabetes that would be caught in the morning were being missed in the afternoon. One reason for the discrepancy is that people tested in the morning typically go for longer than 13 hours on average without food, while those tested in the afternoon fast for only about 7 hours. The NIDDK is now suggesting that different diagnosis standards be developed based on when the test is taken.

Random plasma glucose test

This test is also referred to as a casual plasma glucose test. Both 'casual' and 'random' refer to the fact that you can take the test at any time. No fasting is necessary.

WHAT THE STUDIES SHOW

A recent analysis found that women with menstrual cycles that are very irregular or long (more than 40 days) were about twice as likely to develop Type 2 diabetes as women with normal periods. Obese women with irregular periods faced a nearly four-fold increase in diabetes risk. One possible reason is that women with menstrual irregularities are prone to polycystic ovary syndrome, a hormone disorder characterized by insulin resistance and thus linked to diabetes. The researchers advise women with irregular periods to reduce their risk with weight control and exercise.

How it works The procedure is fairly similar to the fasting glucose test. Blood is drawn and sent to a lab for analysis. But when the results come back, the bar for diagnosis is higher because it is assumed that you may have had glucose from food in your blood. In healthy people, normal insulin response usually keeps blood sugar under 7.8mmol/l even after eating. If a random plasma glucose test shows a blood-sugar level of 11.1mmol/l or higher and you are fatigued, thirsty or are urinating frequently, it is quite likely that you have diabetes.

Why it is used Because it requires no preparation, the random plasma glucose test is often carried out as part of routine blood tests. Your first hint at a diabetes diagnosis may therefore emerge as the result of an annual physical check-up rather than any special effort on your part.

Get confirmation Don't take a single positive result from a random plasma glucose test as the final word. Doctors will almost always insist on confirming such results using a more exact test designed specifically to detect diabetes.

Oral glucose tolerance test

This test is regarded as the gold standard for making a clear-cut diagnosis of diabetes because it assesses blood-sugar levels under highly controlled circumstances, so the results are extremely reliable. But because it is so exacting (and expensive and relatively time-consuming), patients and doctors alike sometimes find the oral glucose tolerance test, or OGTT, to be a less desirable one.

How it works As with the fasting plasma glucose test, you must fast for at least 8 hours beforehand. But in this case, that is only the start. When you get to your test, blood is drawn to provide a point of comparison for additional blood samples that will be drawn at hourly intervals for 3 hours. After the first blood draw, you drink a super-sweet solution containing about 75g of sugar (about three times sweeter than an average soft drink). Each subsequent blood draw helps to plot a picture of how your body handles glucose over time. Results are compared to a normal range at each measure, but the 2-hour mark is especially critical: if your blood-glucose levels at that point are 11.1mmol/l or higher, you definitely have diabetes.

Why it is used A more exact test is sometimes needed when results from other tests are less conclusive than your doctor would like. Let's say you have a strong family history of diabetes and are experiencing obvious symptoms but neither form of plasma glucose test has confirmed a diagnosis. Or a random plasma glucose test comes back showing glucose levels higher than 11.1mmol/l but you have no symptoms. In such cases, your doctor will fall back on the gold standard for an unequivocal result. A version of the oral glucose tolerance test is also the preferred tool for detecting gestational diabetes, although the diagnostic criteria are slightly different for pregnant women.

➲ **Watch what you ingest before the test** Because of the test's sensitivity, OGTT results can easily be skewed by foreign substances in the blood. In particular, you should be sure to inform your doctor if you are taking any kind of medication – including birth-control pills – or herbal or nutritional supplements, since they may boost blood-sugar levels.

Talk of other tests

The three tests summarized above (and in the box, right) – the fasting plasma glucose test, the random plasma glucose test and the oral glucose tolerance test – are the trinity on which doctors commonly depend in order to make a definitive diagnosis. But you may have heard about other tests for measuring blood sugar. Some of these are discussed in Chapter 3, but most are not – and in some cases, should not be – relied upon to arrive at a diagnosis.

DIABETES BY NUMBERS

It is important to know for sure whether or not you have diabetes. Doctors make the determination based on any one of the following measures:

TEST: FASTING PLASMA GLUCOSE

What it does: Measures glucose in blood after an 8 to 10-hour fast

You have diabetes if: Your reading is 7mmol/l or higher in two separate tests taken on two different days

TEST: RANDOM PLASMA GLUCOSE

What it does: Measures glucose in blood at any time, including after eating

You have diabetes if: Your reading is 11.1mmol/l or higher and you have symptoms of diabetes

TEST: ORAL GLUCOSE TOLERANCE

What it does: Following an 8-hour fast, measures blood glucose before and after you swallow a high-glucose solution

You have diabetes if: Your reading is 11.1mmol/l or higher

Glycated haemoglobin Also called the haemoglobin A1c test, this is sometimes carried out after a diagnosis to get a better idea of your blood-sugar patterns, but it is most commonly used to monitor your condition as you continue living with your disease. The main advantage of this test is that, rather than assessing your blood sugar at a specific point in time, it surveys what has happened to your blood-sugar patterns over two or three months by looking at glucose deposits on a specific type of cell. (See pages 80–81 for more information.)

Urine test Do doctors always have to use a needle? It is tempting to wonder why, if glucose appears in urine, they can't simply measure that. High glucose levels in urine can indeed be an indication of diabetes. But the amount of glucose in the blood needed to raise glucose levels in urine varies from one person to the next, and sugary urine does not always correlate with high blood sugar. So a urine test is not sufficiently accurate.

Finger prick Tests in which a small drop of blood is squeezed from a fingertip on to a special test strip that is read by a glucose meter are a mainstay of home monitoring for many people with diabetes.

While these tests give reasonably accurate results for daily tracking, they do not offer the degree of precision needed to make a diagnosis that will affect the rest of your life. Bear in mind that do-it-yourself monitoring devices are reckoned to be between 10 and 15 per cent less accurate than professional laboratory tests – a problem that is primarily attributable to human error. Older, non-digital devices in which the test strip is compared visually to a colour chart are even less reliable.

WHEN TO TEST FOR DIABETES

As yet Britain has no national screening programme resourced through the NHS. However, Diabetes UK recommends regular three-yearly screening for Type 2 diabetes for people who fall into two or more of the following risk categories.

- white people aged over 40 and people from Black, Asian and minority ethnic groups aged over 25 with two or more of the following factors:

  - a parent or sibling with diabetes
  - overweight with a BMI of 25 and above and who have a sedentary lifestyle
  - ischaemic heart disease, cerebrovascular disease, peripheral vascular disease or high blood pressure

- women who have had gestational diabetes which has tested normal following delivery (screen at one year post-partum and then three-yearly)

- women with polycystic ovary syndrome (POS) who are obese with a BMI of more than 30

- those known to have impaired glucose tolerance or impaired fasting glycaemia

- those who have experienced any of the symptoms of Type 2 diabetes (pronounced thirst, frequent urination, tiredness, slow wound healing, tingling hands or feet, weight loss, blurred vision, genital itching).

'Almost' diabetes: Impaired glucose tolerance

The diagnostic thresholds for diabetes seem so clear and complete. Yet there is a grey area in which blood-sugar numbers don't add up to diabetes but don't indicate normal glucose levels, either. This almost-but-not-quite state of affairs used to be called borderline diabetes, but some doctors dislike that term as it seems to dance around the critical yes-or-no question of whether or not you really have diabetes. Instead, in-between numbers are now considered a distinct condition called impaired glucose tolerance, or IGT – another way of saying that your cells are becoming insulin resistant. You have IGT if:

▶ Fasting plasma glucose test results fall between 6.1mmol/l and 6.9mmol/l on two or more tests.

▶ Oral glucose tolerance test results at the two-hour mark fall between 7.7mmol/l and 11mmol/l.

Having IGT does not automatically mean that diabetes is around the corner. One study found that some 17 per cent of those aged 40–65 have IGT. A follow-up study found that 15 per cent went on to develop Type 2 diabetes, 22 per cent remained glucose intolerant and 53 per cent improved. Other estimates give the rate of conversion from IGT to Type 2 diabetes as from 2 per cent to 11 per cent. What makes the difference? A strong family history or membership of an at-risk ethnic group raises your risk. But just as important, the more overweight and sedentary you are, the more likely it is that IGT will eventually develop into something more serious.

A chance for change A diagnosis of IGT is really a window of opportunity; think of it as an early warning that not every person destined for diabetes receives.

The potential power of this opportunity was brought home with the publication of results from a major US clinical trial, called the Diabetes Prevention Program, in early 2002. This study from the National Institute of Diabetes and Digestive and Kidney Diseases tried two main approaches to prevent

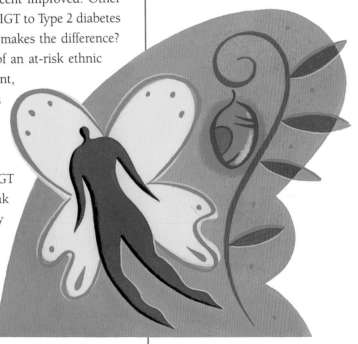

diabetes in people with IGT: lifestyle modifications – diet and exercise – and an oral medication (metformin) used to treat Type 2 diabetes. A third group took placebo (dummy) pills instead of the real drug and made no lifestyle changes.

The study found that over the course of three years, people in the lifestyle group reduced their incidence of diabetes by an incredible 58 per cent – about twice as much as those who made no changes, and far more than those who only took the drug (whose incidence dropped by 31 per cent). These remarkable findings show that taking action can reverse IGT and may allow you to avoid the onset of diabetes if you are at risk.

When diabetes becomes an emergency

What if you simply decided to ignore your diabetes? Of course, you are not going to do that. But it's important to note that – while many complications of diabetes develop slowly over many years – blood sugar that is either too high or too low (due to treatment with insulin) can have immediate effects that may quickly prove dangerous, and in some cases even fatal. Fortunately, these complications can generally be treated easily by either you or your doctor. And close monitoring of your blood-sugar levels can prevent them from sneaking up on you. Later chapters will discuss some of these subjects in more detail, but you will understand diabetes better if you have a working knowledge of these three conditions.

Diabetic ketoacidosis This is mostly a problem for Type 1 patients, whose insulin deficit – barring treatment with supplemental insulin – allows no glucose at all into cells. In order to obtain energy, glucose-deprived cells instead start to burn fat. The fat-burning process, however, produces highly acidic by-products known as ketones. When ketones build up in the blood (a condition known as ketoacidosis), they can cause shortness of breath, mental confusion and vomiting. Eventually, diabetic ketoacidosis, or DKA, can put you into a coma and even cause death.

DKA is rare these days, thanks to insulin treatment and easy-to-use self-monitoring devices, but it is a medical emergency when it occurs. To treat it, doctors immediately replace fluids. This helps to flush out acid and make sure that you receive adequate insulin, which can quickly remove you from danger.

Hyperosmolar syndrome This condition is somewhat similar to diabetic ketoacidosis in that it is caused by extremely high blood sugar. But it affects primarily people with Type 2 diabetes who don't know they have the disease or are not monitoring it effectively. With diabetic hyperosmolar syndrome (DHS), blood sugar becomes so concentrated that it causes the blood to become thick and syrupy. As the body reacts by expelling sugar from the body in the urine, you can become severely dehydrated and experience symptoms such as cramps, rapid pulse, confusion, and even convulsions and coma. Treatment involves fluid replenishment and insulin.

Hypoglycaemia Diabetes is not always about high blood sugar. In fact, the most common acute complication of diabetes is blood sugar that falls too low – a condition known as hypoglycaemia. It is most common in people with Type 1 because blood sugar is most likely to drop from taking too much insulin. But hypoglycaemia occurs in Type 2 patients as well, when glucose levels ebb as a result of insulin or drug treatments, perhaps made worse by other factors, such as going too long without eating.

Hypoglycaemia is rarely life threatening in itself. But it is very unpleasant and can be dangerous because its symptoms – including mental confusion, rapid heartbeat, sweating and double vision – may impair your ability to drive, operate machinery or do your job. Hypoglycaemia must be dealt with at once. Most cases are mild and can be treated by getting some sugar into the system by, say, drinking a half cup of a non-diet soft drink.

CAN DIABETES BE CURED?

Doctors often say that you either have diabetes or you don't, based on your blood-sugar levels. But let's say you have Type 2 and you do everything right. You change your diet, start an exercise plan, lose a significant amount of weight and bring your blood-sugar numbers back to normal. Do you still have diabetes?

In one sense, Type 2 diabetes can indeed be cured if all the measures that define it indicate that the condition at issue – high blood sugar – is no longer present. But this suggests that you can carry on with your life as if you never had diabetes – or that you won't have to worry about developing it in the future. And that would be a mistake.

Diabetes is considered a disease you have for life because, while you can keep it under control and live a normal life, the fact that you are controlling it is significant. The risk of diabetes reasserting itself never really goes away. If you were to stop controlling it – went back to a sedentary lifestyle and a poor diet – your diabetes would inevitably return. Even if you continue with your healthy habits, it is possible that your condition will change as you get older.

Having diabetes is like parenting: Even when your children grow up and move away from home, you still have children. Likewise, even after you have managed to get your diabetes under control, you still have the disease.

The agenda for action

By now, two points should be clear. First, diabetes is a serious, complex illness that has the potential to degrade your overall health in a wide variety of ways. But second, it is well within your power to treat the underlying problem, prevent many – if not all – of the major complications, and live a stimulating, productive and enjoyable life. In order to do this, you will need to implement a big-picture plan in which you:

⟳ **Become a control freak** No, you don't need to be obsessed about your blood sugar. But studies have made it clear that using close monitoring to help you keep your blood sugar as near to a normal range as possible can dramatically reduce your risk of complications arising from diabetes.

⟳ **Lose weight** Just as being overweight is the biggest contributor to the vast majority of diabetes cases, shedding excess pounds is the single most important move you can make in order to gain control over your disease.

⟳ **Eat smarter** The right diet is the first step towards controlling your weight. It is also a tool for managing your blood-sugar levels. This does not mean that you have to stop eating your favourite foods or subscribe to an eccentric eating plan. Instead, you should simply follow a healthy, balanced diet which provides a variety of foods in moderate proportions.

⟳ **Get moving** Equally important to your weight and blood-sugar levels is exercise. As with diet, no extreme measures are necessary. You simply have to get your heart and muscles into action with moderate exercises that are relatively easy to do – and keep doing them. Finding a routine to which you can commit yourself over the long term is the key.

⟳ **Take advantage of treatment** Insulin is an important – even lifesaving – beginning, but a wide range of other medications and treatments

SHOOTING DOWN DIABETES MYTHS

Considering all the factors involved with diabetes, there is ample scope for misinformation. Here are some of the more persistent misconceptions.

Myth If you develop diabetes, you can never eat sugar again.
Truth People with diabetes can eat sweets, but sugary treats must be part of a careful meal plan (as they should be for people without diabetes).

Myth I have just a touch of diabetes.
Truth Either you have diabetes or you don't. Even if your Type 2 case doesn't require insulin injections (Type 1 always does), it still demands medical attention and careful lifestyle choices.

Myth I feel fine, so my blood sugar is fine.
Truth High or low blood sugar does not always produce symptoms. Regular monitoring is the only way to know for certain where you stand.

Myth I'm a pro at self-management; check-ups are simply a waste of my time.
Truth Your treatment programme is never a done deal. Thanks to ongoing research, the medical community is constantly learning more about this complex condition and how best to deal with it. The way to keep up to date with new developments is to keep up your regular visits to the doctor.

Myth If I don't need insulin or drugs, my diabetes isn't serious.
Truth Diabetes is always serious. Even if diet and exercise keep your blood sugar in check, your cells are still insulin resistant and your condition could get worse if you don't control it.

are available today which in some cases may even eliminate the need for insulin. While diet and exercise can go a long way, medical care can make the difference between slowing the progression of the disease and stopping it in its tracks.

In the following chapters, you will find out how you can use all five of these strategies to bring down your blood-sugar levels and help you to lead a full and active life.

Monitoring and measuring

Controlling diabetes is all about vigilance. You can't know if your blood-sugar levels are where they should be unless you check them regularly. The idea of taking several blood samples a day may seem dreary, but sophisticated tools make the task easier than you'd imagine, and they are getting better all the time. Along with results from other tests, your blood-sugar numbers are an all-important window on your disease and a key to managing it – and living with it – successfully.

THREE

3

Tests: the key to success

Everything that you do to treat your diabetes – whether it's exercising, adopting a healthy diet, using insulin or taking medications – serves one primary objective: controlling your blood-sugar levels. But how do you know if you are managing your blood sugar well? Some people rely exclusively on their symptoms to determine how well they are doing.

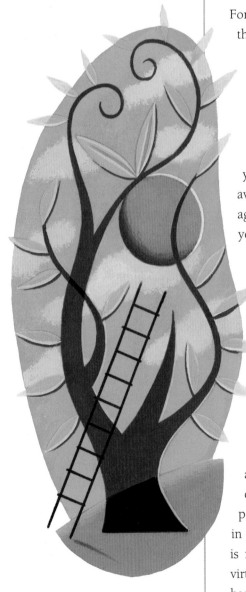

For example, they watch for thirst and fatigue to tell them when their glucose levels are high, or trembling and dizziness to tell them when the levels are low. But gauging your blood sugar by symptoms alone is highly unreliable – and potentially dangerous. Blood sugar can easily soar too high or dip too low without sending any obvious alarm signals, potentially leading to irreversible organ damage.

Fortunately, advances in blood-testing technology allow you to track your blood sugar in ways that were not fully available to people with diabetes as recently as a generation ago. There are two basic methods, and both should be part of your management plan:

▶ Test your own blood at home (or anywhere else) using such convenient devices as test strips and blood-glucose meters – a method known as self-monitoring of blood glucose, or SMBG.

▶ See your doctor regularly for more comprehensive assessment, especially a haemoglobin test that reveals blood-glucose patterns over weeks or months.

Information about your blood-sugar levels is crucial, and the more precise it is, the better. The more you know about the way your blood sugar behaves under specific circumstances, and the impact it has on your health, the more power you wield – power to control your glucose levels and, in turn, your life as a whole. Working without this information is rather like walking in pitch darkness without a torch: it's virtually impossible to know when you're veering off course or heading for a fall. Conscientiously monitoring your own blood glucose – and following up with regular checkups – shines light on your diabetes, providing you with a clear perspective and allowing you to stride ahead with more freedom and confidence.

Worth the effort

Without a doubt, regular monitoring and measuring require a certain amount of dedication and discipline. Some people find it difficult. A recent survey by Diabetes UK of testing habits among its members showed that 11 per cent of those treated with tablets did not test their blood-glucose levels at all – a figure that rose to 17 per cent among those treated with exercise and diet alone. Yet numerous studies have shown that the people who fare best with diabetes are those who do the most to control their blood sugar with the help of careful monitoring.

The most important study in the UK is the United Kingdom Prospective Diabetes Study (UKPDS), completed in 1997. For 20 years it followed more than 5,000 patients newly diagnosed with Type 2 diabetes in 23 clinical centres based in England, Northern Ireland and Scotland. The study showed that tight blood glucose control reduces the risk of major diabetic eye disease by a quarter and early kidney damage by one-third. An earlier study in the USA, the Diabetes Control and Complications Trial (DCCT), which ended in 1993, followed more than 1,400 people with Type 1 diabetes for 10 years, comparing complications in those who closely monitored and controlled their blood glucose with those who took a less vigilant approach. The results showed that close monitoring and control reduced the risk of developing eye disease by 50 per cent, nerve disease by 60 per cent, kidney disease by 50 per cent and cardiovascular disease by 35 per cent.

Inspired by these findings, doctors have developed a form of treatment known as intensive therapy, in which patients, particularly those taking insulin or other drugs, tightly control their blood sugar by carefully adjusting injections, food intake, exercise and medications according to results from very frequent self-monitoring. It is a disciplined approach that may not be right for everyone (and in some Type 2 patients, especially those not taking insulin, may not be necessary). But the idea that everyone with diabetes should monitor and control their blood sugar as best they can has gained wide acceptance. In fact, the US and UKPDS studies show that any consistent reduction in blood glucose reduces the risk of complications.

No matter how much or little testing you do, every bit of information you gather is valuable. You can use this data to:

▶ See how different foods affect your blood sugar, allowing you to adjust your diet as needed to keep glucose in check.

▶ Detect (or rule out) hypoglycaemia – that is, low blood sugar, the most common treatment complication – so that you can deal with it quickly.

▶ Track the effect of medications so that you and your doctor can fine-tune dosages.

▶ Understand how blood-sugar levels swing when you are taking insulin or when you are ill, exercising or drinking alcohol so you can take steps to bring them back in line.

▶ Provide your doctor with a history of day-to-day blood-sugar changes, allowing your entire medical team to give you better-informed treatment advice.

Setting blood-sugar goals

What blood-sugar readings should you aim for? The starting point is to recall what is normal. In people without diabetes, the pancreas releases just the right amount of insulin when it is needed, allowing the body's cells to absorb glucose from the bloodstream and thus keep blood sugar steady at levels that rarely fall below around 4mmol/l or go above around 7mmol/l, even after eating. When you have diabetes, blood-sugar levels can swing erratically from, say, 2.8mmol/l before a meal to around 28mmol/l after eating – or points lower, higher, or in between, depending on the type of diabetes you have, how well your pancreas functions, and many other factors.

Your goal is to bring these wild swings under control and keep your blood sugar as close to a normal range as possible. According to Diabetes UK, you should strive to keep your blood glucose levels at:

▶ 4–7mmol/l before meals

▶ no higher than 10mmol/l after meals

These are average goals for adults that will probably work for you, but they may not be appropriate for everybody. For example, glucose targets for children are sometimes less stringent, while those for pregnant women may be tighter. Your goals may also depend on whether you are suffering from any complications. The best strategy is to discuss with your doctor which blood glucose target levels are right for you.

How often should you test?

How often you need to test depends mainly on what type of diabetes you have and how you are treating it.

For people with Type I If you have Type 1 diabetes and take insulin, you are particularly sensitive to blood-glucose swings because, with the pancreas out of commission, you rely on your insulin injections to keep blood sugar in line. This dependence makes you especially vulnerable to hypoglycaemia, so you should take blood-sugar readings several times a day, usually in tandem with insulin injections before each meal and at bedtime.

Why test before meals and not afterwards? You already know that food will make your blood glucose rise and that your insulin injection will handle it. By testing before the meal

Take-charge tips

Outside of your regular testing regime, it may pay to do some extra self-monitoring at certain times to protect yourself from dangerous blood-sugar highs and, especially, lows. Consider taking additional self-samples:

➲ Before you get behind the wheel for a long motorway drive.

➲ When you make a change in your diet, such as eating more or less food than usual at certain times of day.

➲ When you make a significant change in your insulin treatment.

➲ When you take a medication to treat something other than diabetes.

➲ Before you go into a meeting, make a presentation or take part in a conference with your boss, clients or colleagues.

A testing timetable

You will need to work out a self-monitoring schedule with your doctor based on your individual needs, but these guidelines provide a place to start.

SITUATION	SUGGESTED TEST SCHEDULE
You have Type 1 diabetes and take insulin.	Four times daily, before meals and at bedtime.
You have Type 2 diabetes and take no insulin or medication.	Twice daily, when you get up in the morning and before dinner.
You have Type 2 diabetes and take insulin.	Four times daily, before meals and at bedtime.
You have Type 2 diabetes and take medication.	Three times daily, when you get up, before dinner and at bedtime.

(and at bedtime), you can see how well the amount of insulin in your previous injection maintained blood-glucose levels between meals – the most important consideration. This does not mean that you should completely ignore what happens after eating: Your doctor may also advise you to take readings after meals and, occasionally, in the middle of the night in order to gain additional insight into your blood-sugar patterns.

For people with Type 2 If you have Type 2 diabetes, it is more difficult to generalize about your testing needs. You should discuss it with your doctor. If you are managing your diabetes with just diet and exercise, your blood-sugar levels are probably fairly stable and you may need relatively little testing – maybe twice daily, when you get up in the morning and just before dinner. (Avoiding tests is a good reason to do everything you can to manage your diabetes through lifestyle changes.) Once you understand your blood-sugar patterns, you may find that they don't change very much, and your doctor may allow you to reduce the frequency of your testing even further – perhaps to three or four times a week.

If you are taking insulin, your testing schedule will probably need to mirror the pattern a Type 1 person follows: four times daily, maybe more, depending on your situation. If you are taking medication, you should test at least twice a day. You may need to test more often, especially at the beginning of your regime, when your doctor will want to track how the drug affects your blood sugar.

For people with gestational diabetes If you have gestational diabetes or become pregnant when you have diabetes, keeping blood-sugar levels tightly controlled is especially important for both you and the baby. This means that you will probably have to test your blood two or three times a day – including after meals.

Five steps to success

It is natural to want to see your blood-glucose levels fall into a healthier range as soon as you start treatment. But while it is tempting and can be motivating to set ambitious goals, you must also be realistic. Failing to reach your ideal blood-sugar goals may leave you feeling frustrated and even depressed, which can sap your motivation. To remove the failure factor:

1. Start with no specific goals in mind. Instead, just gather the numbers to show you and your doctor where your blood sugar normally falls, and work from there.

2. If your typical range is excessively high, don't feel that you have to aim for ideal numbers immediately. If they are unrealistic for you, you won't meet them, which will erode your self-confidence and sense of control for the long term.

3. Work with your doctor to set goals which – even if they are higher than the average ideal for adults – are an improvement for you.

4. As you achieve greater control and start bringing down your average blood-sugar levels, consult with your doctor to set new goals, gradually working your way towards healthier numbers.

5. Don't expect to be perfect. Sometimes you will have disappointing readings for no apparent reason.

WHAT THE STUDIES SHOW

Are the blood-sugar records you share with your doctor accurate? One study in which meters with hidden memory were used found that the numbers patients jot down in diaries at home are often lower than the real results. Inaccuracies can easily occur if you forget to write down numbers immediately and have to recall them later on. But there's also a natural tendency to want to make a good report to your doctor. Researchers suggest that some diabetes patients feel guilty if they don't meet their blood-sugar goals or fail to test as often as they should and fudge the numbers to make them look better. But owning up to the truth does the most good in the long run. Discrepancies present a flawed picture of your condition and defeat the purpose of keeping careful records.

Testing your blood sugar

Granted, the job of self-monitoring is not much fun. New devices promise to make the task more pleasant in the near future but, for the moment, it can be difficult accepting that you need to draw blood, and to do it you need to prick yourself – normally in the finger – with a sharp instrument. Still, most people with diabetes find that they soon come to terms with the routine. Here's how to do it.

1. Wash your hands before you prick your finger. Some doctors say this is not crucial if your hands are reasonably clean because people almost never get infections from a finger prick. But washing is still a good idea in case there is something on the skin (sugar residue from a piece of chewing gum, say) that might affect your results. Be sure to dry your hands thoroughly after washing, since excess moisture may also affect your results.

2. Prick your finger with a pin-like (but not all that painful) device called a lancet to draw a drop of blood. You may prefer to prick yourself at other sites instead: the forearms and earlobes are sometimes used as alternatives. However, the majority of people find the fingertips easier, the main reason being that you will probably need to squeeze the targeted site to get a good drop of blood, and that is easy to do with a fingertip.

3. Let the droplet of blood fall on to the pad of a test strip or, if your meter has a built-in test strip, directly on to the meter's sensor. But avoid touching the pad with your finger because it may contaminate the strip with skin oils. (Some test-strip systems are designed to let you touch the blood to the strip if you have trouble keeping your hand steady enough for an accurate drip.) Follow the meter's instructions; with some meters, it is necessary to wipe the excess blood off the test strip.

4. Put the test strip into your blood-glucose meter (if it is not built in). Wait for the meter to make its calculations then check your reading in the digital display.

(5) Write down the number. You might find it easy to over-look this step, but it is probably the most important. If you are trying to develop a record and identify patterns, all the trouble you took to get the number is worth nothing if you don't record it. Even if your meter automatically registers your results, it is a good idea to keep your own record.

Four essential testing tools

This may sound strange, but there has never been a better time to have diabetes. For one reason: there have never been more tools to help you to monitor and manage your condition. The first self-monitoring tests did not appear until the 1970s, and they consisted of test strips that indicated blood-glucose levels by changing into a colour that you had to compare to a colour chart for your result.

Anyone who has painted a room and found that the colour did not seem to match the sample swatch will appreciate that a lot of guesswork could go into matching test-strip colours to colour charts. This kind of colour-match monitoring is still available and can be useful on occasions – say, if your digital monitor's batteries die. But for day-to-day monitoring, there is a better way. The array of devices on offer can be daunting. But rest assured that the basic task is not difficult and the range of choice means you should be able to find equipment to meet your specific needs.

Looking at lancets

Technically, the lancet is the sharp instrument that punctures your skin, while the handheld unit that holds the lancet is called a lancing device. Lancets are disposable both for sanitary reasons and because they can become blunt. Some experts recommend that they be thrown out after each use to ensure that you always use a sterile one, but many people with diabetes (including some doctors) think this is wasteful – not to mention expensive – and re-use their lancets. It goes without saying that you should never use somebody else's lancet.

Many glucose meters come supplied with a lancing device or even with one built in, but you don't have to use what the meter manufacturer provides. Instead, you should find an instrument that is comfortable for you. (Theoretically, you can use lancets by themselves, but a lancing device is easier to manipulate with either hand; it is also less painful to use, being spring-loaded so that penetration is very quick.) Because your skin may not be as thick as, say, the callused hands of a construction worker, most devices allow you to make at least one or two adjustments to how deep the lancet penetrates your skin. Diabetes UK has an extensive list of lancets and lancet devices available in the UK with information on their compatibility. The list is updated as new products come on to the market.

Whichever unit you buy, you will continually need to replenish your stock of lancets. Lancets are not always interchangeable from one device to the next, and costs can vary, so check out lancet price and availability before you buy the lancing device.

Buying a blood-glucose meter

Meter technology and features change rapidly, and the variety of meters to choose from can be bewildering. However, variety also means you should easily be able to find a unit that matches your particular needs and preferences.

Most blood-glucose meters work in one of two ways. Some are still based on a colour-changing process in which glucose in the blood reacts with enzymes on the test strip. But now the meter goes on to read the intensity of the colour and shows you a number in the unit's display window – there is no need to try to match colours by eye. Other meters work by detecting minuscule electrical currents created by the enzyme reactions, with the strength of electron flow depending on the amount of glucose present in the blood. Again, the results are displayed on the meter's digital readout.

To sort through the multitude of meters and find one that is right for you, check first with your doctor, who may steer you towards a particular unit based on experience, reports from other patients, or compatibility with his or her own record-keeping systems. Diabetes UK has information about all the blood glucose meters available in the UK. When evaluating them, you should consider a number of factors, including:

Ease of use Meters come in different sizes and shapes – some as small as credit cards – and you should choose one that is comfortable for you to use. Some require bigger drops of blood

Figuring out features

Manufacturers try to make every meter convenient, but what is handy for you might be an obstacle for somebody else. Here's how several major features stack up:

MAIN FEATURE	PROS	CONS
Built-in memory	Allows you to track your results over time. Some units also automatically average your numbers.	Some meters store as few as 10 readings – not enough if you test four times a day and see your doctor only once a month. Aim for at least a 100-reading memory.
Download capability	Can feed your readings directly into your doctor's database or into diabetes-management software, which can generate useful graphs and charts.	Unit may not be compatible with your doctor's software. May cost more than simpler meters.
It talks	A voice takes you through the self-monitoring process step-by-step to help ensure that you use the proper technique for accurate results.	Annoying. Once you know the process, the voice may prove unnecessary. May cost more than most silent meters.
Siphon-action test strips	Wicking blood up into the test strip is easier than dropping blood down on to it.	Test strips – the major expense in a glucose-monitoring system – may cost more.

for an accurate result than others do, which may be an issue if you have poor circulation. If you have vision problems, look for a meter that features larger displays.

The information you need How much you need to know may depend first of all on which type of diabetes you have. If you are Type 1, or Type 2 taking insulin or medication, you will probably be taking more readings than if you have Type 2 and control your diabetes through diet and exercise. If you are testing frequently, you may want a meter with a built-in memory to help you to keep track of the dozens of results you will accumulate between visits to your doctor. Some units also have data ports that allow you to download this information into diabetes-management software on a personal computer. On the other hand, if you are testing only a couple of times a day or even less frequently, these extra features may be superfluous.

Practical details Points that seem trivial at the outset can become more important to you the more you use your meter. Some units, for example, use standard batteries available at any pharmacy or supermarket, while others take less common (and

METER MISCOMMUNICATION

Glucose tests conducted by your doctor in the surgery (such as the fasting plasma glucose test) measure blood sugar differently from the way that most home meters do. So your home-based readings may be 10 to 15 per cent lower than those your doctor produces. One set of numbers is not more accurate than the other, but you should guard against confusion over the discrepancy, which – if you were to compare the numbers directly – could make you think that your glucose levels are better than they really are.

Why the difference? Many home-based meters measure whole blood – that is, blood that drips, unprocessed, straight out of your body and on to a test strip. Whole blood consists of several ingredients, including plasma (a fluid) and red blood cells. Laboratory tests on your doctor's test samples separate these elements and test only plasma for blood sugar. And blood sugar tends to be slightly more concentrated in plasma than in whole blood.

Some home meters now automatically translate whole-blood numbers into plasma numbers, but there is no need to worry if yours doesn't. When looking at your home-test numbers, your doctor will convert the readings so they are consistent and factor all this into your treatment.

often more expensive) batteries that may be harder to find. A few meters do not even have replaceable batteries, so you have to buy a new meter when yours dies. These units usually last for thousands of readings, but how many thousands will vary from one model to the next. Consider cleaning as well: some meters are easier to maintain than others. Also find out how fast the meter produces a reading: most deliver in less than a minute, but the difference between, say, 40 seconds and 5 can seem significant if you are late for an appointment.

Cost The price of a blood glucose meter varies enormously, from £7 to around £200. The best source of up-to-date information on meters is the Diabetes UK website.

Replacing test strips

In the UK doctors prescribe test strips and lancets on NHS prescriptions. More often than not, the strips are designed to work with your meter and are not useable with other devices. Make sure that the test strips you need are readily available in pharmacies. Generic test strips are available for some systems, especially those based on colour change.

The all-important logbook

Most self-monitoring systems include a logbook in which you can record your results. Recording your blood-sugar levels so that you can track patterns is one of the main reasons you self-test. If you don't like the log that comes with your meter, your doctor may have one more suited to your needs with, for instance, space to write information about medication, insulin or other tests. You can obtain new pages from your doctor or by writing to the meter manufacturer, using the address in your instructions. Alternatively, you can use a notebook to record your numbers (although logbooks provide ready-made columns that may prove more convenient and legible).

Whatever kind of log you use, the crucial thing is to put your numbers down on paper – including the date and time of each reading. Don't simply settle for numbers, though. Remember, you are looking for patterns and associations, making yourself the subject of a little scientific study – and good scientists take plenty of notes. Write down anything unusual about what you eat – any meals that were out of the ordinary, how much you exercise – for example if you have taken a great deal of exercise one day, whether or not you are feeling sick, how much stress you are under. These are the observations that even the best glucose meter cannot store in its memory.

Take-charge tips

Being a 'good bleeder' is a blessing – strange as it may sound – that not everyone shares. If you find that getting blood out of your finger is akin to getting it out of a stone, try these steps to encourage a better flow:

➲ Before testing, do some light exercise or take a warm bath to boost circulation to your fingertips. Or, if your hands are cold (which indicates low blood flow in your fingers), fill a basin with hot water and let your hands soak for a few minutes.

➲ Swing your arms to force blood towards your fingers, then dangle your arms at your sides and shake your hands.

➲ If you have an adjustable lancet, set it for deeper penetration. There is no gain in trying to spare yourself pain with a low setting if you have to repeat the prick to produce any blood.

➲ After pricking, don't try to squeeze blood out right away. Instead, hold your hand below the level of your heart and relax for a moment to let blood pool at the lancing site.

➲ As a last resort, try putting a rubber band on the base of your finger where it connects to your hand to prevent blood from flowing out – then remove the band as soon as you get the blood you need.

Always take your logbook with you when you see your doctor. Although he or she is unlikely to want to page through it all (especially if your meter downloads raw data into the doctor's computer), but if he or she asks you a question based on your numbers – 'Was anything unusual going on two weeks ago Friday?' – your logbook might provide you with valuable clues.

Seven steps to reliable results

To do their job, glucose-monitoring systems must be accurate, but even more important, they need to be consistent. (Even if your readings are off by a certain amount, if you know this and the degree of error is always the same, you can still get a good sense of your blood-sugar levels.) To achieve reliable results, follow these tips:

(1) **Calibrate** Each batch of test strips you buy may have slight chemical variations from other batches, and these can affect your readings, so you need to match your meter to each set of strips before using them. Some meters do this automatically; others require you to go through a calibration procedure each time you open a new box of strips. Check the instructions for either your meter or your test strips.

(2) **Check your strips** If your readings seem strangely inconsistent from one day to the next or out of tune with how you feel, you may have a faulty batch of test strips. Check the expiry date to see if they are past their use-by date and examine individual packages to make sure that they have not been damaged.

(3) **Run a test** Make sure that your meter is accurate by periodically testing it with a solution whose glucose level is pre-determined. If your meter is correctly calibrated, its readings should closely match the expected result. (Most meters come with a control solution for this purpose, but if

Take-charge tips

Although it is impossible to avoid the prick of the lancet's tip, you can minimize the discomfort if you:

➲ Use mild soap and warm water instead of alcohol to cleanse hands before testing. Mild soaps dry your hands less and ease stinging, especially if you tend to use the same site. Warm water brings more blood to your fingertips, making it easier to extract a drop.

➲ Use an adjustable lancing device so that you can set the penetration depth to match the toughness of your skin.

➲ Prick on the sides of your fingers, where there are fewer nerve endings but plenty of blood vessels.

➲ Finish up by applying a little lotion on the prick site to soothe your skin and to keep it moist and pliable.

you lose it or run out, you will find a replacement solution at your local pharmacy.)

④ **Compare at your doctor's surgery** Take your meter with you the next time you have a fasting plasma glucose test at your doctor's surgery. The whole-blood reading from your meter should not vary from the plasma reading by more than about 15 per cent.

⑤ **Check your technique** Are you the problem? Review the meter's instructions and think about your technique. Is there anything you are doing that could throw off results? Are your hands clean? Are you touching the strip with your finger? Are you failing to mop up excess blood using materials specified in your meter's instructions?

⑥ **Check the meter** Maybe your meter needs a clean. 'Needs minimal cleaning' does not mean 'never needs cleaning.' Follow the directions regarding what materials to use (or not to use) to clean the device, paying particular attention to the slot where the test strip goes in. Then check the batteries to see if they are still fresh.

⑦ **Call the manufacturer** If your metering results seem consistently wrong and you are unable to resolve the problem yourself, call your unit's customer service hotline. In many cases, the manufacturer will replace an unsatisfactory meter at no charge.

Advances in testing technology

Self-monitoring technology has come a long way, but it is hard to be satisfied with a routine that is painful, no matter how much you might become accustomed to it. Manufacturers have long sought ways to take the sting out of self-testing procedures and have recently made several advances. These do not necessarily eliminate the need for regular self-testing, but they can reduce the number of finger pricks you need or make them more comfortable.

Laser lancet Instead of drawing blood with the sharp point of a traditional steel lancet, a new device called the Lasette uses a single-shot laser beam to make a small hole in the finger to obtain a drop of blood. Many users report experiencing less pain using the device compared to the traditional lancets, although you can still feel it when the laser breaks the skin. The Lasette available in the UK has eight adjustable energy settings to allow for variations in skin thickness, is smaller than a video cassette and weighs less than 250g (9oz). It carries a CE mark, allowing it to be sold in the European Union. The Lasette is unlikely to be available on prescription in the near future, so anyone wanting to use it will have to pay for the device, which costs around £460.

Less-sensitive site Some meters require less blood than the globule you extract from your fingertip using a standard lancet, thanks in part to siphon-style (also known as capillary) test strips that you can touch to the blood. Because there is no need to squeeze out such a big drop of blood, the lancing devices that come with the meters (some units combine the lancing device and the meter into one product) allow you to break the skin in places, such as the forearm, that are less sensitive than the fingertips. Some diabetes-care professionals say that alternate site testing is less accurate. At times when your blood glucose levels are changing rapidly, such as after a meal or physical activity, it is advisable to test from your finger. Diabetes UK has details of specific alternative site meters. Test strips and lancets for the meters are available on prescription.

No-prick meters The dream is to avoid drawing blood at all, and some devices have moved testing in that direction. The GlucoWatch G2 Biographer uses a sensor worn on the wrist to

measure glucose as it is drawn through the skin with the help of an electric current. The device takes readings of glucose levels automatically up to six times an hour. Alarms can be set to warn the wearer of high or low glucose levels, or if the level will be low in 20 minutes' time. The GlucoWatch G2 Biographer has a memory that can store up to 85,000 records and is intended for home use to supplement, not to replace, information obtained from standard home blood glucose monitoring devices. To ensure continued accuracy, its autosensors must be replaced every 13 hours of monitoring time, and the device must be calibrated against a finger prick blood test each time a new autosensor is used. The GlucoWatch G2 Biographer has carried a CE mark (for sale in the EU) since 1999.

Implants One new device, called the Medtronic MiniMed Continuous Glucose Monitoring System(CGMS), logs a nearly continuous stream of information on blood-glucose levels through a sensor implanted under the skin. The device is used only by hospitals and some diabetes clinics as a one-off to track blood sugar levels over a seven-day period. It is then removed, and healthcare professionals download and read the blood-glucose levels then adjust the care accordingly.

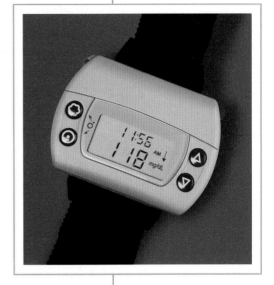

Because the system is expensive, primary care providers are very selective about who they put on this system: it is generally people who are considering using a pump so that the insulin regime can be set up according to the readings obtained by the CGMS.

Eventually researchers hope to be able to keep sensors in the body for longer without their being attacked by the immune system. That could pave the way for combined monitoring and insulin-delivery systems – in effect, an artificial pancreas.

Highs and lows:
why they happen and how to fix them

There would be no need to monitor your blood-sugar levels throughout the day were it not for the inconvenient fact that they change. Figuring out what makes them go up and down is the key to keeping them under control.

Food: the blood-sugar source

Glucose from food causes blood sugar to rise within an hour or two of eating a meal, but the extent and speed of the rise can depend on what you eat and how much – and also on how insulin resistant you are. Testing will help you to gauge your responses to different foods.

➲ **Adjust your meal plan** If the meal plan that you have agreed with your doctor or dietitian fails to keep your blood sugar under control, you may need to go back to the drawing board.

It could be that you are consuming too many total calories in a sitting or eating too many sugars and starches – which raise blood-glucose levels faster and higher than other types of food – at the same time. Mealtime monitoring will help you to determine how your blood sugar changes in response to what you eat, and this will provide your medical team with the information they need to guide you to better choices.

➲ **Be consistent** Using your monitoring data as a guide, try to identify foods that seem better at keeping your blood sugar within your target range. Then try to eat those foods in consistent quantities at the same time every day. The more you control the glucose going into your body, the more you will be able to predict – and control – the rise and fall of your blood sugar.

➲ **Limit alcohol** Try to limit your alcohol intake to one or two drinks a day, preferably with food. Alcohol lowers blood glucose, putting you at risk of hypoglycaemia. And mixed drinks are usually high in sugar and calories.

HANDLING HYPOGLYCAEMIA

If monitoring reveals that your blood sugar has dropped below 4mmol/l your glucose levels are too low and you are in danger of hypoglycaemia. Don't wait for such symptoms as mental confusion, rapid heartbeat, sweating and double vision to occur before you act – they are often triggered only when blood sugar drops dangerously low. Instead, take immediate action.

Eat First of all, consume some fast-acting carbohydrate to get glucose into the blood as quickly as possible. Examples include:

- Five or six sweets
- 50g (1¾oz) chocolate bar
- Three or four glucose tablets
- Half a cup of a sugary drink
- Half a cup of fruit juice

Rest Take it easy for 15 minutes or so while the carbohydrate goes to work.

Test Take another reading to see whether your glucose levels have improved. If you are still below 4mmol/l, eat another snack, rest again for 15 minutes, and take another reading. If your glucose levels have risen to an acceptable level but you have an hour or more before your next scheduled meal, eat another small snack (a few crackers, for example) which will help to tide you over.

Consider medication If your meter readings indicate that you are having trouble keeping your blood sugar within the target range through diet and exercise alone, you may be a good candidate for drug intervention, most likely with an oral antidiabetic drug, such as acarbose (Glucobay), as opposed to injections of insulin.

Exercise: the glucose gobbler

Moving your muscles increases the body's engine revs, boosting its fuel consumption. As a result, glucose levels tend to drop when you are physically active. Overall, this is a good thing, and monitoring can provide insight into ways in which you can strategically use exercise to lower your blood sugar. Be sure to discuss with your doctor an appropriate exercise plan that will form part of your overall approach to diabetes management.

Adjust your drug regime Strenuous exercise can sometimes lower blood sugar for hours after your workout – even for as long as one or two days. If you are tightly controlling your glucose levels with insulin or medication, your

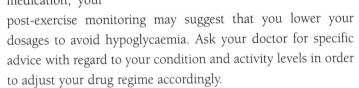

post-exercise monitoring may suggest that you lower your dosages to avoid hypoglycaemia. Ask your doctor for specific advice with regard to your condition and activity levels in order to adjust your drug regime accordingly.

Tank up ahead of time If you are planning to exercise vigorously, you may want to eat more food earlier in the day or take less insulin to ensure that you have enough glucose readily available to fuel working muscles. Aim to work out an hour or two after eating, when blood sugar will be naturally high.

?

DID YOU KNOW

While most types of exercise lower blood sugar, some forms of physical stress, such as illness or even sunburn, can raise it. Be sure to wear sunscreen regularly, especially if you take certain diabetes medications, which can make your skin more sensitive to the sun.

Keep well fuelled afterwards Depending on how strenuous your workout has been, it might be wise to increase your food intake for up to 24 hours after exercising to ensure that your blood-sugar levels don't fall too low.

Use exercise as medicine If you are taking insulin and understand through monitoring how exercise affects your blood sugar, you may find that it is possible to use a workout essentially as an insulin substitute – specifically intended as a way to bring blood sugar down at certain times. (Talk to your doctor before adjusting your drug regime.)

Be alert to the unexpected Certain types of vigorous exercises – weight lifting, for example – that unlock glucose stored in your muscles can cause blood-sugar levels to go up rather than down. Your doctor will suggest how you might adjust insulin or drug treatments accordingly.

Insulin: fine-tuning the control

If you are taking insulin, the point is to keep down your blood-sugar levels, but hypoglycaemia can occur if your insulin injections bring your levels too low. On the other hand, you may experience hyperglycaemia if your doses are improperly timed. Monitoring can help you to work out how to use insulin to keep glucose levels steady.

Inject earlier to bring down highs Patients taking regular (intermediate or long-acting) insulin normally inject it about 30 to 45 minutes before a meal. But if monitoring shows that your blood-sugar levels tend to be high either before or about an hour after you eat, you may want to add more time between injecting and eating to give the insulin a better chance to bring glucose levels down. You might also do some exercise such as a brisk walk for a similar effect. This advice does not apply to patients taking a rapid-acting insulin, such as lispro, which must be injected 15 minutes or less before eating.

Inject later to raise up lows If your blood sugar tends to be on the low side 30 to 45 minutes before you have a meal, you may want to wait until nearer your eating time before injecting insulin. This will prevent your blood sugar from dropping lower before you have had a chance to get some food into your system. Again, this advice does not apply to people taking rapid-acting insulin.

⊃ **Add small snacks** If insulin injections tend to produce hypoglycaemia, you might want to eat a small amount of carbohydrate (such as a handful of raisins) around mid morning and mid afternoon to keep your blood-glucose levels steady between meals. Or discuss with your doctor the possibility of adjusting your insulin regime.

Illness: you're low, sugar's high

Illness and the stress that sometimes precipitates it can boost blood-sugar levels by stimulating the release of hormones that work against the action of insulin and cause glucose to be released from storage sites in the muscles and liver. Naturally, you mainly need to treat the illness, but you also need to take extra steps to keep down your blood-sugar levels.

⊃ **Drink more water** If blood sugar is higher than usual, your kidneys are probably working harder and producing more urine, causing you to become de-hydrated from the unusually high urine output. To keep yourself hydrated you should drink at least 150–200ml (¼–⅓ pint) of water every half-hour or so.

⊃ **Avoid exercise** Even if you think that it might bring down your blood sugar, there is the possibility that exercise will cause the release of glucose from muscles. In any case, it is more important that you rest in order to fight the illness.

⊃ **Consider adjusting insulin** If you are taking insulin, ask your doctor if and when you should take additional or increased doses while you are ill.

Morning: the dawn phenomenon

You would think that blood-sugar levels would be low when you wake up. After all, you have gone the whole night without food. Often, however, blood sugar is high in the morning. The explanation is that your body clock triggers the release of hormones which inhibit insulin so that more glucose is available to the body at the start of the new day. This is natural and not necessarily a problem. But if monitoring reveals that your blood sugar becomes excessively high in the morning, you may want to consult your doctor about what actions you can take.

➲ **Take insulin later** If you are using insulin and take an evening dose, you may find it more effective to inject it closer to bedtime for longer-lasting control during the night.

➲ **Skip the bedtime snack** Try eating less food at night so there is less glucose in the blood the following morning. You may also want to eat less at breakfast.

➲ **Exercise in the evening** Because the glucose-lowering effects of exercise can last for many hours, a brisk walk shortly after supper can help to keep your blood-sugar levels under control the following morning.

Getting the whole story

Self-monitoring tells you a lot about how well you are controlling your blood sugar, but it does not give you the full picture. Each reading you take is a snapshot that shows what your blood sugar was like at that moment. (It could be different 10 minutes later.) It is equivalent to knowing that a high-rise lift was on a certain floor at a given moment when your real concern is that the lift should operate only within a certain range of floors. You need an indication of where the lift is the rest of the time, too. That is where additional tests can help. The most important of these are:

Haemoglobin A1c This test indicates what your average blood-sugar levels have been over two to three months, making it an invaluable tool. If you are taking insulin, your doctor may recommend that you take this test every three months; if not, you may want to have it done every six months or so.

The test provides long-term results because it measures not blood sugar per se, but blood sugar's effect on a particular type of haemoglobin. Found in red blood cells, haemoglobin is a substance that carries oxygen through the bloodstream and clears away carbon dioxide. Red blood cells have a life span of approximately four months, during which glucose gradually 'sticks' to haemoglobin in a process known as glycosylation (the A1c test is sometimes referred to as a glycosylated haemoglobin test). The build-up of blood sugar in haemoglobin reflects how high your blood sugar has been on the whole during that time.

However, because glucose attaches itself slowly to haemoglobin over time, any wild swings in blood sugar that you might experience will not be detected – they will simply show up as tame-looking averages in this test. In other words, the haemoglobin A1c test does not tell the whole story, either. But taken together, self-monitoring and the HbA1c test provide a good overall view of your blood sugar.

Results from the HbA1c test are measured on a percentage scale that goes from 4 to 13. Diabetes UK recommends keeping HbA1c results below 7 per cent. Be sure to discuss the meaning of your results with your doctor though: different laboratories measure haemoglobin A1c in different ways, and results are not consistent between labs. There is a movement afoot to standardize the numbers, but for now you will need your doctor's guidance to interpret the results. A newly approved, pager-sized test kit that allows you to take haemoglobin A1c readings yourself at home can now be bought over the counter, but be sure to consult your doctor first.

Fructosamine The fructosamine test is similar to the haemoglobin A1c test, in that it records how much blood sugar builds up in components of your blood. But it uses proteins as a yardstick, particularly a protein called albumin. This test is less widely used than the HbA1c test because the results are substantially similar, but there is one important difference: the fructosamine test measures blood sugar over a period of two to three weeks. It can therefore be a useful 'bridge' between your short-term home glucose tests and the long-term HbA1c test. Your doctor may order a fructosamine test for an intermediate check on your progress if you make a change in your insulin or medication, or if you are pregnant.

Four more important tests

While blood-glucose monitoring is a crucial part of diabetes management, it is not the only way to keep tabs on your condition – and your risk of complications. The following four tests provide important information about your diabetes and your overall health.

Urine ketones If self-monitoring shows your blood sugar is over 15mmol/l, you may be at risk of ketoacidosis, the condition in which glucose-starved cells burn fat for fuel, releasing acidic ketones into the blood. A urine ketone test, which you can do at home, involves exposing a test strip to your urine. The results indicate whether ketones are present in your body. You should also do a urine ketone test if you experience such symptoms as deep or rapid breathing, nausea or vomiting, fever or stomach pain. Ketoacidosis is a dangerous condition that is especially likely to occur in people with Type 1 diabetes. If your urine ketone test result is positive, contact your doctor without delay.

Lipids At least once a year you should have a blood test to measure a variety of lipids, or fats, in the blood that can raise your risk of cardiovascular disease when present in large amounts. Because people with diabetes are up to five times more likely to develop heart disease than the rest of the population, it is especially important to know your blood-lipid levels. The key lipids you are testing for are:

▶ **LDL (low-density lipoprotein), or 'bad' cholesterol** This waxy, fatty substance can accumulate and harden on artery walls, interfering with the flow of blood and eventually causing a heart attack or stroke. When you have diabetes, your LDL cholesterol should be less than 3mmol/l, which is lower than the norm for people without diabetes.

▶ **HDL (high-density lipoprotein), or 'good' cholesterol** This beneficial form of cholesterol helps to rid the body of 'bad' cholesterol by scouring artery walls and carrying deposits of LDL to the liver and out of the body. High levels of HDL are good. Don't settle for a test that only gives you your total blood cholesterol level: it is the ratio between 'good' and 'bad' cholesterol that is critical, and your HDL should be above 1mmol/l.

▶ **Triglycerides** Most of the fat that you consume is made up of triglycerides, a type of lipid that cells can store and use for energy when required. High triglyceride levels may contribute to hardening of the arteries. Yours should be less than 2.3mmol/l.

Blood pressure This familiar test – performed with a device consisting of a pressurized inflatable cuff that goes around your arm, an air pump and a glass column filled with mercury – should be done every time you see your doctor. It indicates how hard your heart is working to pump blood throughout your body. If your blood pressure is high, your heart is having to work harder than it should, placing too much stress on your blood vessels. The complications that can result are similar to those of diabetes itself – including damage to the kidneys, nerves and eyes.

Blood pressure for people with diabetes should be less than 140/80 millimetres of mercury (mmHg) – a two-part reading that reflects the force that the heart exerts against the walls of the blood vessels when contracting (known as the systolic pressure, which is reflected in the high number of your blood pressure reading) and the residual pressure within the arteries between heartbeats (the diastolic pressure, indicated by the low number of your reading).

Urine microalbumin This test can detect kidney damage – a common complication of diabetes – at its earliest stages. The test looks for minuscule quantities of a protein called albumin, which normally remains within the bloodstream but shows up in the urine when the kidneys are having difficulty filtering wastes properly. If you have Type 2 diabetes, you should have a urine microalbumin test upon diagnosis and then every year thereafter. If you have Type 1 diabetes and were past puberty at the time of diagnosis, you can wait five years after diagnosis

---

WHEN TO TEST

To track your diabetes and its potential complications, have regular examinations that include relevant tests on this suggested timetable:

Every visit to the doctor

■ Blood pressure

Once a year

■ Lipid profile (cholesterol and triglycerides)

■ Eye examination with pupil dilation

■ Urine microalbumin

Every three to six months

■ Haemoglobin A1c

As advised by your doctor

■ Fructosamine

before the first test because it is unlikely that your kidneys would have been silently damaged before that time.

A positive urine microalbumin result may qualify you as a candidate for additional treatment – perhaps with a blood-pressure-lowering medication, since high blood pressure can narrow the arteries leading to the kidneys and damage the delicate blood vessels inside them.

NUMBERS TO KNOW

Ideal blood glucose before eating: . . . . 4 to 7mmol/l

Blood glucose that
indicates hypoglycaemia: . . . . below 4mmol/l

Blood glucose that merits
a ketone test: . . . . above 15mmol/l

A1c glycosylated haemoglobin target: . . . . . . 7 per cent

Low-risk LDL cholesterol . . . . below 3mmol/l

Low-risk HDL cholesterol : . . . . above 1mmol/l

Low-risk triglycerides: . . . . below 2.3mmol/l

Low-risk blood pressure: . . . . . 140/80mmHg or lower

REAL-LIFE MEDICINE

MOTIVATED BY HIS TEST RESULTS

Malcolm Collier, 51, had no idea that he had diabetes until he went for a routine eye test ten years ago which revealed he had retinopathy. 'I hadn't had any symptoms at all,' says Malcolm, from Bristol.

Blood tests led to a diagnosis of Type 2 diabetes, and a wholehearted effort at self-education. 'Diabetes is like a conveyor belt – once you're on it, you can't simply get off again, so I knew I just had to control the disease,' he says.

At the time Malcolm weighed 108kg (17 stone) and did very little exercise. 'I had to get my weight down, so I started to eat sensibly, cutting out a lot of the rubbish, and I got on my push bike,' he says.

At diagnosis he was offered his first HbA1c test, which indicates average blood glucose levels over two to three months. 'The result was very high, at just over 14.5,' says Malcolm, who considers the test one of his most important tools for controlling his diabetes. The level was well above the recommended 7 per cent, but it provided the motivation he needed to bring his levels down.

Malcolm says that because the HbA1c test gives you an average over two to three months, he finds it much more useful than just knowing what his level was on a particular day.

'It's a true reflection of how you have been doing and makes sure that you don't cheat by starving on the day to get a better level. It's basically the proof of everything,' he says.

So Malcolm set out to bring down his HbA1c level. After two years he was put on to tablets to help control his diabetes, but each week he lost a little more weight and as the HbA1c levels came down it gave him the motivation he needed to lose a little more.

Today, 10 years on, Malcolm weighs 86.5kg (13½ stone) and feels like a totally different person. But, he says, you can't be complacent. 'The good thing about the HbA1c test is that it makes you own up to the truth of what your levels really are.' At one point his level came down to 5, but then he put on a little more weight, and as a result his level went up again. 'So I knew I just had to try a bit harder,' he says.

For the past five years Malcolm has done a 115-mile charity cycle ride and he does some kind of exercise every day to make sure his next HbA1c level is better. 'The last test was 6.5, which my doctor is quite happy about,' he says. 'It makes me want to keep fit and carry on cycling as well as eating well. That makes me feel so much better, and you simply can't put a value on that.'

Eat to beat
diabetes

To a large extent, diabetes begins and ends with food, the body's glucose source. Having diabetes doesn't mean that you are condemned to limited food choices and can never enjoy your favourite dishes or desserts again. Rather, the goal is to eat a diversity of nutrients in proper portion sizes, spread evenly throughout the day. Sugar is fine, for example, if eaten in small portions and correctly balanced with proteins, fats and more beneficial carbohydrates. Think of healthy eating for diabetes not as a diet but as a permanent path to better health.

FOUR

4

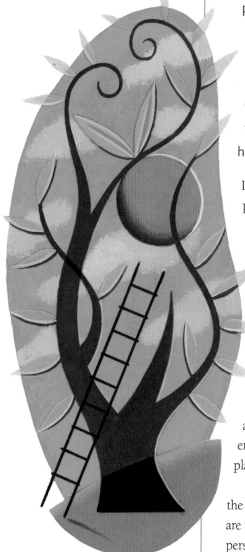

Healthy eating for diabetes

The fact that diet is a key part of managing diabetes is no surprise. After all, glucose comes from food, so it makes sense that what you eat plays a role in making your blood sugar go up. But you shouldn't think of food as the problem. Instead, consider it a big part of the solution. For people with Type 2 diabetes, the right diet could reverse the course of your disease. If you take insulin or other medication it could help you to reduce your dose, or eliminate medication altogether. While for those with Type 1 diabetes, choosing the right diet can help you to manage your condition more effectively.

In the past, a diagnosis of diabetes was followed by 'the talk', a particularly frustrating conversation with the doctor about your future. You'll have to watch your diet much more closely now, the doctor would say. Cut out the sugar. Cut back on carbohydrates. Watch the fat. Lots of steamed green vegetables. No indulgent restaurant meals. No more desserts. It was depressing, disheartening, annoying.

What a difference a few years can make. Thanks to ever-improving research, a whole new mind-set has emerged about eating for diabetes. Blandness is out; flavour is in. Rigid restrictions are out; intelligent moderation is in. The new thinking is to eat delicious, healthy, creative food, with a sensible eye towards the right mix of nutrients and the right portion sizes. It's a more open-ended food plan, but with proven results.

Another aspect of diabetes management that has changed is the demise of a 'one size fits all' nutritional programme. Not only are the scope, impact and cause of the condition different for each person, but each person's lifestyle and priorities differ as well. So it's far more important that if you are newly diagnosed, you ask your GP to refer you to a state-registered dietitian to help craft a unique plan for you. If possible, keep a food diary of everything you eat for seven days before your appointment with the dietitian. You should also show your dietitian your daily log of blood-sugar readings. The eating plan that you devise with your dietitian should take into consideration the need for weight loss, the intensity of the condition, personal food tastes and lifestyle issues.

Yet there are core truths about nutrition and diabetes that transcend individual needs and preferences. The key rule is that you must be sensible about your mix of foods, how they are cooked and how often you eat. People with diabetes should eat a balanced healthy diet – low in saturated fat, sugar and salt, with plenty of fruit and vegetables and the right amounts of starchy foods, such as bread, potatoes, cereals, pasta and rice.

What's on the menu?

Surprisingly, all the foods you eat fall into only a handful of basic food categories that make up the building blocks of your diet. While the total number of calories you consume is a major consideration, it also matters which building blocks those calories are derived from. Why? Because while food raises your blood sugar within an hour or two of eating, the level and speed of that increase depends on both the quantity and types of foods you consume.

This pictorial food guide, published by the Food Standards Agency, shows the proportion and types of foods that are needed to make up a healthy balanced diet. Foods can be divided into five main groups:

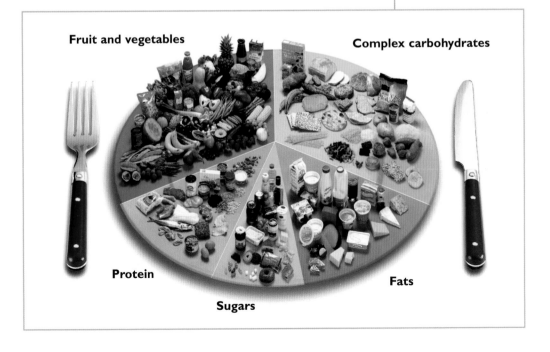

▶bread, cereals such as rice, and potatoes (complex carbohydrates)

▶fruit and vegetables

▶milk and dairy foods

▶meat, fish and alternatives (nuts, pulses, eggs and proteins)

▶foods containing fat

▶foods containing sugar.

Foods from the largest groups should be eaten most often and foods from the smallest group should be eaten least often. The guide is shaped like a dinner plate to make healthy eating simpler to understand. Because no single food provides all the nutrients the body needs, a healthy balanced diet is likely to include a large variety of foods, to achieve adequate intakes of all the nutrients.

We need energy from food to live, but we also need the right balance between carbohydrate, fat and protein to remain healthy. Too little protein can interfere with growth and other body funtions, too much fat can lead to obesity and heart disease. Adequate intakes of vitamins and minerals and dietary fibre are important for health, and there is evidence that several bioactive plant substances (phytochemicals) found in fruit and vegetables are important in promoting good health. Here is an overview of the key nutrients that a person with diabetes should consume to help give you a better grasp of how to eat healthily for diabetes.

Carbohydrates

The body's main source of energy is carbohydrates. They come in two forms. Simple carbohydrates are the kind that are easily digested into glucose, such as table sugar and sugary drinks. Complex carbohydrates are starches made up of more complex sugars, fibre and a rich assortment of other nutrients. These carbohydrates take longer for the body to digest and contain more beneficial ingredients. They make up the bulk of whole grains and vegetables.

Carbohydrates are easily broken down into sugars, so they have the most impact on your blood-glucose levels. Simple carbohydrates, such as sweets and cakes, are so easy to digest that they almost instantly flood your body with blood glucose. It's no wonder, then, that carbohydrates have long been seen as the enemy of people with diabetes. But different carbohydrates affect our blood glucose levels in different ways. It is therefore important to try to understand the glycaemic effect of different foods (see the Glycaemic Index and Guide on page 101), so that you can enjoy your favourite foods while still looking after yourself.

Following a low-carbohydrate diet may actually do more harm than good because carbohydrates are the best source of fuel for your body. And since carbohydrates, gram for gram, provide only about half the amount of calories of fat, an eating plan that includes complex carbohydrates also gives you much wider food choices with less risk of gaining weight.

The trick is to avoid reducing 'carbohydrates' to a single category of food. Both bagels and broccoli are mostly carbohydrate, but many low-carbohydrate diets do not differentiate adequately between these very different foods. Many eating plans limit all carbohydrates, regardless of the source.

The problem with simple carbohydrates isn't just that they are high in sugar – most people with diabetes can handle such treats every now and then in small portions. Rather, it's that such foods are often high in fat and low in vitamins, minerals and other healthy nutrients.

Diabetes UK and the Diabetes Research and Wellness Foundation recommend that starchy carbohydrate foods should be the basis of all your meals. This is because these foods help you to keep your blood-glucose levels steady. There are specific starchy foods that are particularly recommended for those with diabetes – these include cereals, potatoes, breads, pasta, rice and oats.

CAN I EAT ALL THE SUGAR-FREE FOODS I WANT?

You would think sugar-free foods such as sweets and soft drinks would have less impact on blood-glucose levels than regular sweets or soft drinks. But you can't eat sugar-free foods with impunity.

The reason for this is that common sweeteners, such as maltitol, sorbitol and xylitol, may not be sucrose (the technical name for sugar), but they do contain carbohydrate, each gram of which can raise blood glucose just as much as sugar does. Non-nutritive sweeteners such as saccharin and aspartame contain no carbohydrate or calories, but products that contain these sweeteners (such as yoghurt and soft drinks) might.

The best advice is to pay no attention to 'sugar-free' claims on the packaging. Look instead at a product's total carbohydrate count.

!

CAUTION

Foods such as beans and broccoli are notorious for producing gas in the intestines, but the effect is temporary and your body will adjust if eating more fibre becomes a habit. Meanwhile, you may feel more comfortable if you add fibre gradually over a period of weeks to give your system a chance to get used to it. Start by adding about 5g a day until you reach the 25–30g daily target. Your body will also handle added fibre more effectively if you drink more water.

Sugar in context

There is actually no need for people with diabetes to avoid sugar completely. The effect that any sugary food or drink has on your blood-glucose levels depends not only on how much sugar it contains, but also, for example, on how the food is cooked, what else it contains and what you eat with it. A sugar-rich drink taken between meals is absorbed quickly and causes a sharp rise in blood glucose. However, when you eat sugar as part of a meal, blood-glucose levels do not react in the same way because the sugar is absorbed much more slowly.

Sugar substitutes such as aspartame and acesulfame potassium do not affect blood-glucose levels. You can use them to sweeten foods after cooking or to sweeten drinks. If you regularly use artificial sweeteners, you should choose a variety of different types.

Complex carbohydrates

By nature, these contain slower-to-digest sugars and tend to have more beneficial nutrients than simple carbohydrates. In particular, they contain lots of fibre.

Fibre, simply put, is the stuff in plants that your body can't digest. It's the husks on the grains, the stringy threads in celery. So what's so good about fibre?

Insoluble fibre (found, for example, in wholegrain cereals and in the skin on potatoes) is bulky and absorbs water, so it fills you up faster. It also slows down digestion, prolonging feelings of fullness. This is critical for maintaining a healthy weight. Insoluble fibre also binds together waste, keeping you regular. It 'sweeps out' your digestive tract, keeping it clean.

Soluble fibre (such as that found in beans and lentils) has been shown to help to reduce cholesterol in your blood, protecting your heart. It also helps to keep blood-glucose levels steady. (see box on page 93 for ways to add fibre to your diet).

Fibre is not the only beneficial constituent of complex carbohydrates. Compelling new research suggests that eating the right vegetables, whole grains and beans every day may play a role in preventing disease. For instance, the phytochemicals in broccoli may help to prevent certain cancers; onions' allium compounds may help to reduce cholesterol, an important factor for people with diabetes; oats and some soya products may also be helpful in reducing cholesterol.

HOW TO GET YOUR FILL OF FIBRE

Fibre is critical in weight control, as it makes you feel full and keeps you regular. It also helps to keep blood glucose levels steady and reduce blood cholesterol. Here's how to increase fibre in your diet.

■ **Don't skimp on breakfast** A modest meal of whole grains and fruit provides up to a third of your daily fibre. Choose a breakfast cereal with 3g of fibre per serving (check the salt and sugar content), or muesli or porridge – they contain lots of soluble fibre with a low Glycaemic Index. Eat whole-grain bread rather than wholemeal or white, and add fruit to your cereal.

■ **Eat the skins** Scrub and eat the edible skins on fruit and vegetables (when you peel a potato, you lose a third of the fibre). The seeds in berries, kiwis and figs also supply valuable fibre.

■ **Opt for beans and lentils** Dried or canned, pulses are a great source of fibre. Try to keep them whole: their skin needs to be broken down in the body before they can be digested, so blood glucose rises more slowly. Baked beans contain sugar, but are a good source of soluble fibre and have about the same Glycaemic Index as a banana, so there is no need to opt for sugar-free varieties.

■ **Add vegetables** Vegetables such as carrots and celery are good sources of fibre. Add them to casseroles, soups, salads, sandwiches and pasta. Fresh, frozen or canned – all are good. Instead of discarding the fibre-rich stalks of broccoli, for example, chop and cook them a bit longer, adding the florets slightly later.

■ **Boost your fluid intake** When you eat more fibre, you need to make sure that you are drinking sufficient amounts of fluid (see page 109).

Fatty foods

Fats are a class of organic chemicals known as fatty acids or lipids. When digested, they make almost double the energy of the same amount of carbohydrate or protein. Fat is only a problem when you eat too much, especially of the less healthy type. Fat molecules are easily stored, leading to weight gain. The build-up of fat-related molecules in the bloodstream is bad for the heart and circulatory system.

Not all fats should be avoided. There are three main types of fats. Two of those offer health benefits so important that you might wish to add them to your diet – in appropriate amounts.

Saturated fat The type of fat that is least healthy for you is the kind that maintains a solid shape at room temperature. Primarily, this means butter, hard cheeses and the fat on meat. While this kind of fat (known as saturated fat) offers incredible amounts of fuel, it has few other health benefits and has the most detrimental effect on your blood cholesterol, which in turn makes you more prone to heart problems.

HOW TO REDUCE YOUR SATURATED FAT INTAKE

Fat is a beloved dietary staple because it's both tasty and versatile. But while no one needs to forgo all of fat's pleasures, a lot of the fat in our diet comes hidden (and unbidden) in cooking or eating habits that can easily be changed without sacrificing taste.

■ **Opt for leaner meat** Whenever possible, choose lean meat or mince and be sure to trim off any visible fat before cooking. (If you put the meat in the freezer for 20 minutes beforehand, it will firm up the meat for closer cutting and make marbled fat more visible.)

■ **Skin your chicken** About half of the fat in poultry is concentrated in the skin, which you can leave on while cooking in order to keep the meat moist but should remove before eating – especially if you like drumsticks, which contain more than twice the fat of chicken breast, even with the skin removed.

■ **Skim soups and stews** When preparing casseroles, stews or curries, cook them ahead of time, allow to cool and skim the congealed fat off the top. The same goes for soups or stocks: chill the broth overnight and skim any fat from the surface.

■ **Switch to skimmed milk** Whole milk gets almost half its calories from fat. By contrast, skimmed milk has almost no fat, and only half the calories of whole milk (although its vitamin and mineral content is almost as high). If you don't like the taste of skimmed milk, semi-skimmed milk is a good compromise.

■ **Eat low-fat dairy foods** When buying dairy foods such as yoghurt or ice cream, choose low-fat versions. Some cheeses are very high in saturated fat and should be eaten sparingly. Cheddar, for example, contains six times as much saturated fat as sirloin steak, weight for weight. Cottage cheese is a good low-fat option.

■ **Avoid creamy sauces** Whenever possible, choose tomato-based rather than creamy sauces, and avoid creamy-style soups.

■ **Cook with oil** Rather than cooking with butter or other hard fats, choose olive oil, rapeseed oil and groundnut oils, or spreads made with monounsaturated oils.

■ **Choose healthy snacks** Salty snacks such as potato crisps and tortilla chips can be high in saturated fat. Better options are unsalted nuts, fresh fruit, a handful of dried fruit or fresh-cut vegetables with salsa,

Polyunsaturated and monounsaturated fats Fats that are in liquid form at room temperature (primarily plant oils, such as corn, olive or rapeseed oil) are split into two categories: polyunsaturated and monounsaturated. Both have benefits, but the latter are best for you. There is evidence that monounsaturated fat raises your HDL ('good') cholesterol – important for people with diabetes because they have an increased risk of heart disease. Monounsaturated fat also has been shown to reduce insulin resistance.

Fish oils, or omega-3 fatty acids These are essential to the body and are found in fish such as salmon, herring, mackerel, trout and sardines. Research shows that eating oily fish as part of a healthy lifestyle can help to lower the risk of heart disease. You should eat two portions of oily fish a week.

GREAT SOURCES OF 'GOOD' FATS

- Olive oil
- Rapeseed oil
- Almonds and other nuts
- Avocados

Trans fatty acids are generally used in the food industry to make unsaturated fatty acids firmer. They are found in manufactured foods such as biscuits and cakes. Studies show that these fats, like saturated fats, can raise your blood cholesterol levels. So watch out for foods that have 'hydrogenated vegetable oils' high up on the ingredients list.

Protein

Although protein is essential for most of the body's vital functions, including the growth, maintenance and repair of cells, in general we all eat too much of it. Excess protein intake is counterproductive: the body can't store it for later use and instead converts it into glucose and by-products such as urea, which have to be excreted, putting an extra strain on the liver and kidneys. Diabetes already increases your risk of kidney damage, some doctors believe that eating too much protein may impair kidney function faster than a low-protein diet.

If you are already controlling your fat and carbohydrate balance: protein will account for the rest of your calories. For most people with diabetes only 10-15 per cent of calories should come from protein – with 35 per cent from fat and 50 per cent from carbohydrates. You can easily get all the protein you need in just a few servings of protein-rich foods, such as meats, fish, eggs, and plant foods such as pulses, nuts and soya products. Smaller amounts are also found in vegetables and grains.

Aim to replace some of the meat in dishes with beans and pulses. Eating pulses regularly can help you to control your blood glucose levels. Soya products, such as tofu and Quorn, are low in fat and make excellent low-fat alternatives to meat in many recipes. Pork pies, sausage rolls, Scotch eggs and other meat products contain hidden fat, so limit these to occasional treats.

The body absorbs iron less well from vegetarian foods than from animal foods. However, you can improve iron absorption if you include with your meal foods or drink that are rich in vitamin C (such as tomatoes or oranges).

The importance of fruit and vegetables

Most of us are not good at eating our full quota of fruit and vegetables. Fresh produce rarely plays a dominant role in our meal planning. Yet it is an extremely important part of a balanced eating plan. Research studies have consistently shown that eating regular amounts of fresh fruit and vegetables can bring immense – and easily-achieved health benefits.

WHAT IS A PORTION?

- I medium-size fruit, such as an apple, banana or orange

- I large slice of melon or pineapple

- 2 plums, apricots or satsumas

- 2-3 tbsp fresh fruit salad or canned fruit

- I tbsp dried fruit

- I glass (150ml/5fl oz) fresh fruit juice

- 2-3 tbsp raw or cooked vegetables

- I dessert bowl of salad

Orange and yellow-coloured fruits are higher in beta-carotene, which is converted into vitamin A in the body. All fruits contain some vitamin C, especially the citrus variety. The antioxidant vitamins found in fruit (A, C and E) are thought to protect against numerous infections and possibly even against some cancers. Fruits also tend to have a low Glycaemic Index, raising blood glucose slowly (see page 101).

Vegetables don't raise blood glucose very much and so add few calories. In fact, they are generally the most nutrient-dense, low-calorie foods you can eat. And if you fill up on vegetables, you will have less room for less healthy, calorie-loaded foods.

SALT

Eating too much salt is linked with high blood pressure so it is advisable to cut down on salt intake to prevent heart disease. It's estimated that people in the UK eat at least 10g of salt each day. Because most of the salt you eat comes from manufactured foods, it is very likely that you are taking in far more than this amount each day, especially if you consume a lot of processed meals and snacks.

For good health it is recommended that you keep your total daily salt intake to 6g (just over a teaspoon). Remember that food labels only give you the sodium content (usually per 100g), so you need to multiply this figure by 2.4 to get the amount of salt in 100g of food.

Some tips for cutting down on salt:

■ **Measure the amount of salt** you add in cooking and gradually reduce it. When recipes suggest adding salt, use an amount that imparts just enough flavour. You will soon get used to eating less salt.

■ **Don't add salt** at the table.

■ **Experiment with herbs and spices** using, for example, dried and fresh herbs, paprika and freshly milled black pepper. If you find it hard to get used to a less salty flavour, try a salt substitute. Low-salt products (such as unsalted bread and butter) can be used as replacements for salt-rich foods.

■ **For varied flavours**, try adding lime juice, balsamic vinegar and chilli sauce.

■ **Read food labels carefully**. Salt may apear as sodium, sodium chloride, monosodium glutamate or bicarbonate of soda.

■ **Cut down on salty foods** such as crisps, salted nuts, savoury biscuits and salty pastries. Instead, eat fresh fruit, unsalted nuts and unsalted popcorn.

■ **Processed and smoked foods**, such as bacon, sausages, smoked fish, some canned fish and other processed convenience foods are often loaded with salt. Whenever possible, eat fresh fish, meats and vegetables. They contain only a small amount of salt naturally.

▶ **How long can I store fruit and vegetables before all the goodness goes?** Heat and light can destroy the vitamins in fruit and vegetables. Store fruit in the fridge or in a cool, dark place and don't keep it too long. It is most nutritious when fresh. Once you start peeling and chopping fruit, nutrients can be lost, so eat it whole if you can.

▶ **Will mashing or juicing fruit and vegetables affect the nutrients?** Mashing disrupts the fibre and changes the inherent physical make-up of the fruit or vegetable. This raises the Glycaemic Index, which reduces some of the benefits. But as long as you eat the fruit or vegetable (or drink its juice) quickly, you're still maintaining the nutritional value. Drink fruit juice, even unsweetened varieties, with a meal. This helps to slow down the rise in blood glucose.

▶ **How much fruit and vegetables do I need to eat to get a benefit?** For good health, you should aim to eat 440 g (just under 1lb) of vegetables and fruit each day. This equates to about five 85g (3oz) portions, Remember that potatoes are classified as starchy carbohydrates, so they don't count.

▶ **Do juice, dried fruit, and vegetables in ready meals 'count' towards my five daily portions?** Dried fruit and fresh fruit juice do count (see box What is a portion? on page 96). However, it is best to choose juice as only one of your five portions, since the valuable fibre has been removed. Pulses such as beans and lentils are also counted just once a day. This is because they don't contain the range of nutrients you get from other sources such as green, leafy vegetables, carrots and tomatoes. So, 85g (3oz) about half a can) of baked beans counts as a portion, and interestingly, since there might well be 85g of tomatoes in aserving of canned tomato soup or 85g of vegetables in a bought stir-fry, then you can, in theory, achieve your five portions a day by eating bought ready-prepared foods. However, it makes good nutritional sense to have a mixture, so that you get a variety from different food sources.

▶ **Can I eat as much fruit as I like?** This will depend on individual circumstances. If you test your blood glucose levels, you need to be aware of how different foods react in your bloodstream. Fresh fruit is brimming with natural sugars, and so can raise blood glucose levels more quickly and to a higher level than vegetables. The trick is to determine how fruit raises your own glucose levels. One way to do that is to eat a standard portion of fruit, then test your glucose level a couple of hours later. Some fruits may raise your blood glucose more than others. Careful monitoring is the only way to know for sure

Milk and dairy foods

Milk and dairy foods are good sources of calcium, which you need for healthy bones and teeth. You also need an adequate calcium intake to help regulate your blood pressure. However, some dairy products are very high in saturated fats.

Choose lower-fat versions of milk and dairy foods. Many cheeses are high in saturated fat, especially hard cheeses such as Cheddar or Leicester, and blue cheeses. Look out for lower-fat cheeses such as reduced-fat Cheddar, Brie, Edam, Camembert, cottage cheese and reduced-fat cheese spreads. Limit high-fat foods such as cream and crème fraîche in favour of some of the lower-fat alternatives such as fromage frais, low-fat yoghurts, reduced-fat Greek yoghurt and light crème fraîche.

Getting enough vitamins and minerals

As a rule, if you eat a wide variety of foods, you'll have no trouble getting all the nutrients you need. However, people with diabetes appear more likely to be deficient in certain micro-nutrients – something your dietitian can evaluate. Nutrients you may need more of include:

Vitamin C Evidence for diabetes-related deficiencies is most clear for vitamin C, which, like glucose, requires insulin to help it enter cells. It's not hard to add more vitamin C to your diet. Just one cup of steamed broccoli contains 123mg – a whole day's supply.

Magnesium The most common mineral deficiency, especially in people with Type 1 diabetes, is of magnesium. Getting too little of it may promote eye damage, a common complication.

Vitamin E An antioxidant, vitamin E may protect against such complications as eye, nerve and kidney damage. But amounts in food tend to be small, so you may want to take a supplement. Check with your doctor first.

Vitamin B$_{12}$ Some diabetes medications, such as metformin, may interfere with the body's absorption of B$_{12}$ from food, potentially leading to deficiencies.

WHERE THE NUTRIENTS ARE

Vitamin C
Citrus fruits, tomatoes, spinach, red peppers, broccoli, strawberries

Magnesium
Leafy green vegetables (like spinach), whole grains, dairy products, brown rice, apricots and bananas

Vitamin E
Many nuts, such as almonds, Brazil nuts, and peanuts, as well as whole-wheat flour

Vitamin B$_{12}$
Poultry and a variety of seafood, including clams, crabs, scallops and prawns

Before taking any dietary supplements, check with your doctor. As a rule, if you suffer from deficiencies in any nutrients, it's best to derive the nutrients you need from dietary sources. Supplements are generally considered less desirable because some vitamins and minerals can be harmful in high amounts; in addition, supplements lack other nutrients or elements, such as fibre, that may make it easier for the body to absorb and use what it ingests.

Finally, there's one mineral you may need less of: sodium. High blood pressure is common among people with diabetes, and studies suggest that eating less sodium can help bring blood pressure down. Use table salt sparingly and avoid canned or packaged foods, which tend to be high in sodium. Rely more on herbs and spices when cooking.

How nutrients heal

Many natural foods are filled with micronutrients – organic chemicals with healing powers and important benefits to your body. Since having diabetes may increase the rise of high cholesterol, heart disease, kidney problems and high blood pressure, you'll want to be sure to eat foods that play a role in the prevention of these problems. Examples include:

Garlic This can lower cholesterol levels and blood pressure. It contains a phytochemical called allicin. In fact, members of the allium family – onions, garlic, leeks and shallots – can all contribute to lower cholesterol and lower blood pressure.

Red wine It is widely reported that red wine may play a role in preventing heart disease. But drinking alcohol regularly may not be the best idea for a person with diabetes (see page 109). Scientists now suspect that the benefits of red wine are actually from the non-alcoholic flavonoids, particularly the grape skins. The phytochemical in the skins is called resveratrol. So there seems to be some benefit in including a small portion of red grapes or a small glass of grape juice, or indeed a glass of red wine with your meal.

Oatmeal and soya The evidence for eating oatmeal and soya to lower cholesterol is strong.

Lutein The phytochemical, found in spinach and other dark green leafy vegetables, may help to fight macular degeneration, a major cause of vision problems.

Folic acid (from fruit, vegetables, pulses and whole grains) acts to lower the levels of a chemical known as homocysteine in the blood. High levels of homocysteine are a risk factor for development of heart disease, stroke and peripheral vein disease.

What is the Glycaemic Index?

How fast or slowly your blood sugar goes up after eating depends on what you eat. Developed in the 1980s by Canadian researchers, the Glycaemic Index (GI) is a ranking of foods according to their effect on blood glucose levels. The faster a food is broken down during digestion, the quicker the rise in blood glucose levels.

Since a primary aim in treating diabetes is to keep blood glucose levels steady throughout the day, it is best to limit your consumption of foods that cause sharp rises in blood sugar (except in special circumstances, such as when you are ill or taking heavy exercise). Foods that cause a rapid rise in blood glucose will have a high GI, so the key is to consume foods with low GIs on a regular basis.

It was previously thought that if you ate the same amount of carbohydrate, regardless of the food, it would have the same effect on your blood levels. But we now know that different carbohydrates have different effects on blood glucose levels. For instance, 25g (1oz) of bread does not have exactly the same effect as the same weight of fruit or of pasta.

Using the GI

Each food is given a GI number according to its effect on blood glucose levels. But it's not as simple as just choosing foods with a low number. The GI only tells you how quickly or slowly a food raises blood glucose when it is eaten on its own. In practice, we usually eat foods in combination: bread is eaten with butter or margarine; potatoes are eaten with meat or fish and vegetables.

Foods with a high GI are not bad foods. The key to healthy eating is to get the right mix of foods, which will both ensure better control of your blood glucose levels and also help you to obtain the wide variety of nutrients needed for good health. Think about the balance of your meals, which should include starchy foods and be low in fat, salt and sugar.

Glycaemic Index

Here's a rough guide to the Glycaemic Index (GI) of popular foods. Note that the formulations of processed foods can vary, and this will affect the GI

Low GI foods
Muesli, porridge
Multigrain bread
Rye bread
Fruit loaf
Pasta (made of durum wheat)
Lentils and beans (including baked beans)
Sweetcorn, sweet potato
Oranges, apples, pears, peaches

Medium GI foods
Weetabix
Shredded wheat
Pitta bread
Rich tea biscuits
Digestive biscuits
Basmati rice, white
Couscous
New potatoes, boiled
Ice cream
Honey
Jam

High GI Foods
Cornflakes, Rice Krispies, puffed wheat, sugar-rich breakfast cereals
Bagels
White or wholemeal bread
Morning coffee biscuits
French fries
Mashed of baked potato
Rice, white or brown (except Basmati)
Glucose drinks
Sports drinks

The good news is that you can lower the overall GI of a meal by including more low GI foods. Combining foods with different GIs alters the overall GI of a meal, so you should try to incorporate a low GI food into each meal you eat.

Making weight loss work

The most consistent advice over the years for people with diabetes is the need to keep your weight down. The reason is simple: the more fat you carry, the more insulin-resistant your cells become. Since the vast majority of people with Type 2 diabetes are overweight, this is a key issue. For many people, losing even 4.5kg (10lb) is enough to produce beneficial results in blood glucose levels. But as anyone who has tried to lose weight knows, it's easy for the best laid dietary plan to go awry – at least temporarily. Don't worry. This is a long-term project, and occasional lapses are to be expected. The important thing is to find a few key strategies to help you to shed unwanted pounds and keep them off.

The diet industry in the UK is estimated to be worth more than £1 billion a year, and most of us are likely to have contributed to this in one way or another. In recent years there has been an explosion in weight-loss plans and theories, yet we are not getting any slimmer as a population – quite the contrary.

Recently, high-protein, low-carbohydrate diets have been all the rage. The idea is this: when you cut out carbohydrates from your diet, your body no longer has glucose to burn as energy. So instead it burns body fat, leading to weight loss. The trouble is, protein foods are often rich in saturated fats, and many dietititians and nutritionists claim that this type of diet is likely to have long-term health implications. Recent research has suggested it may lead to kidney problems. Since people with diabetes are more prone to kidney problems, it is not advisable to opt for a high-protein diet.

If you continue to go for the latest quick fix or published diet, you'll continue to fall into the dieting trap. You are lured by the headlines; told that the diet is revolutionary, that you'll be slim for ever. You'll be promised a huge weight loss in days or weeks – far more enticing than the sensible weight loss the dietitians and doctors will encourage. But, you know the facts – it's the steady, weight loss that works, and is far healthier for you.

7 DIET MYTHS

Weight loss can be difficult, no thanks to popular myths that have the ring of truth but can actually work against you. These are some of the more common ones.

1 DESSERTS ARE FORBIDDEN

The truth is, there's room in your diet for any kind of food, especially the ones you love most — as long as you control your total caloric intake. Denying yourself your favorite foods can lead to binge eating and, ultimately, discouragement.

2 YOU HAVE TO LOSE A LOT OF WEIGHT TO MAKE A DIFFERENCE

The closer you can get to an ideal weight, the better, but small, sustained improvements at the beginning of a weight-loss pro-gramme have the biggest impact on your health. Studies show that losing between 2kg and 5kg (5 to 10lb) can improve insulin resist-ance enough to allow some peo-ple with Type 2 diabetes to quit medication or injections.

3 WHAT YOU EAT MATTERS MORE THAN HOW MUCH

Both matter, but recent research finds that the number of calories in your food is more important than where they come from. For example — a bagel might seem healthier than a doughnut ring, but dense bagels have the calorie content of six slices of bread. As long as you're not eating too much fat in other foods, the doughnut ring wins.

4 IF YOU WORK OUT, YOU CAN EAT WHATEVER YOU WANT

That's robbing Peter to pay Paul. You can't lose weight if you reduce calories in one way but increase them in another. To lose weight you must burn more calories than you consume.

5 SKIPPING MEALS MAKES YOU LOSE WEIGHT FAST

Actually, studies show that people who skip breakfast tend to be heavier than people who don't. And skipping meals tends to make you overeat later. If you have diabetes, it's important to keep up a steady intake of small portions of food throughout the day to keep your blood-sugar levels stable and reduce the risk of hypoglycaemia.

6 STARCHES ARE FATTENING

If you are insulin resistant, your body may find it easier to convert carbohydrate calories to fat than to burn it as energy, but

the fact remains that starches (and other carbohydrates) are less dense in calories gram for gram than other types of food. The main issue is calories, so if you load starchy foods with fat — sour cream and butter on a baked potato, for instance — or eat them in large quantities, the caloric load can add up.

7 YOU SHOULD NEVER EAT FAST FOOD

Never say never. Fast food can be worked into your meal plan if you choose well. Opt for grilled foods instead of fried, avoid or scrape away high-fat dressings like mayonnaise, and share those chips to keep portion size down.

Then, there is the simple theory of weight loss: simply burn more calories in a day than you consume and you'll soon lose weight. To do that, simply exercise a little more, and eat a little less. In this simple approach, you eat a well-balanced diverse array of food: lots of complex carbohydrates, healthy oils, lean meats and fish. Not only does this theory work, it is also almost perfectly in tune with the latest thinking about healthy eating for diabetes.(For more on exercise, see Chapter 5.)

Calorie counting and willpower

So how many calories should you eat in a day? Requirements vary, depending on body size, physical activity and basal metabolic rate. But any diet plan that is set below 1,200 calories a day can make it extra hard to get all the vitamins and minerals you need, and is often not filling enough, so you abandon the diet. Eating too little can lead to fatigue, which in turn only leads to more over-eating.

BOOSTING YOUR WILLPOWER

Try these tips to help you to keep to your weight loss plan. Perhaps the most important strategy is to set targets, but not ones that are over-ambitious so that you get discouraged too easily.

1 WEIGH YOURSELF ONLY ONCE A WEEK

Your weight fluctuates from day to day and it is not helpful to weight yourself more often. A steady loss of 500g to 1kg (1–2lb) a week will give you better long-term results than a diet that promises you'll lose a stone in a month.

2 SET REALISTIC TARGETS

Don't aim to lose more than 2.5–3kg (6–7lb) a month. Reward yourself with treat such as a trip to the theatre or a new book, when you reach your target.

3 EAT AT THE TABLE

Make your meal more of an occasion by eating at the table. Limit night-time snacking and avoid eating in front of the television.

4 USE A SMALLER PLATE

It will make your meals look bigger.

5 DISTRACT YOURSELF

When you feel like over-indulging, go for a stroll, take a bath or read a book.

6 EAT BEFORE FOOD SHOPPING

Do your grocery shoppping after you've eaten a meal or a snack – you're less likely to buy quick-fix snacks. Use a shopping list and compare the calorie and fat content of foods.

7 MAKE ACTIVITY PART OF YOUR DAILY LIFE

Remember that physical activity can be therapeutic, so tackling those garden weeds can have more benefits than you think. The more calories you burn, the faster you'll lose weight.

Essentially, 500g (1lb) equals 3,500 calories. So to lose 500g in a week you should burn an extra 500 calories a day through exercise, or cut 500 calories from your diet, or come up with some combination. To lose 1kg (2lb) a week, you'll need a 'caloric imbalance' of 1,000 calories a day, achieved by exercise, diet or both. It's a pretty simple formula.

You can only achieve your ideal weight if you really want to. So the first step is to make up your mind that this is what you really do want. Then take action that is likely to lead to the result you want. It took time to reach the weight you are now, and it will take time to shed it, so be patient.

Think slim, visualize yourself at that ideal weight, feeling energetic, taking part in all the activities that you would love to, with that increased sense of confidence, while enjoying your food as part of a new, healthier lifestyle.

Keep portions under control

The perfect meal is one in which you are served a reasonably sized portion of wonderful, surprising, delicious food. You shouldn't feel overfull at the end of the meal, but you shouldn't be hungry either. You should feel satisfied and content.

⮑ **Eat smaller portions** Eating smaller portions of your favourite foods works in many ways. First and foremost, you get to eat the foods you love. It's fine for people with diabetes to eat sugary food, for example: it just needs to be restricted to small portions and eaten after a meal. You'll begin to have a healthier view of food, too.

Although the food guidelines today allow people with diabetes to choose from a wide array of foods, portion size still matters. It may seem unlikely that just one extra chicken wing or another teaspoon of oil makes a difference, but they do. Those extra 100 calories make it that much more difficult to lose weight or manage blood glucose.

Here are some examples of a 'correct' portion:
- ▶ 3 tablespoons breakfast cereal, or 2 tablespoons muesli.
- ▶ 80–100g (3–3½oz) roast beef, ham, lamb or chicken.
- ▶ 115–140g (4–5oz) cooked fillet of white or oily fish (not fried in batter)

WHAT THE STUDIES SHOW

Staggering your food intake throughout the day helps keep blood sugar on a more even keel, but it also appears to lower cholesterol, according to a study at the University of Cambridge. Researchers surveyed more than 14,000 people about how often they eat meals and snacks and matched responses to results of cholesterol tests. They found that those who ate more than six times a day had total blood-cholesterol levels about 4 per cent lower than people who ate only three times a day, and about 5 per cent lower than those who ate only once or twice a day.

▶ 2 heaped tablespoons boiled rice or pasta

▶ 1 medium-sized potato or sweet potato.

▶ 25g (1oz) Cheddar cheese, or 40 g (1½oz) low-fat Cheddar cheese.

▶ 1 small pot of yoghurt.

▶ Fruit and vegetables (see box page 96)

Eat more frequently Another guideline is to eat more frequently. Instead of having three big meals a day, eat smaller meals more frequently, plus lots of healthy snacks. Studies indicate that staggering your food throughout the day not only helps to stabilize blood glucose levels but may also lower cholesterol levels (see What the studies show, page 105)

Of course, your body is unique, and the nature of your diabetes will affect the frequency with which you should eat. Work with a registered dietitian to come up with a good plan for dividing your meals up throughout the day.

Eight steps to healthy eating

Diabetes UK recommends the following steps to help you to control your blood glucose levels, blood fats and blood pressure, as well as your weight.

Eat complex carbohydrates Eat regular meals based on starchy carbohydrate foods such as bread, pasta, chapatis, potatoes, rice and cereals. This will help you to control your blood glucose levels. Whenever possible, choose wholegrain varieties that are high in fibre, such as wholemeal bread and wholemeal cereals, to help maintain a healthy digestive system and prevent problems such as constipation.

Cut down on fat This applies especially to saturated (animal) fats, the type of fat that is linked to heart disease. Choose monounsaturated fats, such as olive oil and rapeseed oil. Eating less fat and fatty foods will also help you to lose weight. Cut down on butter, margarine, cheese and fatty meats. Choose low-fat dairy foods such as skimmed milk and low-fat yoghurt. Grill, steam or oven-bake instead of frying or cooking with oil or other fats.

Eat more fruit and vegetables Eat more fruit and vegetables. Aim for at least five portions a day to provide you with vitamins and fibre as well as to help the overall balance of your diet. A portion is, for example, a single piece of fruit or a medium-sized serving of a vegetable.

⮌ **Reduce sugar** Cut down on sugar and sugary foods This does not mean that you have to adopt a sugar-free diet. Sugar can be used as an ingredient in foods and in baking as part of a healthy diet. However, you should choose sugar-free, low-sugar or diet squashes and fizzy drinks, because sugary drinks cause blood glucose levels to rise quickly.

⮌ **Use less salt** A high intake of salt can raise your blood pressure. Try flavouring food with herbs and spices instead of salt.

⮌ **Drink alcohol in moderation** Limit your alcohol consumption: It should not exceed two units of alcohol per day for a woman and three units per day for a man. (One unit is a small glass of wine, for example, or half a pint of normal-strength beer.) Never drink on an empty stomach, because alcohol can increase the likelihood of hypoglycaemia (low blood-glucose levels) occurring.

⮌ **Lose weight if you are overweight** This will help you to control your diabetes and will also reduce your risk of heart disease, high blood pressure and stroke. Aim to lose weight slowly over time (500g–1kg (1–2lb) per week) rather than crash dieting. Even if you don't manage to achieve your ideal weight, losing a small amount, and keeping it off, will help you to control your blood glucose and improve your overall health.

⮌ **Avoid 'diabetic' foods** Don't be tempted by 'diabetic' foods or drinks They are expensive, unnecessary and have no added benefit for people with diabetes.

Fluids

Every system in your body needs fluid – in fact, your lean muscle, blood and brain are each more than 70 per cent water. Water is the most important ingredient your body needs every day. It regulates body temperature, transports nutrients and oxygen, carries away waste, helps to detoxify the kidneys and liver, dissolves vitamins and minerals, and cushions the body from injury.

MANAGING YOUR CARBOHYDRATE

A programme of five-day training courses is being introduced in the UK to help people with Type I diabetes to manage their condition by teaching them the skills to estimate the carbohydrate in each meal and to inject the right amount of insulin.

Run by trained nurses and dietitians, the Dose Adjustment for Normal Eating (known as DAFNE) course includes such topics as carbohydrate estimation, blood glucose monitoring, insulin regimens, hypoglycaemia, illness and exercise. The programme is based on the Intensive Insulin Therapy education programme developed in the late 1970s by a team at the WHO Collaborating Centre for Diabetes in Dusseldorf. The approach has been widely adopted in Germany and other parts of Europe. Following a successful trial from February 2000 to July 2001, it will be gradually implemented on a national level. (More information from Diabetes UK or the DAFNE website www.dafne.uk.com)

SNACK IDEAS

To stabilize your blood glucose levels, spread your carbohydrate intake over the day by having regular meals. Whether you snack between meals will depend upon your lifestyle, activity levels, personal preferences and the diabetes medication you are taking. Thinking of new snack ideas that are not high in fat can be challenging. Try some of the ideas below.

FRUIT

■ Make the most of seasonal fruit. The mini fruit now available in some supermarkets are excellent for snacks or go for exotic fruits such as kiwi fruit or mango.

■ Individual tins of fruit in natural juice (with a ring pull) such as Fruitini.

■ Dried fruit with raisins, apricots and tropical mixes are available in individual packets.

BREAD AND TOAST

■ Stuff a warm pitta bread with proteins such as ham, chicken or cold beef. Add plenty of salad leaves and a mustardy dressing.

■ Make mini pizzas on halved rolls or muffins.

■ Toasted crumpets or English muffins are delicious with a savoury topping such as low fat cream cheese or a sliver of smoked salmon.

■ Try toasted teacakes or currant buns, or portions of fruitcake or sponge and malt loaf.

■ Savoury or fruit scones

■ Sandwiches – a single slice of bread with a tasty filling is enough for a snack.

■ Mini buns or American style muffins

CEREALS

■ A bowl of non-frosted flakes or bran with milk and extra fruit.

■ Chewy or crunchy cereal bars.

BISCUITS

■ Some sweet biscuits are lower in fat than others. Good bets are garibaldi, ginger nuts, rich tea and Hob Nobs.

■ Low calorie rice cakes are excellent energy boosters and come in a wide range of sweet and savoury flavours.

YOGHURTS AND FROMAGE FRAIS

■ Stick to low fat and diet varieties to get the maximum fill-up for minimum calories.

MILKSHAKES

■ Home made milk shakes are easily made with semi-skimmed milk, low fat yoghurt and fruit whizzed up in the liquidiser.

POPCORN

■ Home popped corn (use a microwave) can be sprinkled with a little sweetener or salt or flavoured with some chilli powder, paprika or celery salt.

DIPS

■ Fruit wedges and raw vegetable sticks are delicious with salsas or reduced fat dips.

SOUPS OR CUP-A-SOUPS

■ Make the most of the wide range of snack soups now available.

CRISPS

■ If you crave crispy snacks, 'French fries', Quavers and Twiglets are lowest in fat.

Even mild dehydration can lead to problems such as fatique and constipation. Drinking adequate amounts of water may also help to prevent some diseases such as kidney stones, and may be associated with a lower incidence of colon cancer. And yet, most people do not drink enough.

Water is best, but milk, unsweetened fruit juices, low-calorie squash, tea and coffee all contribute to your fluid intake. Alcohol does not count, as it acts as a diuretic and can increase fluid loss. In fact, add an extra glass of water for each glass of alcohol you drink.

Develop a regular routine by keeping water bottles near you as a reminder, or get into the habit of leaving your desk at work to go for a refill. And don't wait until you are thirsty. You may already be de-hydrated. You'll need to drink extra water in dehydrating conditions such as hot, humid or cold weather or at high altitudes, and when you are doing heavy exercise that makes you perspire.

Is there room for alcohol in your diet?

Yes – unless your GP has asked you to avoid it for a specific medical reason. In moderation, alcohol may even help to prevent cardiovascular problems associated with diabetes. But bear in mind two points. First, alcohol lowers blood glucose levels owing to its effect on the liver. Secondly, it is high in calories – almost as high as fat – but with few nutrients. Here are some useful tips on alcohol consumption.

○ **Pair alcohol with food**. Food acts like a sponge, helping to absorb some of the alcohol and in turn minimizing its effect on blood glucose. Sip your drink slowly to further slow absorption, or add a sugar-free mixer to make the drink go further.

○ **Don't drink when your blood glucose is low.** By taking consistent daily blood-glucose readings you will be in a good position to make a decision whether to drink or not. If your blood glucose is already low, don't drink alcohol.

○ **Observe the safe drinking limit** Guidelines for people with diabetes are a maximum of 21 units a week for men (3 units a day) and 14 units a week for women (2 units a day). Drinking far less is preferable. Try to space your drinking throughout the week and to have a couple of alcohol-free days each week.

One unit of alcohol is equal to:
- half a pint of beer or lager
- 1 pub measure of aperitif, sherry, liqueur or spirit
- 1 standard glass of wine

➲ **Risk of hypoglycaemia**. Alcohol can cause hypoglycaemia if you are taking insulin or certain medication for your diabetes; the higher the alcohol content (for example, in spirits), the greater the likelihood of hypoglycaemia. The following guidelines may help to prevent it occurring:

▶ Avoid drinking on an empty stomach. Always have something to eat with a drink and especially afterwards if you have been out drinking – the hypoglycaemic effect of alcohol can last for several hours.

▶ Choose low-alcohol drinks. Avoid special diabetic beers or lagers, as these are higher in alcohol.

▶ If you enjoy spirits such as vodka and gin, try to use the sugar-free/slimline mixers.

▶ If you track the carbohydrate you eat, do not include the carbohydrate from alcoholic drinks.

➲ **Drink less alcohol** if you are trying to lose weight and be sure to stay within a maximum of seven units of alcohol a week.

REAL-LIFE MEDICINE

SO MUCH FITTER – THANKS TO DIABETES

Marilyn Horner, 51, can thank her diabetes diagnosis for making her fitter and healthier than she was several years ago. 'I am ashamed to say I weighed 143kg (22½ stone), and I'm only 5ft tall,' says Marilyn, from Manchester.

Six years ago she was admitted to hospital with a severe chest infection. 'The doctor asked if I had my insulin with me. "I don't have diabetes!" I told him. But it turned out that my blood-sugar levels were 19.5, so I was definitely diabetic. It was quite a shock, and only then did I connect all the other symptoms I had. I'd been drinking more, feeling tired all the time, going to the toilet a lot and my weight was fluctuating.' She was immediately put on to insulin injections, which brought her blood-sugar level down to 9. She was then put on to tablets which she has been taking ever since.

Marilyn is in no doubt that her obesity was the main cause of her diabetes as there is no family history of the disease. 'The weight just had to come off for my own well-being and to control the diabetes,' she says. 'I started to read the food-labels at the supermarket and was amazed how much fat and sugar there was in the canned and processed food I'd been eating. I began to eat a lot more fresh food.' Before her diagnosis Marilyn didn't bother with breakfast. In the morning she'd have chocolate biscuits with her coffee. Lunch would be meat with plenty of potatoes, bread and maybe a cake for dessert. During the afternoon she'd snack on crisps and for supper she'd have sandwiches, and biscuits later on if she felt hungry.

Today, Marilyn has cereal for breakfast with skimmed milk, then nothing until lunch, which is usually a salad in summer and on colder days fish or chicken with vegetables, a baked potato and fruit or a fat-free yoghurt. She no longer snacks in the afternoon, and supper is usually soup or a salad and then an apple or banana later on if she's hungry. Marilyn lost 6.5kg (1 stone) in the first three months, then 1 or 2 pounds a week ever since. She has now lost 44.5kg (7 stone).

It has made such a difference to her life. 'Now I can walk 3 or 4 miles at a time. I go swimming and ballroom dancing. I do more socializing and I'm meeting new people. I can buy clothes that fit me – I couldn't do that before.' Marilyn now has a full-time job as a receptionist at a Salvation Army Homeless Hostel. 'I didn't have the confidence to apply for jobs before. I feel better than I have in years. I have a way to go, but I'm happy as long as my weight continues to go down steadily.'

Exercise as medicine

Being active trims fat from your body and helps you to tip the scales in the right direction – two key ways to control diabetes. But there's more. Exercise is almost like insulin in its ability to bring down blood sugar. It also helps the body to use insulin. All this makes physical activity one of the single most effective ways to control your diabetes – not to mention reducing your risk of having a heart attack or stroke. Adding workouts to your schedule needn't take a lot of time or effort. It can even be fun!

FIVE

5

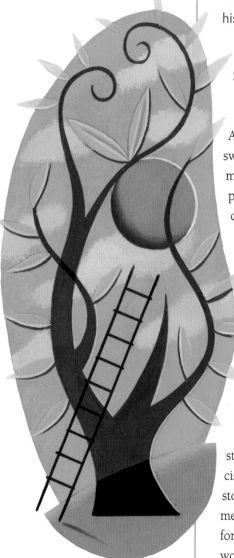

Powerful treatment

Say a dramatic treatment hit the market that could lower your blood sugar from 18 to 6.5mmol/l and help you to lose a stone and a half (9.5kg). Would you be interested? Surjeet Soin from Luton certainly was – and those were his results. But it wasn't a powerful new drug that the 60-year-old took. His secret weapon was exercise.

Soin walks five or six miles a day in the countryside near his home. 'I took up walking six years ago and in all I do about 25 miles a week,' he says. He also does a lot of gardening. Alongside the exercise, he eats a healthy diet. 'I cut out the sweet dishes and cream cakes and gave up alcohol. I feel so much better than I did when I was diagnosed ten years ago. I'm proof that if you exercise and have a healthy diet, you really can control your diabetes.'

We all know that exercise is good for our health. But it has specific benefits for people with diabetes – a fact that was recognized centuries ago by healers in the ancient cultures of India and China. Since then, scientists have discovered exactly how exercise works its magic. Here's what it does:

Lowers blood sugar Putting your muscles into action is like using your car's accelerator: it instantly boosts the demand for fuel – namely, glucose. Once your muscles exhaust their own supply of glucose, they use up the stores in your liver, then draw glucose straight from the bloodstream, lowering your blood-sugar levels. When you stop exercising, your body gives top priority to replenishing glucose stores in the liver and muscles rather than the blood, which means that your blood sugar will stay lower for hours – perhaps for as long as a couple of days, depending on how hard you worked out.

Boosts insulin sensitivity If you exercise regularly, you can actually lower your level of insulin resistance. That's because exercise forces muscles to use glucose more efficiently by making cells more receptive to insulin. It's as if getting physical gives your cells a kick start: if they absolutely must have more glucose, they will work harder to get it. Exercise also boosts the number of insulin receptors. If you exercise regularly you will perpetuate good blood-sugar control. In fact, the effect won't entirely fade away unless you go for about 72 hours without a workout. Even if you have been a committed couch potato for years, you can raise your insulin sensitivity with exercise in as little as one week.

Burns fat What happens when muscles use up the glucose in the liver and blood? After about 30 minutes of continuous exercise, the body turns to fatty acids both in flabby storage sites throughout the body and in the blood. Using fat for energy helps to clear the blood of harmful fats, such as LDL cholesterol and triglycerides. It also boosts 'good' HDL cholesterol and helps to trim abdominal fat, which is linked to a higher risk of diabetes and complications.

Sheds surplus pounds The more active you are, the more energy you use, and if you control your diet as well, you'll end up with a calorie deficit that eventually tips the scales in the right direction. As a bonus, exercise also builds up your muscle mass. And since muscle burns energy faster than other types of tissue (especially fat) do, that means you'll burn more calories all the time – even when you're relaxing in front of the TV.

Protects your heart Exercise reduces your chances of having a heart attack, stroke or other cardiovascular problem linked with diabetes by helping to improve your risk profile. In one study, Type 2 patients who took part in an aerobic-exercise programme lasting only three months saw their triglyceride and HDL cholesterol levels improve by about 20 per cent, along with a significant drop in blood pressure. And the benefits are not limited to those with Type 2 diabetes. Researchers at the University of Pittsburgh in the USA found that the risk of dying from cardiovascular illnesses was three times higher among sedentary people with Type 1 diabetes than among those who regularly burn about 2,000 calories a week through exercise.

Makes you feel good Don't underestimate this. Dealing with a chronic disease day after day can sometimes feel discouraging, stressful, or even depressing. Exercise helps by producing feel-good chemicals in the brain that can boost your mood, relieve stress and alleviate the blues. It also does wonders for your sense of confidence and self-esteem. When you finish a workout, you're justified in feeling that you've accomplished something

WHAT THE STUDIES SHOW

According to the British Heart Foundation, seven out of ten adults in the UK do not take enough regular physical activity. A 2004 Department of Health (DoH) report stated that up to two-thirds of men and three-quarters of women report activity levels so low that they substantially increase their risk of contracting a range of chronic diseases. DoH guidelines are that adults should take a minimum of 30 minutes of at least moderate activity on at least five days a week, either in a single daily session or separate 10-minute bouts.

important. You might feel that if you can do this, maybe you really can get your health under control. And you would be right.

Makes you look better Although not the most important health benefit, it is certainly a strong motivator. Without a doubt, if your fitness improves, your appearance does, too. You lose flab and gain muscle, strength and energy, and as a result you seem livelier, more capable and maybe even younger.

Fringe benefits

Exercise helps to control diabetes and reduce the risk of heart attack and stroke. In addition, it:

► Helps to prevent certain diseases, such as colon cancer.
► Improves or maintains the blood flow to sex organs, potentially enhancing sexual function and enjoyment.
► Preserves cognitive functions, such as memory.
► Retards bone loss that can lead to osteoporosis.
► Boosts the ability of immune-system cells to fight invaders.
► Slows physical decline that accounts for most impairments associated with ageing.
► Eases arthritis pain by strengthening and stretching the muscles, tendons and ligaments that support joints.
► Guards against back pain by strengthening muscles that support the spine.
► Aids digestion and helps to prevent such ailments as irritable bowel syndrome (IBS).
► Promotes good sleep.

Tailor-made training

Exercise is so powerful it's almost like taking medicine. But a prescription that works for you won't be ideal for everybody with diabetes. Your exercise plan should fit your circumstances, including which kind of diabetes you have and how you are treating it now. That's why it's important to discuss your exercise plan with your doctor or your diabetes care team.

Whichever strategy you choose, you'll want to bring blood sugar down – but not too far. To keep close tabs on it, test an hour before your workout, then again a half hour later to find out if your levels are rising or falling. If they're falling and on the low side, you may want to eat about 15g of carbohydrate before you start exercising. If your blood sugar is high and rising, you may need more insulin. Once your blood sugar becomes more stable, your doctor may allow you to monitor less often, but self-testing following a workout is always a good idea.

The readings you get will help to clarify how exercise should fit into your overall diabetes-management plan, which will vary from one situation to the next.

If you have Type 1 diabetes

People with Type 1 diabetes need to approach exercise with extra caution. If you work out too soon after taking insulin, the glucose-lowering team of insulin plus exercise can be too much of a good thing and lower your blood sugar to dangerous levels. On the other hand, having too little insulin in your blood while you exercise can make blood sugar build up and potentially cause ketoacidosis. To ensure your safety, check with your doctor about taking steps such as the following:

➲ **Avoid peak hours** Try to time your workout so that you're not exercising when insulin activity peaks, often within the first hour or two of an injection, depending on which type you use.

➲ **Adjust your dose** You may be able to drop your daily insulin requirements by up to 20–30 per cent if you cut your dose before a workout. Ask your doctor how much of an adjustment to make based on your current dosage and how hard you exercise – then be sure to actually do your workout.

➲ **Exercise after eating** You're less likely to become hypoglycaemic if you wait to work out until an hour or two after a meal, when your blood sugar will be naturally high and plenty of glucose will be on hand to fuel your muscles.

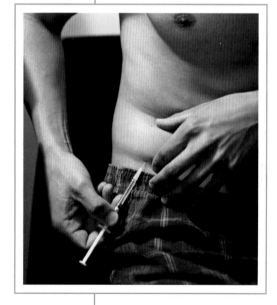

➲ **Inject into the abdomen** If you inject insulin into muscles you'll be using, they will absorb it faster and send your blood sugar plummeting. So unless you are going to do sit-ups immediately, inject into the softer folds of your midsection. If you're exercising your abdominal muscles, wait to exercise until about an hour after your injection to allow the insulin to disperse throughout the body.

⊃ **Have a snack** Eating a small, low-fat snack containing about 20g of carbohydrate during your workout can help to prevent blood sugar from falling too low, especially during vigorous exercise or workout sessions lasting an hour or more.

If you have Type 2 diabetes and use insulin

The great promise of exercise for people with Type 2 diabetes is that – unlike with Type 1 – it can actually put the condition into reverse. Boosting your insulin sensitivity could bring your blood sugar back into the normal range, especially if you're controlling your diet as well, and could permanently reduce the amount of insulin you need – or even stop you needing insulin altogether. Some practical advice:

⊃ **Proceed with caution** While keeping your eyes on the prize – less insulin or none at all – remember to keep your goals reasonable at first. If you're taking insulin, you stand the same risk of hypoglycaemia during exercise that a Type 1 person does. Take a look at the list of recommendations for people with Type 1 – they also apply to you.

⊃ **Try not to snack** If you're in danger of hypoglycaemia during exercise, you may need a snack to bring your blood sugar back up. But this solution can ultimately work against you because it adds calories you're probably better off avoiding. So instead of relying on snacks to head off hypoglycaemia, be diligent about planning to exercise after a meal so blood sugar is high during your workout.

⊃ **Stick to your meal plan** If you do eat an unplanned snack during your workout, don't make up for it by subtracting calories from your after-exercise meals. It's just as important to keep calories up after a workout as before, since exercise can make blood sugar dip dangerously for as long as a day.

If you have Type 2 and use medication

If you take a drug such as metformin to control your blood sugar, you may be able to reduce the amount you need – or stop taking it altogether – by adding more physical activity to your life. Once you figure out how exercise affects your blood sugar, you should discuss with your doctor how to adjust your drug regimen accordingly. Bear in mind, though, that exercise and diet are not automatic substitutes for diabetes drugs – and

!

CAUTION

Talk to your doctor before starting an exercise programme. If a stress test indicates heart trouble, you may be advised to walk, not run, for exercise. If you have high blood pressure or eye or kidney damage, you should avoid the strain of weight lifting. And if your feet have suffered nerve damage, you may be better off doing a low-impact exercise like swimming rather than pounding the pavement.

taking drugs doesn't excuse you from working out. In fact, drugs often work their best only when combined with other measures, such as meal planning and exercise. Some advice:

⮕ **Time your workouts** If you're on medication, avoid exercising when the drug is reaching its peak effectiveness so that your blood sugar doesn't drop dangerously low. If you're working to cut back on or eliminate your drug use, your doctor may start by having you take less (or none) before your workout. In effect, you may be able to exercise instead of taking your medication if the effects on blood sugar prove to be similar.

⮕ **Be alert to side effects** Some diabetes medications can cause muscle ache or fatigue, while others can make you dizzy or nauseous. You and your doctor both need to be clear about how intensely you intend to exercise and how your medication's side effects may limit your activities.

⮕ **Drink plenty of water** It takes about eight large glasses of water a day to keep the body hydrated – and you'll need more when you're sweating. Don't wait until you feel thirsty before drinking; that's a sign of high blood sugar and could bring your workout to a halt while you check for hyperglycaemia. Instead, drink 300–500ml (10–18fl oz) 15 minutes before exercising, then 150–250ml (5–9fl oz) every 15 minutes during your workout, and at least 500ml (18fl oz) afterwards.

THE EXERCISE–BLOOD SUGAR PARADOX

Why does blood sugar sometimes go down but other times go up after exercise? Muscles use glucose for energy, so as a rule, blood sugar goes down when you're active, as the body moves glucose from the liver and bloodstream into the cells. But that's assuming that there's enough insulin on hand to help with this transfer. If you take insulin and your dose is too low, glucose can build up in the blood during exercise and cause hyperglycaemia. That's why it's important to consult your doctor for advice on exercising and to check your blood sugar before and after (and perhaps even during) exercise to understand how physical activity affects you.

If you have impaired glucose tolerance

Recent evidence has shown that increased physical activity in conjunction with dietary changes can prevent individuals with impaired glucose tolerance from progresssing to Type 2 diabetes. Studies suggest that people who take exercise have a 35–50 per cent lower risk of developing Type 2 diabetes. The greater the amount of exercise taken, the lower the risk of developing the disease. To take advantage:

⮕ **Get started immediately** Just because full-blown diabetes may seem a very distant possibility doesn't mean that you have

WHEN TESTING MEANS RESTING

As long as your blood sugar is under control, there is no 'bad' time to exercise. But blood-sugar testing can tell you when it might be better to hold off, at least until your glucose or insulin levels can meet your muscles' demands. Here are some guidelines to follow.

■ To protect against hypoglycaemia, don't exercise if your blood sugar is below 4mmol/l. Instead, have a piece of fruit or other snack containing at least 15g of carbohydrate, then test again about 20 minutes later. Keep snacking until blood sugar rises above the 4mmol/l mark.

■ To protect against hyperglycaemia, test for ketones (using a urine ketone test strip) if blood sugar before exercise is above 15mmol/l. If the test detects ketones, don't start to exercise until you have taken more insulin to handle glucose uptake during your workout.

■ If ketones are absent, don't exercise if blood sugar is above 22mmol/l if you have Type 2 diabetes or 16mmol/l if you have Type 1 diabetes.

time to spare. If you don't start making changes now, insulin resistance is only likely to get worse. But if you start to exercise straight away, you can boost your cells' insulin sensitivity within a week, even if you're obese, giving you a good chance of avoiding a diagnosis of diabetes.

◗ **Track your blood sugar** Don't assume that because you haven't developed diabetes you don't have to worry about blood sugar. You may not need to test as often as a person with a diabetes diagnosis, but you should still keep track of your glucose levels with self-monitoring and regular checkups to ensure that your condition remains under control.

◗ **Keep it up** It's just as important for you to keep workouts regular and consistent as it is for a person with diabetes. Controlling the risk of developing the disease will never be easier than it is now – and you should aim to keep it that way.

How to sweat safely

You'll avoid most hypoglycaemia problems with proper planning (by matching exercise to your drug, insulin and meal regimens) but you should always be prepared for surprise bouts of low blood sugar.

◗ **Know when to stop – now** The second you detect symptoms of hypoglycaemia, such as shaking-confusion, lightheadedness or difficulty speaking, stop exercising immediately – not after 'just one more minute'. Be alert to all symptoms, and understand that some of them, such as sweating and rapid heartbeat, overlap with natural responses to exercise.

◗ **Take a snack with you** A quick snack can rapidly bring falling blood-sugar levels back up again in an emergency – but only if you remember to bring one along.

◗ **Get a workout partner** Because it is not always obvious when hypoglycaemia is setting in, it's wise to work out with somebody else or in a place where other people are available if you need help, especially if you're exercising vigorously.

◗ **Carry ID** Even if you're working out with a friend, you should carry identification with your name, address and phone number – and those of your doctor. Also have the name of some-one to call in an emergency as well as your insulin or drug dosages.

⮑ **Stay alert afterwards** Blood sugar can continue to fall long after you've exercised, so be alert for signs of hypoglycaemia until 24 hours after your workout.

The aerobic prescription

How will you spend the next 20 minutes? Sprawled in front of the TV? At your computer? Chatting on the phone? Passive pleasures, to be sure, but consider an alternative. Twenty minutes of brisk walking, cycling, swimming or dancing can improve cardiovascular fitness, bring your blood sugar into line and help to trim fat off your belly.

Aerobic exercises such as these should be the mainstay of your exercise programme. They keep the body moving for sustained periods of time, which taps all of its glucose stores and does the most to bring blood sugar down. They pump up your heart and breathing rate, which boosts blood circulation and oxygen delivery throughout the body and helps to keep your heart and blood vessels in good shape. And they are the most efficient way to burn body fat.

Aerobics generally involves repetitive movement of large muscle groups, such as the legs, that demand lots of oxygen (the term *aerobic* means 'with oxygen'). Any activity that gets your pulse going and quickens your breath qualifies. Obvious examples are running, cycling and swimming. But you can also get an aerobic work-out through hobbies such as hoeing your garden, hiking or dancing.

Getting started on an aerobic exercise programme is not difficult – getting off the sofa and out of the door is a great beginning. But if you want to put together a more meaningful plan, follow the FIT formula – Frequency, Intensity and Time.

The FIT formula

To get the most out of the time you spend exercising, you need to plan a programme that gives you enough sessions that go on for long enough at a high enough level of intensity to make a difference to your fitness levels.

➲ **Frequency: the calendar consideration** How often should you exercise? Unless you are doing vigorous training that requires time for rest and recuperation, you should feel free to exercise as often as possible, if your doctor okays it. But holding yourself back is probably not the issue. The latest Department of Health guidelines are that you should exercise for 30 minutes on five days a week. If you're just starting to exercise and this seems overwhelming, remember that any increase in activity will do you good. If you're totally sedentary, you can improve your cardiovascular condition significantly with as little as one work-out a week. Once you get into the habit, it will take at least three workouts a week for you to challenge your muscles consistently enough to continue improving.

Take-charge tips

To know if you're hitting your target heart rate, you will need to take your pulse during your workout.

➲ Locate an artery either on the palm side of your wrist or at either side of your neck just under your jawbone.

➲ Press lightly with your index and middle fingers to feel your pulse.

➲ Timing with your watch, count the number of beats you feel in 10 seconds.

➲ Don't bother counting for a full 60 seconds: the longer you stop to count, the slower your heart will beat, which skews your reading. Instead, multiply the 10-second count by six to find your heart-beats per minute.

➲ Alternatively, calculate in advance how many beats should occur within 10 seconds by dividing your target rate by six. For example, if your target rate is 90 to 153 beats per minute, you should count 15 (90 divided by 6) to 25 (153 divided by 6) beats in 10 seconds. If you remember the target 10-second numbers, you can skip doing the sums during your workout.

➲ As a totally maths-free alternative, take the talk test. If you're sweating steadily and somewhat short of breath while exercising but can still carry on a conversation without gasping for air, you're probably within your target heart-rate range.

Calculate your target heart rate

AGE	25	30	35	40	45	50	55	60	65	70	75	80
Maximum heart rate	195	190	185	180	175	170	165	160	155	150	145	140
50% of max (low intensity)	97	95	92	90	87	85	82	80	77	75	72	70
85% of max (high intensity)	166	162	157	153	149	145	140	136	132	128	123	119
Beats per 10 seconds at 50%–85% of max	16–27	16–27	15–26	15–25	15–25	14–24	14–23	13–23	13–22	13–21	12–20	12–20

⭢ **Intensity: how hard to push** The exercise you do must be intense enough to give your body a good workout, but not so intense that you can't keep it going for a sustained period. Naturally, your intensity tolerance will be different from the next person's. Some people can run a mile in 10 minutes, while others might feel winded by a walk around the block. It's important to find the level of exertion that is right for you and your current physical condition, not only to gain the maximum benefit for your health but also to make sure you don't overdo it.

The gold standard for measuring how hard you're working is your heart rate, or how fast your heart is beating. Aim for a heart rate that's 50 to 85 per cent of your maximum – the point at which your heart can't pump any harder. At the beginning of your exercise programme, you should start at the low-intensity end of this spectrum and gradually work toward a more vigorous workout as you become better conditioned.

Maximum heart rate tends to be fairly consistent from one person to the next, although it declines gradually as you get older. That makes it easy to come up with a target heart-rate range that is specific to your age. To calculate your target heart rate:

▶ First calculate your maximum heart rate by subtracting your age from 220. For example, if you are 40 years old, subtract 40 from 220 to get a maximum heart rate of 180 beats per minute.

▶ Multiply this number by 0.50 and 0.85 to get the lower and upper limits of the 50 to 85-per cent range. In this example, a maximum heart rate of 180 results in a target heart rate of 90 (180 x 0.50) to 153 (180 x 0.85) beats per minute.

WHAT THE STUDIES SHOW

Children of diabetes sufferers can significantly reduce their risk of developing the disease by exercising more, according to the British Heart Foundation. Preliminary results from a study at the University of Glasgow show that people whose parents have Type 2 diabetes – and are thus genetically susceptible to the disease – can reduce their risk of developing it to that of someone with no genetic link simply by doing regular exercise.

Be sure to confirm with your doctor that the target heart rate you calculate is safe for you. Then check your pulse when you exercise (see 'Take-charge tips' on page 122). If it is within your target range, every pump of your heart is beating back your diabetes and its potential cardiovascular complications. But don't feel that less strenuous activity has no value. Even small bouts of exertion help to burn calories (although to a lesser extent), and any amount of activity is better than none.

⮕ **Time: the long and short of it** The third FITness factor is how long each workout should last. As a rule you should aim for 20 to 40 minutes – long enough to give your heart and lungs the workout they need to improve, but not so long that you get tired and start to slow down. The more conditioned you become, the longer you should be able to go.

If you don't have 20 to 40 minutes, try cutting your workout in half but doing it twice – once in the morning and once in the evening (or any other time that is convenient). Research shows that you can get almost as fit with shorter bouts of activity sprinkled throughout the day as with a single session. For example, in a study at Stanford University, men who exercised three times a day reaped similar gains in oxygen uptake (a measure of cardiovascular fitness) as men who exercised for 30 minutes in a single session. This is in line with the Department of Health advice that 30 minutes' activity spread throughout the day, in bouts of 10 minutes or more, has as many health benefits as a single 30-minute session.

Intensity and energy expenditure

Here are the approximate levels of intensity and the number of calories you'll burn when doing the following activities:

ACTIVITY	Intensity	Intensity (METS)	*Energy expenditure
Ironing	Light	2.3	69
Cleaning and dusting	Light	2.5	75
Walking – *strolling 2mph*	Light	2.5	75
Painting/decorating	Moderate	3.0	90
Walking – *3mph*	Moderate	3.3	99
Hoovering	Moderate	3.5	105
Golf – *walking, pulling clubs*	Moderate	4.3	129
Badminton – *social*	Moderate	4.5	135
Tennis – *doubles*	Moderate	5.0	150
Walking – *brisk, 4mph*	Moderate	5.0	150
Mowing lawn – *using power mower*	Moderate	5.5	165
Cycling – *10–12mph*	Moderate	6.0	180
Aerobic dancing	Vigorous	6.5	195
Cycling –*12–14mph*	Vigorous	8.0	240
Swimming – *slow crawl (50m/min)*	Vigorous	8.0	240
Tennis – *singles*	Vigorous	8.0	240
Running – *6mph (10 minutes/mile)*	Vigorous	10.0	300
Running – *7mph (8.5 minutes/mile)*	Vigorous	11.5	345
Running – *8mph (7.5 minutes/mile)*	Vigorous	13.5	405

MET = Metabolic equivalent
1MET = metabolic rate (rate of energy expenditure) when at rest
2 METs = a doubling of the resting metabolic rate
* (Kcal equivalent for a person of 9½ stone (60kg) doing the activity for 30 minutes)

That means you have great flexibility to exercise when it's most convenient. If you vacuum the floor in the morning, go for a walk around the block at lunchtime, and rake some leaves in the evening, you can satisfy a day's workout requirements without changing into gym clothes or needing to take a shower.

Getting the right FIT

Don't feel like pushing yourself today? Did you skip a workout last week? It's not a problem. If you happen to change one of the FIT variables, simply adjust another one to compensate. For example, if you exercise at a lower-than-usual heart rate (less intensity), you can add to the duration of the workout (more time) so you come out even. If you miss a workout (less frequency), you can boost either the intensity or the time during your next session – as long as you don't overdo it.

Put the muscle on blood sugar

If you're going to give priority to one form of exercise, it should be aerobic. But there's another weapon in the exercise arsenal that's worth launching against diabetes: resistance training, also known as weight lifting. While aerobics builds endurance, resistance training builds strength and muscle mass – important because just like bigger cars, bigger muscles burn more fuel, which lowers your blood sugar. It also boosts your metabolism, even when you're at rest. And when you're stronger you'll look better, be less prone to injury, and simply find it easier to do daily tasks, from carrying groceries to climbing stairs.

Unlike aerobics, resistance training – so called because muscles work against a resisting force, such as the weight of a dumbbell – involves exercises that make muscles tire quickly. So they can only be sustained for a brief period. The idea is to consistently stress muscles, adding resistance as you become stronger to build them up even more.

Don't assume that pumping iron is only for fitness freaks with rippling muscles or that you're too old to lift weights. Studies show that even adults approaching their 90s can firm up their muscles with resistance training, reaping bonus health benefits such as stronger bones and more vitality.

(Continued on page 128)

GOOD WAYS TO GET GOING

No one form of exercise is inherently better than another. Your only goals are to move your body, pump up your heart rate – and have fun doing it. What you choose to do is a matter of preference, although some aerobic activities may be more appropriate than others in the light of any complications you may have. Here's what some of the most popular forms of exercise have going for them.

WALKING

Benefits

It costs nothing, won't harm your joints, and you can do it virtually anytime, anywhere – down your street, in a shopping centre, or in a park. Its low intensity makes it a good starting point for any exercise programme, but if you increase the pace (especially on hills), it delivers a solid cardio-vascular workout.

Tips

Start by just walking out of the door. Breathe the air. Let your mind wander. Try to walk for at least 10 minutes at first, and gradually lengthen your walks as you feel more comfortable. Keep the pace easy until you hit the 20 to 30-minute mark, then start building up the intensity. Work towards a pace of about four miles per hour (a mile every 15 minutes). A simple gadget called a pedometer, available from sports shops, can keep track of your mileage for you.

A WALKING PLAN FOR BEGINNERS

Not used to exercise? Walking is an easy, non-intimidating way to start. Try this six-week plan to get you going. By week six, you'll be walking enough to help control your blood sugar.

	DURATION	INTENSITY	FREQUENCY
Week 1	10–15 minutes	As slow as you want	3–5 times
Week 2	15 minutes	50–60% of your maximum heart rate	3–5 times
Week 3	20 minutes	50–60% of your maximum heart rate	5 times
Week 4	20 minutes	60% of your maximum heart rate	5 times
Week 5	25 minutes	60–70% of your maximum heart rate	5 times
Week 6	30 minutes	60–70% of your maximum heart rate	5 times

JOGGING

Benefits

Jogging is almost as inexpensive and convenient as walking, but it's more intense, so you can get a better workout in less time. Jogging also feels (and looks) more serious than walking, which can bolster your sense of accomplishment.

Tips

Instead of setting out for a run, go for a walk-jog. Start out by walking briskly, then progress into a run. When you feel winded, walk again. As you become better conditioned, you'll find yourself jogging more and walking less. If your joints start to bother you, rest for a day or two or go back to walking. To minimize the risk of injury, avoid jogging on hard pavements and opt, whenever possible, for soft, even surfaces, such as running tracks in schools and smooth expanses of grass.

BICYCLING

Benefits

Biking delivers fitness benefits plus a bracing rush of speed – at least if the bike is real, not stationary. Both types exercise your heart and your leg muscles without putting undue stress on your knees.

Tips

Start at a moderate pace of about 50 revolutions per minute (rpm). Digital readouts on stationary bikes often show the rpm; on a real bike, count how many times one pedal reaches the top of its arc in 30 seconds, then multiply by two. When it feels comfortable, gradually boost your rpm to somewhere between 60 and 90. From there, you can adjust the programme on your stationary bike for more resistance or (on a real bike) start shifting into higher gears or head for the hills.

SWIMMING

Benefits

By taking the load off joints, swimming is one of the most effective, yet safe sports, especially if you're overweight. It's also highly aerobic, depending as much on heart and lung capacity as muscle power.

Tips

Start at a leisurely pace with strokes that keep your face out of the water. When your aerobic conditioning improves, you can start holding your breath more. Make it a goal to do 10 lengths without stopping. You might also decide to take a water-aerobics class if one is offered at a gym near you.

ROWING

Benefits

Works the arms and the legs (along with most other muscles in the body) while also providing an excellent aerobic workout.

Tips

For proper form, use your arms and legs simultaneously, sliding back in the rolling seat without throwing your back into the action. Once you've grasped the correct motion (if you're at a gym, ask a trainer for instructions), start with 5-minute sessions and gradually work up to the 30-minute target, then adjust the resistance to make the exercise more difficult.

How to make a muscle

Resistance exercises don't work the entire body at once, as aerobic exercises do. Instead, you do different exercises that target specific muscle groups. If you go to a gym, you'll find machines designed to help you to do this. But you can also do resistance training at home, using basic exercises such as press-ups and pull-ups and possibly some hand weights or dumb-bells, obtainable from any sporting-goods store. (If you don't want to buy dumbbells, you can improvise using everyday objects such as milk jugs filled with water or sand, or even cans of soup or baked beans.) How much weight you need depends on what you can comfortably lift, and that will vary from exercise to exercise, so you'll need more than one set of dumb-bells. Sets of 1, 2 and 5kg (around 3, 5 and 10lb) should suffice. Use the exercises on page 132–3 to get started. And follow these basic principles.

➲ **Lift to fatigue** Rather than building endurance, with weight lifting you want to quickly make muscles so tired that they just can't do much more. As a rule, you should have enough resistance during any exercise to make muscles feel fatigued after 8 to 12 repetitions. At the beginning of your programme use light weights, that you can easily lift for 12 repetitions, until your muscles become accustomed to being worked.

➲ **Make gradual progress** Don't try to do too much at once. Building muscle is a long-term construction project that moves ahead slowly. Tackling more weight than you can comfortably handle will only make muscles sore and discourage you from continuing your workouts. If you can easily lift a given weight 12 times, add weight to make 8 repetitions easy, but 12 hard. (Don't add more than 2.5kg (5lb) at a time.) Then, keeping to that amount of weight, gradually add more repetitions to your workouts until 12 repetitions feels easy. At that point, add more weight so that 8 repetitions are easy but 12 are hard… and so on.

➲ **Move slowly** Avoid quick, jerky movements with weights, which can stress muscles, ligaments and joints. Slow, controlled movements ensure that you are working muscles at every point in your range of motion and not letting momentum do any of the work for you. As a general guideline, take two seconds to lift the weight and four seconds to let it down again.

⮑ **Breathe evenly** Don't hold your breath when lifting weights – you need to keep oxygen flowing to working muscles. Breathe out when you lift and in when you let the weight down.

⮑ **Go from big to small** Work large groups of muscles such as the chest, legs and back first, saving smaller muscles, such as the biceps and triceps, for last. That way, you won't tire smaller muscles that support the bigger muscles during their workout.

Taking the first steps

If you're a stranger to exercise, the idea can seem intimidating. And starting anything new requires motivation. If you're having trouble getting going, take the easiest action possible – stepping out of the front door for a walk. Once you conquer inertia, you can start to think about a more structured exercise plan.

Experts have discovered that people go through several distinct stages when they make fitness a fixture in their life. In the beginning, there's ignorance or lack of interest – exercise is simply off your radar – followed by a period of 'contemplation', in which you're interested but take no action. Next comes 'preparation', in which you begin to get moving but aren't physically active enough. It's common in this stage for barriers – everything from lack of time to lack of confidence – to hold you back. The mantra is often 'I could never do that.' And 'that' could be anything from exercising for 20 minutes continuously to joining an exercise class. But the question is: What can you do? Can you be physically active for two minutes by, say, walking around instead of sitting down while waiting for someone at the station? Then start there. The more you move, the more easily you'll progress to the next two stages: 'action', in which you exercise regularly as a new habit, and 'maintenance', in which you reinforce that new habit to make it stick.

Planning for action

Crossing the line into the action phase can be so gradual, you may not be sure when you have arrived. One sign: You feel a need to organize your efforts. All your exercise doesn't have to

?
DID YOU KNOW

An alternative to hand weights is resistance bands, sold in sporting-goods shops. Like giant rubber bands, they provide resistance for your muscles as you perform various exercises. The bands are often colour-coded for different levels of resistance, so when an exercise becomes too easy, simply switch bands to make it harder.

be written into your diary, but scheduling it can ensure that the time you need is not swallowed up by other activities. It can also help you to work toward specific goals that will keep you improving. The ideal plan is a mix of aerobic workouts lasting at least 20 to 30 minutes three to five days a week and resistance training at least two days a week. That sounds like a lot of exercising, but here are two basic strategies for fitting it all in.

Alternating workouts Do your aerobic exercise three days a week, leaving a day between each workout. Use the two intervening days to do your resistance training. That way, you can fit a comprehensive fitness plan into a five-day schedule, giving you two days off. This plan will also give muscles – which are worked differently in aerobics and in resistance training – a day to rest between each form of exercise.

Combination workouts If you can only find time for workouts a few days a week, do one workout that incorporates both aerobics and resistance training – but don't do it two days in a row. These sessions will be longer than if you worked out five days a week, but many people find that once they have committed a block of time to exercise, adding another 20 to 30 minutes is not a huge hurdle. Start with aerobics, which will warm and limber up muscles, and follow with resistance. (Exhausting muscles with weights first would make your aerobics workout more difficult.) If you're really pushed for time, skip the resistance training on one of the days.

Seven steps to success

When you start an exercise programme, it's common to feel nagging doubts – that it's too hard, you're no good at it, you're too out of shape.

BEFORE YOU JOIN A GYM

Potentially, the world is your workout facility. But if you want access to quality resistance machines, aerobics classes and trained staff, a gym may be worth the money – especially if it helps you to commit to an exercise programme. But gyms make their money because many of the people who pay for them rarely show up to use them. Here are some tips to make sure you'll get your money's worth.

■ Find a gym that is no more than 15 minutes from home or you'll have trouble getting there regularly.

■ Take a tour before signing anything, and ask to have a trial workout. If possible, talk to clients (out of your tour guide's earshot) and ask their opinion of the place.

■ Make sure that fitness instructors are qualified to recognized standards. You can check this through the Register of Exercise Professionals (www.reps-uk.org).

■ Check out the other gym users, especially at times you're most likely to be there. Will you be comfortable working out with these people?

■ Be clear about your needs. Some gyms and health clubs offer only fitness equipment and classes, while others go further, with tennis or squash courts, swimming pools and even social activities. Don't sign on the dotted line if you think you might want something different in six months' time.

To help yourself stay focused and boost your confidence:

(1) **Make it fun** Some people think that exercise has to be unpleasant to do any good. Don't be one of them. You're more likely to persevere with activities you enjoy – maybe because you like seeing what's going on in the neighbourhood during your walks, you feel like a child when gliding on your bike, or you enjoy spending time with your workout partner.

(2) **Forget the old days** You may have been a star footballer or tennis player at school, but say 'thanks for the memories' and move on with reality. Dwelling on how your body has changed will only make you see setbacks. Instead, focus on how you can change again – for the better.

(3) **Set firm goals** It helps to have goals, especially clear, immediate ones. Keep your goals specific and oriented towards what you will actually do, not where you'll end up if you do it. Saying 'I'll run five minutes longer next time' is better than 'I want to be able to do five miles by the holidays.'

(4) **Be your own benchmark** Pay no attention to the next person's six-pack or lack of cellulite. What you're doing has nothing to do with anybody but you. Stay focused on your goals. If you achieve a small success, even if it's just walking three times this week instead of twice, then celebrate!

(5) **Make a note of it** Tracking your progress in a notebook can help you realize how far you've come – or haven't. If you're walking or running, record your time or distance. If you're resistance-training, jot down how much weight you're lifting and how many repetitions you're doing.

(6) **Involve friends** Try to enlist likeable companions as workout partners: With a friend to back you up, you'll feel validation, support and maybe even a little competitiveness to spur you on. You are also more likely to stick to an exercise schedule if skipping a workout means letting down a friend. And don't forget the value of having someone at your side if your blood sugar crashes.

WHAT THE STUDIES SHOW

Short on time for strength training? Twice a week should be enough. Researchers at the University of Arkansas had one group of women do a weight workout three times a week and another group only twice a week. The twice-a-week group lifted slightly lighter weights and did six more repetitions of each exercise, spending about five extra minutes on their workout. The study showed that the twice-weekly group reaped almost the same benefits as the other women after eight weeks, boosting strength by at least 15 per cent and losing more than 2 per cent of their body fat.

(Continued on page 134)

AN ALL-YOU-NEED ROUTINE

These seven exercises provide a full-body workout that targets all the major muscle groups. Start by doing just one set of each exercise. Once your muscles are accustomed to the routine, do at least two sets to gain maximum benefit. Eventually, you may want to add or substitute exercises with help from a trainer or a good fitness book. Remember, always ask your doctor to approve any exercise programme to make sure it's safe for you.

LEGS
Lunges

1 Stand with your feet shoulder-width apart. Keeping your back straight, take a large step forward with your right foot so that your right leg is bent at a 90-degree angle and your knee is aligned over your right foot but not beyond your toes. Your left foot should remain in the starting position, although your left knee can bend to within a few inches of the floor and the heel can come off the floor.

2 Push yourself back firmly with your right leg to return to the starting position, then repeat with the left foot, and so on.

CHEST
Dumbbell chest press

1 Lie face up on a bench with your knees bent to protect your back. Grasping a dumbbell in each hand with palms facing each other, exhale as you press the weights straight above your chest until your elbows are straight, but not locked.

2 Inhaling, slowly lower the dumbbells to your chest, with your elbows just below the level of your torso.

Safety pointer: Maintain a firm grip on each dumbbell, with fingers wrapped around one side of the bar and your thumb around the other, to keep weights under control at all times.

BACK
One-arm dumbbell row

1 With your left knee resting on a bench or low table, place your left hand on the bench and your right foot on the floor, knee slightly bent. In your right hand, hold a dumbbell straight down at your side, eyes facing the floor and back straight. Exhale as you draw the weight to your torso.

2 Inhale as you lower the dumbbell back to the starting position. Repeat 8–15 times. Then repeat the exercise on the other side of your body.

Safety pointer: Keep your back straight and your torso motion to a minimum to avoid straining your back, especially as you get tired.

TRICEPS
Dumbbell kickbacks

1 Rest your right knee on a bench or low table, your right hand on the bench, and your left leg extended behind you, knee slightly bent. To get the weight to the starting position, hold a dumbbell in your left hand, palm toward your body, and bend your arm at a 45-degree angle.

2 Without moving your elbow, straighten your arm, extending the weight behind you. Then return to the starting position. Repeat on the other side.

BICEPS
Biceps curl

1 Sit on a chair, feet flat on the floor a little wider than shoulder-width apart. Grasp a dumbbell in each hand, with your arms straight at your sides, your palms facing your legs.

2 Keeping your elbows pressed against your sides, raise the weights in an arc towards your shoulders, turning your wrists so that your palms face your shoulders. Then lower the weights until your arms are straight, but elbows are not locked.

ABDOMINALS
Crunches

1 Lie face-up on the floor or an exercise mat, knees bent and feet on the floor about six inches apart. Point your toes up to provide extra back support. Lightly hold both hands behind your head or ears. Starting with your head a few inches off the floor, exhale as you curl your upper torso towards your thighs, raising your shoulders up but keeping the small of your back pressed against the floor.

2 Hold briefly, then, inhaling, slowly lower your upper body to the floor, keeping your head lifted a few inches at your lowest position.

SHOULDERS
Lateral raises

1 Stand with feet shoulder-width apart. Grasp a dumbbell in each hand with arms at your sides, elbows slightly bent and palms facing your body.

2 Keeping your back straight and tensing your abdominal muscles for back support, raise both dumbbells straight out from your sides until they are at shoulder level. Keep your elbows unlocked and your wrists, elbows and shoulders in a straight line. Pause, then lower the weights.

⑦ **Keep your priorities straight** Life is about choices. And what's really more important: cleaning the bath or fulfilling your exercise quota for the day? In the long run, exercise can save your life. In the short run, it can make you feel great. While cleaning the bath might seem critical at the moment, it may not seem important a week from now.

How to be a perpetual-motion machine

If you can't manage a steady schedule of workouts, don't feel that you've failed. Instead, look for opportunities to make movement a part of everyday life – you'll find them. Studies show that taking a lifestyle-based approach to exercise can improve fitness almost as much as a programme of gym work-outs, with sedentary people able to gain 30 minutes of activity five days a week just by sneaking it into their normal day. Here are some ways to achieve this.

➲ Next time you go to a sporting event, get up and walk around at halftime. Climb the stairs if there are any – and stay clear of the hot dog stand.

➲ Instead of waiting for the lift, take the stairs – you may actually get where you're going faster.

➲ If you're going to sit in front of the TV, make it a stationary-bicycle seat. Aim to pedal your way through a 30-minute programme. If you don't have an exercise bike, do star jumps, a few press-ups or march on the spot during the commercials.

➲ Instead of fighting for a parking place close to the theatre, find a car park some way off and walk the rest of the way.

➲ Take the dog out for a walk (if you don't have one, borrow a neighbour's). Let the dog decide where to go, and follow wherever it leads.

➲ Get up to change TV channels instead of always using the remote control.

➲ Instead of meeting a friend for coffee, go for a walk in the park together.

REAL-LIFE MEDICINE

WALKING AWAY FROM DIABETES

When Frank Jones, 64, suddenly lost about 3kg (7lb) in one week, then a further 1.5–2kg (3–4lb) the following week, he thought he might have cancer. 'We were due to go on holiday to Scotland and I had been trying to lose weight at the time, but that kind of weight loss was highly unusual,' he says.

Frank and his wife went away on holiday and he found that he was thirsty all the time and couldn't stop drinking. Upon his return he made an appointment with his GP. The doctor did a urine test and confirmed what Frank was now starting to suspect: he had Type 2 diabetes. It turned out that his blood sugar levels were incredibly high, at around 38 mmol/l.

That was 10 years ago, when Frank was 54. His doctor put him on tablets and Frank also started to eat more healthily, but 12 months later he still was unable to control his blood-sugar levels.

He then started to take insulin and his levels finally started to come down. But he felt he could do more himself. 'I was often reading in the magazine from Diabetes UK about the benefits of exercise and how important it is in controlling diabetes,' he says. So he and his wife came up with the idea of walking their neighbours' dogs while they were out at work. 'We walk three dogs every day for about one and a half hours and at weekends we still go, but without the dogs,' he says.

Frank and his wife live on the edge of Rochdale, so within five minutes they can be walking along the footpaths in the foothills of the Pennines. They venture out every day, rain or shine. 'Of course the dogs need their exercise, so we go whatever the weather.'

Frank has combined the walking with a healthy diet. 'Our living room looks like a permanent harvest festival – there's always plenty of fruit and vegetables around,' he says. His wife bakes, but uses a combination of wholemeal and self-raising flour with just a little sugar and dried fruit.

Frank's BMI is now 25 and his weight has settled at 71kg (11 stone 2lb). Significantly, two years ago his HbAIC level was 8.9, but his latest test showed that it had come down to 7.6. He still takes his insulin twice a day and is committed to following a healthy diet, but Frank believes that it is the walking that has really made the difference.

'It's a question of habit, really,' says Frank. 'It's so easy to say "I haven't got the time", but you very soon get into the routine of going out. Now, if for some reason we don't go out I feel very sluggish.'

Drugs and surgery

Less than a century ago, there was no treatment for diabetes. Then came insulin and the first medications for Type 2. Now the new treatment options available offer unprecedented flexibility, with shorter and longer-acting forms of insulin to choose from and an assortment of drugs that can be mixed and matched to meet your own specific needs. Meanwhile, new devices deliver insulin without needles, and surgery, although not risk-free, offers a solution for some people.

SIX

6

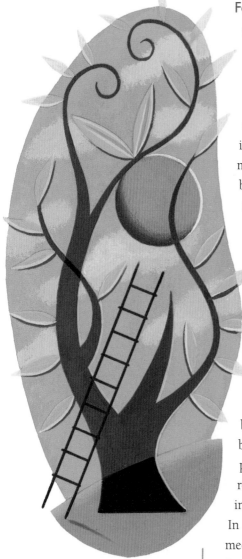

Treatment options

You're on a healthy diet, you're taking exercise – but your blood sugar is still too high. What now? Diet and exercise go a long way towards controlling blood sugar, but there will be times when you'll need some extra help. For people with Type 1 diabetes, insulin is actually a key to survival. People with Type 2 can benefit from insulin, too, but injections may still be a long way down the road if you can get a grip on glucose with pills.

In the not-so-distant past, the medical options for controlling diabetes were limited. Initially, there was only insulin and, starting in the 1950s, a single class of oral medications (known as sulphonylureas) that could help to bring down blood sugar. It was not until the mid-1990s that new classes of drugs began to emerge. Now if you have Type 2 diabetes, you and your doctor can choose from several types of oral medications – all of which attack high blood sugar in different ways. This has vastly expanded your treatment options, not only because each type of drug represents an advance in itself but because the various types can be used together in dozens of different combinations that best suit your individual needs.

It's important to note that diabetes pills are not simply oral forms of insulin. Acids in your digestive tract would break down insulin and render it useless before your body could use it, which is why insulin has to be injected instead of swallowed. And pills don't work for people with Type 1 diabetes because such medications often rely on the ability of the pancreas to produce at least some insulin – which doesn't happen with most Type 1 patients. In fact, being able to use oral medications as a first line of medical therapy is a key distinction between Type 2 and Type 1 diabetes.

Medications have helped thousands of people with Type 2 diabetes to lead healthier and more fulfilling lives, but they are not a cure for Type 2 diabetes any more than insulin is a cure for Type 1. And you certainly can't abandon your meal plan or regular exercise just because you're taking medication. If anything, the reasoning goes the other way: If your doctor prescribes drugs, achieving better glucose control with diet and exercise may get you off medication again.

When do you need medical help?

Whatever the miracles of medication, controlling blood sugar naturally with diet and exercise will always be a priority. Drugs, after all, often have side effects. Yet sometimes doctors put patients on medication immediately after diagnosis. What makes you a candidate for drugs?

It all begins with your blood sugar. Remember that a diagnosis of diabetes is made when fasting blood glucose is more than 7mmol/l and you're trying to bring it down to around 6.5mmol/l. Beyond that, your long-term haemoglobin HbA1c test results should come in below 7 per cent – and many endocrinologists say 6.5 per cent is a better goal. These are the benchmarks your doctor will consider first.

There are no hard and fast rules about when to start taking medication because everyone's body is different and each case must be treated individually. But doctors tend to follow some rough guidelines, as outlined below.

Deciding who needs drugs

Generally, doctors will let you try to bring blood sugar under control with diet and exercise alone as long as your fasting glucose is 7.7 to 8.3mmol/l or less. But here's where the HbA1c results come in. If your haemoglobin number is holding at around 7 per cent, there's a good chance you'll succeed with lifestyle changes alone. If this number creeps up to 7.5 or above, however, you are likely to need extra help. Still, at this level your doctor will usually allow you to try diet and exercise alone for a three-month trial period. Then, if your HbA1c number is still above 7 per cent, you'll probably need to take medication.

If you start off with fasting blood-glucose levels higher than 8.3mmol/l or your HbA1c results hit 8 per cent, your doctor may give you drugs immediately. That doesn't mean you'll need them for ever. Often, doctors prescribe drugs so that they can gain immediate control over blood sugar until changing diet and increasing exercise have a chance to produce results. After that, you may no longer need drugs.

Blood-sugar numbers are not the only factor that dictates whether you need medication. Say your numbers suggest that diet and exercise alone would help you, but you're not overweight (true of about 10 per cent of people with Type 2) or you already follow a healthy diet and work out. In each case, it's unlikely that depriving yourself of a biscuit or exercising an extra 10 minutes will make a significant difference, so your doctor may prescribe medication sooner than he would someone with similar numbers who is overweight and very sedentary.

On the other hand, your doctor may steer clear of prescribing certain drugs if you have complications or other health problems that make them inappropriate for you. For example, metformin, one of the most popular diabetes drugs, can cause a potentially fatal build-up of lactic acid in the blood (a condition called lactic acidosis) in people who have kidney, heart or liver disease, and it should not be taken by these patients.

Bringing in the big gun: insulin

Even after you're on medication, your doctor will keep a sharp eye on your blood sugar. If one prescription isn't working adequately, your doctor may try other drugs or drug combinations. You might go through five or six different regimens before insulin is prescribed. Once it is clear that drugs, diet and exercise are not doing enough to keep your blood sugar under control, your doctor may add an evening or bedtime dose of insulin to offset the glucose released by the liver at night.

For some people with Type 2 diabetes, it makes sense to go straight to insulin therapy. Doctors may advise this strategy for patients who don't tolerate other drugs well, have diseases of the kidneys or liver, or have a greater need for immediate insulin due to injury, infection or severe stress.

People with Type 2 diabetes often don't need to give themselves as many injections as people with Type 1. This is because the body can still manufacture insulin (or use the insulin it does produce) to some extent. But the longer you have Type 2 diabetes, the less your body can do on its own, generally, and the more likely you are to need to take insulin. It doesn't mean that you have failed to manage your diabetes. It simply means that your disease has progressed to a point at which other types of therapy just can't help you as much as they should be able to.

The medication menu

No fewer than 13 basic drugs for diabetes are now available, and they are grouped according to how they work. Some make the body produce more insulin, others make cells better able to take in glucose or slow the release of glucose into the blood, and some drugs perform several functions at once.

Choosing which drugs to use can be a complicated business, and you'll need to trust your doctor to help you to make the right choices. But you should educate yourself in order to have an input into these decisions and understand your options if the drugs you are prescribed don't work well for you.

Bear in mind that medication works best in people who have had diabetes for less than 10 years. That is because drugs build on the body's ability to produce some insulin, but this ability tends to dwindle as diabetes progresses. You can also expect drugs to become less effective the longer you take them. That's why it is good to have choices; often your doctor can add a different drug to your regimen.

Sulphonylureas: the old and the new guard

Sulphonylureas are the longest-standing diabetes drugs. Some of them have been around for more than 50 years and are still among the most widely prescribed treatments.

All sulphonylureas bring blood sugar down in the same way. They bind to beta cells in the pancreas and stimulate them to produce more insulin. They differ from each other mainly in how much of them you need to take, how often you take them, how quickly they work and how long they last. For example, the more recently introduced drugs are far more powerful than their predecessors, so much lower doses are required. They are also less likely to interact with other medications.

Side effects Most people do well on sulphonylureas, but it's possible that these drugs will upset your stomach or cause skin reactions as a result of increased sensitivity to the sun. You should inform your doctor if these problems persist. Some people are allergic to sulpha drugs (which include sulpho nylureas and some antibiotics), so, although these reactions are rare, be on the look out for skin rashes, hives or swelling,

Sulphonylurea drugs

These drugs stimulate cells in the pancreas to make more insulin, and help it to work more effectively. Possible side effects include nausea, stomach upsets, skin rashes. Avoid sulphonylureas if you have liver or kidney problems or are pregnant. Some may cause hypoglycaemia.

DRUG	BRAND	Initial daily dose	Min/max daily dose	COMMENTS
Chlorpropamide		250mg	100–500mg	Long-lasting, staying active in the body for 24 hours of more. May cause hypoglycaemia. May also contribute to water retention and cause your face to flush if you drink alcohol.
Glibenclamide	Daonil Semidaonil Euglocon Diabetamide Gliken	5mg	2.5–15mg	A long-acting drug, usually taken before meals, but may be taken as a larger dose once daily, immediately after breakfast.
Gliclazide	Diamicron Diaglyk	40–80mg	40–320mg	Medium-acting drug, usually taken with the two main meals of the day.
Glipizide	Glibenese Minodiab	2.5–5mg	2.5–20mg	Takes effect in one hour. Usually taken before meals to control after-eating glucose spikes.
Glimepiride	Amaryl	1mg	1–6mg	Long-acting. Usually taken only once, at breakfast, to keep blood sugar steady throughout the day.
Gliquidone	Glurenom	15mg	15–180mg	Short-acting. Usually taken up to 30 minutes before a meal, two or three times a day.
Tolbutamide			500–2000mg	Takes effect after about an hour. A good choice if you have difficulty keeping blood sugar down after meals.

especially of the airways. You should also avoid sulphonylureas if you have liver or kidney problems or if you're pregnant.

Mighty metformin

Metformin – branded as Glucophage – has become the drug of choice for overweight patients in the UK – and it's no wonder, when you look at the amazing diversity of effects packed into each two to three-times-daily pill. Metformin reduces the amount of glucose released from storage sites in the liver. This keeps blood sugar low not only after eating but between meals and during the night as well. It also hinders the absorption of glucose from food. By itself, metformin will not cause hypo glycaemia because it does not make cells draw glucose out of the blood. Because it attacks the problem from a different angle, it makes a perfect companion to sulphonylureas. Combining the two is one of the most common forms of drug therapy.

There is another plus. People often tend to lose weight when taking metformin, although the reason is not yet fully understood. It may reduce the appetite by irritating the gastro-intestinal tract or by giving food a strange taste (often with a metallic tang). Whatever the reason, this makes metformin a boon to Type 2 patients who are overweight and need to shed a few pounds anyway.

Furthermore, metformin brings down LDL ('bad') cholesterol and triglycerides (while raising 'good' HDL cholesterol) and may make muscles more insulin sensitive. It works so well, in fact, that it reduces the risk of diabetes in people with impaired glucose tolerance by 31 per cent, according to a major US study.

Side effects Metformin sounds like a miracle medicine, but it's not perfect. Besides the unappetizing taste it lends to food and such gastrointestinal symptoms as nausea, bloating and gas, some patients find that it causes skin rashes. These side effects often disappear after several weeks and are less likely to crop up if you start on low doses and take the drug with food. You should avoid metformin if you're pregnant or have kidney disease, severe liver disease or congestive heart failure – conditions in which the drug can promote lactic acidosis, a potentially fatal build-up of lactic acid in the blood. Drinking a lot of alcohol while on metformin can also promote this condition, so be honest with your doctor about your alcohol intake when considering this drug.

Sensitivity training for cells

Another class of drugs wins the tongue-twister award for its scientific name: thiazolidinediones. But the idea behind these drugs is simple. They attack high blood sugar from a third angle – by boosting the insulin sensitivity of cells so that they are better able to take in glucose and clear it out of the blood. This makes the drugs especially useful for keeping blood sugar down immediately after a meal, so your doctor may add one of them to your regimen if other drugs fail to do this. If you are Type 2 and use insulin, these medications (usually taken once a day) may also allow you to reduce your dose.

? DID YOU KNOW

The sulpha-drug class includes antibiotics that were new to battlefields during World War II. When a French army doctor noticed that the antibiotics made some patients act as if they had low blood sugar, he wrote about it to a colleague, who began experiments that showed sulphas could bring down blood sugar in animals. From these discoveries, the first oral medications to treat diabetes, the sulphonylureas, were developed and made available in the decade after the war.

WHAT THE STUDIES SHOW

Some doctors are so enamoured of metformin that they fail to consider its potential side effects sufficiently seriously. In 2001 a Scottish study of 1,847 patients taking metformin found that 24.5 per cent had a contraindication. A recent US study found that almost a quarter of people on metformin shouldn't be taking the drug because they have health conditions, such as kidney disease or heart failure, that make them prone to the potentially fatal side effect of lactic acidosis.

Sometimes called glitazones, thiazolidinediones have had their share of controversy. Troglitazone, marketed in the UK as Romozin, the first of these drugs to become available, was withdrawn from the UK and US markets after it was linked with liver damage in a very small number of patients. This has not proved to be a problem with the two drugs still on the market, rosiglitazone (Avandia) and pioglitazone (Actos), which both have a different chemical structure from Troglitazone. There have been no reports of liver damage or failure in any of the clinical trials for Actos or Avandia.

Don't expect instant results. It takes several weeks and sometimes up to three months for muscle and fat cells to respond fully to these drugs. Like metformin, however, they may bring down cholesterol and triglyceride levels and they won't cause hypoglycaemia.

Side effects It's no surprise that metformin is more popular than thiazolidinediones. These drugs make many people gain weight and often cause swelling from water retention, especially around the ankles. They may also cause such gastrointestinal problems as nausea and vomiting, yellowing of the skin and headaches. As with most drugs, you should not use thiazolidinediones if you are pregnant. They are also best avoided if you don't want to become pregnant: thiazolidinediones may improve fertility (probably because insulin resistance, which the drugs help to correct, makes you less fertile), and pioglitazone can render hormone-based contraceptives less effective.

The sugar stopper

The drug acarbose (Glucobay), technically known as an alpha-glucosidase inhibitor, works to prevent enzymes in the intestines from breaking down carbohydrates into glucose, leaving them to be digested later by bacteria in the lower gut. This slows the release of glucose into the bloodstream and restrains the rise in blood sugar that follows a meal. Usually taken at the start of each meal, acarbose may be a good choice if you have difficulty keeping blood sugar steady after eating, especially if thiazolidinediones don't work well for you. Hypoglycaemia is not a problem with acarbose unless you combine it with other drugs, such as sulphonylureas. If you do experience a bout of hypoglycaemia while on these drugs, however, treat it by taking glucose tablets, which are less responsive to the medication than the sucrose found in sweet snacks or fruit drinks.

Side effects Because it leaves carbohydrates to be fermented by bacteria in the lower gut, acarbose produces a lot of gas, bloating and other gastro-intestinal problems, including diarrhoea, and some people find it intolerable for those reasons. In many cases, however, these effects will ease up over time. It helps to start on a low dose and gradually take more as your body adjusts. Still, acarbose is a poor choice if you have a gastro-intestinal condition such as irritable bowel syndrome or ulcerative colitis or if you suffer from liver or kidney disease.

Fast workers

Known as prandial glucose regulators, the drugs in this category, repaglinide (NovoNorm) and nateglinide (Starlix), work in the same way as sulphonylureas – by wringing more insulin out of the pancreas. But they differ chemically from sulphonylureas and take effect more quickly, so you can take them with your meal (or up to half an hour beforehand) to keep blood sugar down after eating. Their effects are short-lived. For instance, nateglinide's concentration in the blood drops sharply as soon as 90 minutes after taking it. For that reason, these drugs are less likely to cause hypoglycaemia. And because they go to work so quickly, they give you the freedom to eat impromptu meals. They are often combined with metformin for longer-term control.

Side effects Like sulphonylureas, these drugs can cause hypoglycaemia, but because they are designed to work when your blood sugar is already high after eating, this tends to be less of a problem than with the older drugs. You might also

AVOIDING DRUG INTERACTIONS

Before your doctor prescribes a diabetes drug, be sure to tell him about any other drugs you are taking. Likewise, make sure that doctors treating other conditions know you have diabetes. Many drugs can make diabetes worse by raising blood sugar. Others can lower blood sugar and may need to be factored into your dosage. Among medications to watch out for are:

DRUGS THAT MAY RAISE BLOOD SUGAR

Blood-pressure drugs beta-blockers, calcium channel blockers, minoxidil, thiazide diuretics

Drugs for HIV megesterol acetate, pentamidine, protease inhibitors

Antipsychotics lithium, phenothiazines

Tuberculosis medications isoniazid, rifampicin

DRUGS THAT MAY LOWER BLOOD SUGAR

Pain relievers aspirin, acetaminophen

Blood-pressure drugs alpha blockers, angiotensin-converting enzyme (ACE) inhibitors

Infection fighters cibenzoline, gancyclovir, mefloquine, pentamidine, quinine, quinolones, sulfonamides, tetracyclines

Antidepressants doxepin, MAO inhibitors, tricyclics

experience nausea, minor weight gain, itching and skin flushing, but these effects are usually mild. Do not take repaglinide or nateglinide if you are pregnant or nursing, and you should be cautious about using them if you have liver or kidney damage.

Medication marriages

Sometimes two drugs are better than one, especially if they work in different ways. Here are some drug combinations that you and your doctor might consider, especially if taking one drug alone does not control your blood sugar sufficiently. Be aware that when you take a combination of drugs, you have to watch out for possible side effects from all the active ingredients.

▶ **Metformin plus a sulphonylurea**
Why you might use it To make the pancreas produce more insulin while keeping baseline blood sugar low. It's the most popular – and probably the most effective – drug combination for diabetes.
What to watch out for Hypoglycaemia, gastrointestinal troubles (mild diarrhoea, stomach upset).

▶ **A sulphonylurea plus a thiazolidinedione**
Why you might use it If sulphonylureas begin losing their ability to stimulate your pancreas into increased insulin production, it can be helpful to bring in rosiglitazone or pioglitazone to boost insulin sensitivity.
What to watch out for The dual action of producing more insulin and making cells more receptive to it makes you especially susceptible to hypoglycaemia.

▶ **A sulphonylurea plus an alpha-glucosidase inhibitor**
Why you might use it Using acarbose to delay glucose absorption can help to keep blood sugar low after meals if the sulphonylurea fails to accomplish this on its own.
What to watch out for Digestive discomfort, hypoglycaemia.

▶ **Metformin plus an alpha-glucosidase inhibitor**
Why you might use it Not every drug combination has been subjected to detailed study. However, this one has, and results show the two drugs together are better than metformin alone at keeping blood sugar under control, specially after eating.

What to watch out for Mainly gas, bloating and other effects from bacterial breakdown of carbohydrates.

▶ **Metformin plus a thiazolidinedione**

Why you might use it This combination may be especially useful if sulphonylureas are no longer effective, particularly if being overweight has led to you being insulin resistant.

What to watch out for Gastrointestinal problems.

▶ **Metformin, a thiazolidinedione and a sulphonylurea**

Why you might use it If you're taking metformin plus a thiazolidinedione, or metformin plus a sulphonylurea, and your blood sugar is still too high, a third drug may be added to your regimen.

What to watch out for Hypoglycaemia.

Drugs and their dosages

Most drugs come in a variety of dosages, so your doctor can fine-tune your regimen according to your condition and how well you respond to what you take. Expect to start on a low dose and move to higher doses the longer you stay on the drug.

CLASS	DRUG	BRAND NAME	INITIAL DAILY DOSE	MIN/MAX DOSE DAILY
Sulphonylurea	Diamicron		250mg	100–500mg
	Glibenclamide	Daonil, Semi-daonil Euglucon, Diabetamide Gilken	5mg	2.5–15mg
	Gliclazide	Diamicron, Diaglik	40–80mg	40–320mg
	Glipizide	Glibenese, Minodiab	2.5–5mg	2.5–20mg
	Glimepiride	Amaryl	1mg	1, 2 and 4mg
	Gliquidone	Glurenorm	15mg	15–180mg
	Tolbutamide			500–2000mg
Biguanide	Metformin	Glucamet, Glucophage	500mg	500–3000mg
Thiazolidinedione	Rosiglitazone	Avandia	4mg	4–8mg
	Pioglitazone	Actos	15–30mg	15–30mg
Alpha-glucosidase inhibitor	Acarbose	Glucobay	5mg x 3	50–600mg
Prandial glucose regulators	Repaglinide	Novonorm	0.5mg	0.5–16mg
	Nateglinide	Starlix	60mg	60–540mg

Insulin: who needs it?

Insulin can be a lifesaver if you have diabetes, and it is considered one of modern medicine's true breakthroughs. When it first became available in the 1920s, there was only one kind of insulin, still known as 'regular' insulin. Today there are many more options – some of them available only since the 1990s.

Whether it comes from a vial or from insulin-producing cells in the pancreas, everybody needs insulin, of course – not just people with diabetes. But if your pancreas cannot supply it you need to take over its job yourself. That's not only a task for people with Type 1 diabetes. In fact, 30 per cent of those with Type 2 need insulin as well – usually because the beta cells of the pancreas cannot manufacture enough insulin to meet the body's needs (even with medication) or cells become more insulin resistant.

Normally, the pancreas pumps just the right amount of insulin necessary to help cells take up the glucose in your blood. Although a healthy pancreas constantly makes subtle adjustments, there are two basic insulin patterns you need to mimic artificially whether you have Type 1 or Type 2:

▶ A continuous, low-level baseline of insulin to keep blood-sugar levels stable between meals (this is sometimes referred to as basal insulin).

▶ Extra bursts of insulin (known as boluses) when blood sugar rises above this baseline level, especially after a meal.

If you have Type 1 diabetes, you'll typically take doses of different insulins throughout the day to cover all your needs. If you have Type 2 diabetes, the number of doses you take (and the type of insulin you use) will vary according to how well your pancreas is functioning.

Choosing the right insulin

Insulin has improved in both quality and variety over the years, starting with the way it is made. Until recently, most insulin was extracted from animals, such as cows and pigs, and purified for use in humans. It worked well for most people, but others had allergic reactions, such as redness, itching, swelling or pain at the injection site. Animal insulin is increasingly rarely used, thanks to genetic engineering. Today scientists can insert human DNA with insulin-making instructions into bacteria to make them generate bona fide human insulin as they reproduce.

What matters most about insulin, however, is how it behaves. Available today are insulins that differ in how fast they start working, when their action peaks, and how long they stay active. Insulins are organized into four categories based on how long their effects last. A fifth type is a mixture of short-acting and long-acting insulin.

Short-acting insulin Regular insulin is now officially classified as 'short-acting'. This means that it starts to work quickly but doesn't last very long. You can use short-acting insulin to provide a burst of glucose control when you need it, particularly in time for a meal. Regular insulin starts to work in 30 minutes, has its best effect in 2 to 5 hours, and stops working in 5 to 8 hours.

Rapid-acting insulin If you don't want to wait half an hour to eat while your injection takes effect, you don't have to. Two new insulins (sometimes considered a subset of short-acting insulins) have been chemically altered to work even faster. They are insulin lispro (Humalog) and insulin aspart (NovoRapid). Insulin lispro starts working in 5 to 15 minutes, has its best effect in 45 to 90 minutes and stops working in 3 to 4 hours. Insulin aspart starts working in 10 to 20 minutes, is most effective for 1 to 3 hours and stops working in 3 to 5 hours. These patterns are closer to what you'd experience after eating if you had a healthy pancreas. Besides allowing you more freedom to eat when you want, rapid-acting insulin is less likely than regular insulin to cause hypoglycaemia because it doesn't stay in your system after the glucose from your meal is used up.

Very long-acting insulin At the opposite extreme are the very long-acting insulin glargine (Lantus) and insulin detemir (Levemir), which have distinct advantages. They take effect gradually over the first few hours and last all day and night, offering relatively constant action with no pronounced peak over 24 hours. In other words, they closely mimic the pancreas's background insulin production by holding insulin levels steady over the long haul.

Intermediate-acting insulin The two offerings in this category are insulin zinc suspension (Hupurin Bovine Lente, Monotard, Humulin Lente, Ultratard, Humulin Zn) and isophane insulin (Hupurin Bovine Isophane, Hypurin orcine Isophane, Pork Insulatard, Humulin 1, Insuman Basal). These insulins start to work in 1 to 4 hours, are most effective from 4 to 12 hours and stop working in 16 to 35 hours. Designed to give you good half-day insulin coverage, they are often combined with short-acting insulin.

The ins and outs of insulin therapy

You can combine different types of insulin, just as you can combine drugs to take advantage of their different effects. The plan that you and your doctor work out together will have to take into account several factors – including how much you exercise (and when), what is on your meal-plan menu, and whether you are able to eat meals at a regular time each day.

Expect there to be a certain amount of guesswork at first. Everyone's body responds to insulin differently, so your personal onset, peak and duration times may be slightly different from the averages. You will always need to keep a close watch on your blood sugar with self-monitoring to find out exactly how you respond to the therapies you try.

In the end deciding on an insulin plan comes down to two concerns:

▶ Ensuring that your body has enough insulin readily on hand to respond to blood-glucose levels as they rise and fall throughout the day

---

INSULIN AT A GLANCE

Insulins fall into four basic categories, with the following characteristics:

Rapid-acting
insulin lispro, insulin aspart

Starts	5–15 minutes
Peaks	45–90 minutes
Lasts	3–4 hours

Short-acting
regular insulin

Starts	30 minutes
Peaks	2–5 hours
Lasts	5–8 hours

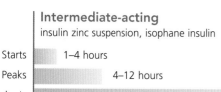

Intermediate-acting
insulin zinc suspension, isophane insulin

Starts	1–4 hours
Peaks	4–12 hours
Lasts	16–35 hours

Very long-acting
insulin glargine, insulin detemir

Starts	2 hours (glargine), 2 hours (detemir)
Peaks	12–18 hours (glargine maintains steady levels)
Lasts	24 hours or more

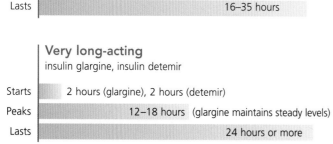

▶ Ensuring that you don't get caught with too much insulin in your system during times when your blood sugar is low – a recipe for hypoglycaemia

It's a tricky balance, but one worth striving for. Remember that the breakthrough Diabetes Control and Complications Trial in the USA, first initiated 20 years ago, found that people who kept their blood sugar in tight control reduced their risk of such complications as eye, kidney and nerve disease by half or more. But the study also underscored the fact that tight control makes it easy for blood sugar to plummet too low.

The trick to keeping blood sugar low but not too low largely comes down to timing. The insulins you choose need to peak when your blood sugar is high. There are various ways to achieve this, and the plan you choose depends partly on how many shots you want to administer each day. Although few people are keen on additional daily shots, as a general rule better control – which equals better health – requires more injections Here's how insulin plans can vary, depending on how often you inject.

One shot a day

Frankly, you can call this the 'dream on' plan. One injection is sometimes adequate for people with Type 2 diabetes, but it won't be enough to meet your needs if you have Type 1. Consider your theoretical options:

▶ A short or rapid-acting insulin at breakfast would take effect quickly and handle the glucose from your orange juice and cereal, but it would pass its peak by lunchtime and leave your blood sugar unacceptably high for the rest of the day and night.

▶ An intermediate-acting insulin at breakfast would be active by lunch but leave you with no coverage for breakfast – unless you like eating midmorning. By evening, the dose would be fading, and you would still have the night ahead.

▶ Taking a long-acting insulin at the beginning of the day would not start taking effect quickly enough to keep your blood sugar from spiking after you eat.

▶ You could mix short-, intermediate-, or long-acting insulins in the same syringe (check with your doctor for the proper procedure), but you would still find yourself short at some point later in the day or night.

Two shots a day

With twice the shots comes twice the coverage – but there are still some gaps that you would be better off filling. Your doctor may advise against settling for a two-shots-a-day plan, but your success depends on how well you comply with your regimen, and the choice is ultimately up to you.

The split dose With a 'split dose' programme, you inject yourself with intermediate-acting insulin twice: once in the morning (half an hour or more before breakfast) and again in the evening (half an hour or more before dinner). That way, as the action of the first dose is fading, the second dose is taking effect. Unfortunately, this means there's a point at which neither dose is up to full power – typically, just around dinnertime, when you could use more, not less, insulin. Still, because the second dose peaks in the evening, you will get the night-time coverage you need, although the insulin starts to fade as dawn approaches. Again, you may have to delay breakfast until the insulin starts to take effect.

The mixed split dose For better coverage, you have a second option called the 'mixed split dose', which follows the same injection schedule as the split dose. The difference is that instead of taking just an intermediate-acting insulin such as isophane insulin, you add some short-acting regular, lispro or aspart insulin to your syringe. It will keep blood sugar under control when you inject at breakfast (which means you can eat sooner) and dinner, while the intermediate peak covers lunch.

You can mix the short and intermediate-acting insulins in any proportions according to your responses or needs – say, if your blood sugar is extra high before a meal or you want to have a second piece of pie and need more insulin to handle it. For the sake of convenience, some insulin products come premixed, typically combining 70 to 75 per cent isophane insulin with 25 to 30 per cent regular or lispro.

In theory, these plans sound good. In practice, however, few patients who follow them manage to achieve good enough blood-sugar control to meet currently recommended glucose targets. And although they free you from more injections, they can be limiting in other ways – particularly by locking you into specific mealtimes every day.

Three shots a day

This really is the minimum standard of care for Type 1 diabetes. More shots means more control because you can use short-acting insulin to counteract the effects of a meal or snack, you have more freedom to eat when you want, and you can quickly correct blood-sugar highs revealed to you by self-testing.

Three-shot plans take a various forms that you will want to discuss with your doctor. One is similar to the mixed-split-dose plan except that you take the second dose of intermediate-acting insulin at bedtime instead of dinner for better coverage at night. At dinner you take a third shot of short-acting insulin. Another option is to use long-acting insulin in the morning to cover your basal needs for the rest of the day and night, plus a short-acting insulin at every meal.

Intensive therapy

Even people who take three shots a day often find themselves adding a fourth or even a fifth injection to achieve ideal control. This is the pinnacle of insulin treatment, sometimes referred to as intensive therapy or management. It's not for everyone because of all those shots, plus the extra finger-sticking glucose monitoring that goes along with them. But if you are intent on doing all you can to control your diabetes, these regimens usually work the best.

Freedom and flexibility The aim of intensive therapy is to make your life easier, not more difficult. The underlying assumption is that you're not a robot following a regimented programme of eating and activity that is identical every day. Rather, you might have a late lunch if you've been out shopping, eat a bit more with your coffee when the in-laws come to visit – and even skip a workout. An intensive therapy programme allows you to do all this.

One traditional approach to intensive therapy is to take an intermediate-acting insulin (typically, isophane insulin) twice a day: in the morning (with a short-acting insulin to cover breakfast) and at bedtime. Added to that are two short-acting insulins that you inject whenever you choose to eat. The exact dosages of the four shots should be adjusted according to how physically active you are or how much carbohydrate you eat. Many doctors now favour replacing isophane insulin in this plan with the new

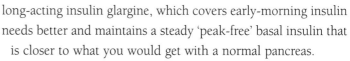

long-acting insulin glargine, which covers early-morning insulin needs better and maintains a steady 'peak-free' basal insulin that is closer to what you would get with a normal pancreas.

Pumping up your options Not keen on injections? Consider an insulin pump, which provides a continuous infusion of insulin. These pager-like devices, which can be hung on a belt or worn around the neck, hold a small reservoir of insulin that is dispensed through a catheter in your abdomen. (See Insulin pumps, pages 157–159.)

Intensive therapy's main drawback is the added risk of hypoglycaemia that comes from keeping blood sugar consistently lower. You will need to be alert to signs of dropping blood sugar (sweating, nervousness, rapid heartbeat) and be prepared to treat them in the short term with carbohydrate snacks. If you have persistent problems with hypoglycaemia, see your doctor about adjusting your insulin dosage.

Insulin and Type 2 diabetes

Studies find that intensive blood-sugar management is just as helpful in preventing complications with Type 2 diabetes as it is with Type 1. Fortunately, the experience will probably feel a little less intense if you have Type 2 because you'll probably be able to get by with fewer insulin injections, at least to begin with.

Remember, if you have Type 2, the pancreas is usually still able to produce some of the insulin your body needs, so injections are most often started as a last resort after diet, exercise and drugs no longer suffice. But you may want to talk to your doctor about starting insulin before your blood-sugar control deteriorates to that degree. Some research suggests that taking it sooner can help to preserve the function of insulin-producing beta cells in the pancreas.

If you follow standard treatment patterns, though, your insulin therapy will typically begin with an evening dose of intermediate or long-acting insulin, often combined with a sulphonylurea to cover your daytime needs – a therapy sometimes called BIDS, for 'bedtime insulin, daytime sulphonylurea'.

Eventually, most people with Type 2 will need to step up their insulin regimen so that it resembles treatment for Type 1, although this may not happen until you've had diabetes for 15 or 20 years. Most likely, treatment will then consist of two injections a day – usually a mix of short and intermediate-acting insulin at breakfast and bedtime. If that is not enough to meet your blood-sugar targets, you will need to work out a multiple-injection plan with your doctor. Because blood sugar naturally tends to be more stable with Type 2, your risk of hypoglycaemia with intensive therapy is not as great as it is with Type 1.

Calling the shots

Injections can seem scary at first, but most people quickly get used to them. The thin, small-gauge needles available today are specially coated and extremely sharp, so they slide easily into the skin with minimal pain. With a little practice and attention to a few details, shots soon become just another problem-free part of your daily routine.

When it comes to deciding where to inject, you have plenty of options. Anywhere that you have a layer of fat just below the skin is fair game – the abdomen, the tops and outer sides of your thighs, your buttocks and your upper arms. But the all-around winner is the abdomen, which usually has the most ample folds of fat and absorbs insulin faster and more consistently than other areas do.

As a rule, you shouldn't inject in the same site from one shot to the next. This can make the skin harden, create thick lumps, or cause small indentations to form. But neither do you want to move to a new part of the body with each shot, since insulin is absorbed more slowly in some areas than others, so it would be more difficult to keep the effects of your injections consistent. The solution is to inject in the same general area, but place consecutive shots about an inch away from each other, rotating the sites as you go. If you're injecting at several different times of day, you might want to take, say, your morning shots in one area of the body and your

A WEIGHTY SIDE EFFECT

Intensive therapy gives you tight control over your blood sugar and is therefore the best way to ward off complications. You may, however, have to deal with an effect you hadn't anticipated: weight gain. Why? Because close glucose control makes cells better able to use glucose for energy (calories), so the body excretes less of it in urine. Weight gain can be more of an issue with Type 2 people who are already struggling to keep their weight down.

The first thing to be aware of with the weight issue is that the benefits of better blood-sugar control far outstrip any harm from a few extra pounds. Studies find, for example, that even when insulin therapy causes weight gain, cardiovascular risk factors such as blood pressure either don't change or, in the case of cholesterol and triglycerides levels, actually improve. If metformin still works for you, its weight-reducing properties can help. So can adding one workout per week to your exercise plan, or adjusting your meal plan.

evening shots in another, but still rotate the shots at those times within their designated areas.

Minimizing the pain

Fine, sharp needles go a long way towards keeping shots prick-free, but you can take additional steps to minimize the pain.

⮕ Relax. Tense muscles can promote tightness that makes it more difficult for the needle to penetrate your skin.

⮕ Clean the injection site ahead of time with plain soap and water. If you use alcohol as a disinfectant, wait until it dries before going ahead with your injection, or the needle may push alcohol into the skin, causing stinging.

⮕ Insert the needle quickly. As with tearing a bandage off sensitive skin, slowness and hesitation make it hurt more.

⮕ Keep the angle of the needle steady as it goes in and out so it's not swivelling around under your skin.

⮕ Choose a fresh site with each injection so you're not putting the needle into tissue that is still sensitive from your last shot.

⮕ Avoid giving shots in the inner thigh, where rubbing from leg movement can cause soreness at the injection site.

SHOTS MADE SIMPLE

Giving shots may seem like something only someone in a white coat should do, but you're perfectly qualified to handle it on your own. The following guide covers the steps involved in administering a single dose of insulin. (Mixing doses is slightly more complicated but involves the same basic techniques.) First, wash your hands with soap and water and check the bottle to make sure you're using the right insulin if you take different kinds at different times of day. Got your insulin, syringe and some alcohol wipes? You're ready to go.

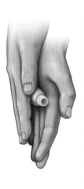

① Gently roll the bottle between your palms (shaking it can make the insulin less potent). Check its appearance. Except for regular insulin, which is clear, the contents should look uniformly cloudy. Don't use it if it's clumped or settled at the bottom or if the bottle has a frosty look.

② After wiping the stopper with an alcohol wipe, take the cover off the syringe and pull the plunger back until it reaches the dose you need, as marked by the lines printed on the side.

③ Stick the needle through the stopper and press down the plunger so all the air in the syringe goes into the bottle.

Injection alternatives

Needles are the tried and tested way to deliver insulin. They are reliable, consistent and relatively easy to use. But if you're looking for other options, you'll find plenty in a range of newer devices. Are these gadgets right for you? The only way to know is to find out more.

First, think about what you believe are the main drawbacks of needle-and-syringe delivery. Do you hate needles? Do you feel that it's inconvenient to stop what you're doing to give yourself a shot? Do you feel that there's just too much paraphernalia to carry around with you? You'll find alternative delivery systems to address all of these issues.

Insulin pumps

What if there was a way to deliver insulin in a slow and steady trickle all day, like a pancreas does? That's the idea behind electronic insulin pumps. These wearable devices hold a one or two-day supply of short-acting insulin that is dispensed continuously for basal coverage while providing a pre-programmed spurt of insulin at the touch of a button before meals. Pumps allow close

CAUTION

When giving yourself shots in the abdomen, avoid injecting in the area 2 inches around the navel, where tougher tissue can make insulin absorption inconsistent. You should also avoid injecting into moles, scar tissue or hard muscles, such as the shoulders.

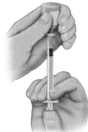

④ Turn the bottle and syringe upside down so the tip of the needle is submerged in insulin. Now pull the plunger back out again, drawing insulin from the bottle until you reach your dose mark.

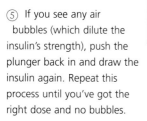

⑤ If you see any air bubbles (which dilute the insulin's strength), push the plunger back in and draw the insulin again. Repeat this process until you've got the right dose and no bubbles.

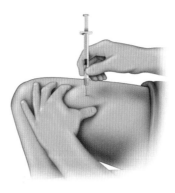

⑥ After cleaning the injection site, pinch a fold of skin and push the needle in at a 90-degree angle. If you're thin, think about using a short needle or inserting it at a 45-degree angle to avoid injecting into muscle. Push the plunger down; release the skin and pull the needle out, pressing a cotton swab near the needle as you pull. Keep pressing (but don't rub) with the swab for a few seconds.

control of blood sugar without the need for lots of injections. Every two or three days, you need to change the site of the catheter that connects the pump to your body, which involves inserting a small needle just under the skin.

Insulin pumps are becoming increasingly popular among people with Type 1 diabetes because the instant adjustments allow considerable flexibility, they provide excellent glucose control, and their precise delivery often allows you to use less insulin than with injections. In addition, new water-resistant pumps can be worn almost anytime, anywhere – even when swimming. Pumps can also be quickly disconnected for, say, sexual activity. Fail-safe controls keep the unit from giving you an insulin overdose, beep if flow ceases due to a clog, and signal when the batteries are running low. Yet only an estimated 0.19 per cent of people with Type 1 diabetes in the UK use pumps, compared with about 8 per cent in the USA, 10 per cent in Germany and 12 per cent in Sweden.

Pumps in the UK cost £1,000 to £1,500 each. Guidelines from the National Institute for Clinical Excellence (NICE) state that 'the cost of ongoing consumables and, in due course, replacement pumps, should be funded by the NHS for established pump users'. Yet pumps are often not available on prescription (it depends on the local Primary Healthcare Trust), and consumables – tubing, plasters and so forth – are not available on prescription at all. Diabetes UK estimates the cost of these at £2 a day.

Some doctors are finding that the new insulin glargine, with its rapid onset and steady action, can control basal glucose almost as well as a pump, at less cost. Problems such as clogs and infections at the injection site can sometimes interfere with your insulin delivery, although patient education and practice can minimize these problems – as can more frequent self-monitoring with blood tests, which you'll find are still necessary. The new generation of pumps have been improved with additional safety features.

Talk to your doctor about whether or not an insulin pump is a good idea for you. According to Diabetes UK, people most suited to using a pump must:

⮑ have a good knowledge and understanding of diabetes
⮑ be motivated and willing to take control of their diabetes

WHAT THE STUDIES SHOW

A 2002 study at Strong Children's Hospital, in Rochester, New York, found that, with only a couple of exceptions, 53 children aged under 13 were safely able to achieve better glucose control with less hypoglycaemia using pumps than they did with injections. Insulin pumps are being used successfully by children and teenagers in the UK, although only by a small number. To help train and advise paediatric diabetes teams with little experience of the therapy, a network of health professionals experienced in pump use has been set up, known as Pump Management for Professionals (PUMP).

➲ be prepared to test blood-glucose levels at least four times a day and be confident in acting on those results

➲ have a sound understanding of how insulin, exercise and food intake affect blood-glucose levels.

A voluntary organization for pump users which campaigns for all pumps and consumables to be available through the NHS is INPUT, 9 Grafton Gardens, Lymington, Hampshire SO41 8AS; 01590 677911; www.webshowcase.net/input

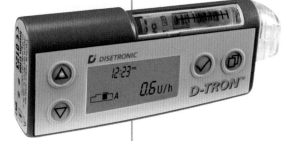

Two more options

If you conclude that a pump is not right for you, there are other options to consider.

Insulin pens These devices don't eliminate needles, but they make injections more convenient by prepacking the insulin, needle, and syringe into one small unit that looks like a fountain pen. In this case, the 'ink' cartridge is a vial that contains insulin, which you inject using a needle at the pen's tip – no insulin bottle or syringe-filling procedure are necessary. When it's time to take your shot, you uncap the pen, choose your dose by turning a dial that clicks into place (the pen holds multiple doses), then press a button to inject the insulin. Pens are available on prescription in the UK.

Jet injector If you don't want to use needles at all, you might try a jet injector. This device uses a powerful burst of air to shoot a fine spray of insulin directly into your skin. Jet injections are not entirely pain-free. You'll feel a nip from the pressurized blast, and some people find that the jets cause bruising. But they can be a good option for children and anyone who would rather not stick needles into themselves. Like pen injectors, jets can carry multiple doses at a time, and you choose the amount of insulin you want by turning a dial. The only jet injector available in the UK, the mhi-500, is available on prescription (together with the nozzle, piston and vial adaptor, known as consumables) for people in England and Wales. To buy, the device costs £120 and replacement consumables around £1–£1.50 per week.

SAFE DISPOSAL

Guidelines from the Environment Agency and the Health and Safety Commission state that containers of used needles, syringes and lancets (known as 'sharps') must not be thrown out with domestic waste.

Sharps bins are available on prescription in England and Wales. People with diabetes should ask a member of their health care professional team for advice on the most appropriate methods of storage and disposal for their area.

How sharps are disposed of varies across the UK. Local authorities are obliged to collect clinical waste such as sharps boxes from householders on request, but may make a charge for this service.

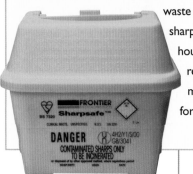

Should you consider surgery?

Going under the knife is always a big decision because it poses so many risks – of complications during the procedure, problems with anaesthesia, and post-op pain and disability, to name a few. But what if an operation could dramatically improve your blood-sugar control and reduce your diabetes-related risks? Surgery may indeed offer solutions for some people.

Diabetes is not like heart disease or cancer, in which the problem to be attacked is often clearly visible as, say, a clogged artery or a tumour. How do you surgically correct an imbalance that exists at the molecular level within the blood flowing throughout your body? New techniques are on the horizon, but at present there are two ways.

For Type 1: pancreas transplants

The most obvious surgical solution to diabetes is to get a new pancreas, an option that is mainly considered for Type 1 patients because they can't produce any insulin naturally. A pancreas transplant provides a replacement source of insulin, with the donated organ (or part of one) typically installed in the pelvis just above the bladder. The old pancreas is usually not removed because it can still make digestive enzymes.

When successful, a pancreas transplant can eliminate the need for supplemental insulin, bringing glucose under normal control. Furthermore, there is evidence that the progression of complications such as diabetic retinopathy (a disease of the retina that causes protein leaks, haemorrhages and new blood vessel formation over the surface of the retina) may be slowed and perhaps even arrested thanks to the new pancreas. But the procedure can have drawbacks.

Beyond the very real difficulty of finding donors, the body's immune system is naturally inclined to reject foreign tissue and thus wants to attack the new pancreas (rejection occurs in about one-third of transplants). Fending off this attack requires taking potent immunosuppressant drugs, which make you more vulnerable to infection from viruses and bacteria and less able to fight other diseases, including cancer. Other potential problems are clotting of the blood supply (in 5 per cent of transplants) and inflammation of the pancreas. About 4 in 10 patients will need a second operation to fix a problem that occurs early after the transplant. Overall, results of pancreas transplants are good, with 70 to 80 per cent working a year on from the operation and lasting an average of eight years.

With a view to meeting national demand by 2009, in November 2003 the government pledged to treble the number of pancreas transplants carried out in England and Wales to 150 in five years, and the commissioning and funding of pancreas transplants is now controlled at a national level.

Combined pancreas and kidney transplants are generally recommended for people with Type 1 diabetes who have kidney failure from damage caused by high blood sugar. When successful, such a double operation removes the need for insulin injections, frequent blood tests and kidney dialysis, and arrests the damage that diabetes does to your eyes, nerves and arteries. The improved blood-sugar control also appears to protect the newly transplanted kidney from the recurrence of diabetic kidney failure. In rare cases (fewer than 5 per cent) patients do not survive a combined pancreas and kidney transplant.

For Type 2: weight-loss surgery

Because obesity is so closely tied to diabetes and its cardio vascular complications (especially in people with Type 2), some doctors (very few in the UK) think that weight-loss surgery offers a quick way to solve a number of serious health problems in one fell swoop. Other doctors are more cautious, stating that it is unwise to undergo major elective surgery when you can choose far less drastic options.

The goal of weight-loss surgery is to reduce the amount of food the stomach can hold. The most common way to do this is with gastric bypass surgery, usually by means of an operation called vertical banded gastroplasty. In this procedure, a special band and staples crimp the upper portion of the stomach into a small pouch. The contents of this pouch are rerouted, through a narrow outlet, to the small intestine, allowing the digestive system to handle only a tiny amount of food at a time. (Eventually, as the pouch stretches, it can handle about 115g/4oz) Often the surgery is combined with a bypass that diverts the stomach contents around the upper part of the small intestine, where much of the breakdown and absorption of food normally takes place. Although bile and secretions from the pancreas work to break food down further along the small intestine's pipeline, food is incompletely digested, so fewer calories are absorbed into the body.

In the UK there is very little NHS funding available for such surgery, which would be used only as a last resort in cases of morbid obesity – that is, a BMI of more than $40kg/m^2$.

REAL-LIFE MEDICINE

PUMPING UP CONTROL

Wearing an insulin pump is an excellent way to control blood sugar, as Mina Joshi, 54, has discovered. She was diagnosed with Type 2 diabetes when she came to the UK from Africa in 1980, aged 30. She believes she had probably been suffering from diabetes since childhood. 'I think I have had diabetes from the age of six or seven, but it was never picked up,' she says.

When her GP diagnosed diabetes, her blood glucose levels were very high at 20.2mmol/l. She immediately started taking tablets, but these didn't bring her levels down, and she was soon put on insulin. That worked until 2000, then everything went wrong again. 'I just couldn't keep my levels under control,' she explains. 'At that stage my diabetes nurse experimented with various kinds of insulin – in all I tried 13 different kinds, but they didn't work.' In fact, her HbAlc level just kept climbing until it reached 13.9

It was at this point that she started to look into insulin pumps. 'I had read about them in the magazines I receive from Diabetes UK, but my nurse at the clinic didn't know much about them. So I did some research for myself.' This led her to Guy's Hospital. She had a consultation with the diabetes specialist there and convinced him that the pump was worth a try. Eventually, in 2001, she got her pump. Initially the effect was slow. Her first HbAlc test didn't show great results – probably, she says, because of the high levels of blood sugar circulating for such a long time. But then her second test was 5.2. 'Can you imagine! I went from 13.9 to 5.2 in six months!' she says.

Mina believes she found the pump just in time. 'Poor control of my blood glucose levels was seriously threatening my health. I already had two cataracts and a heart condition. The pump was exactly what I needed.' Mina found the pump itself easy to use and understand. 'It came with a very good booklet. The first adjustment is made by the diabetes nurse, then I was monitored for three months to make sure I was using it correctly,' she says. But, she warns, the pump does not replace monitoring. 'It's vital when you use an insulin pump to monitor your levels. I test six times a day, before and after meals. With insulin pumping slowly into your body at all times, if you don't do the blood tests you won't know to adjust the levels and you could end up in a much worse situation.'

Mina doesn't find wearing the pump awkward at all. 'I know some ladies keep the pump in their bra or men wear it on their tie or waist. I wear mine on a hook on my trousers. I'm proud of my pump. After all it's helped me so much!'

Preventing complications

By itself, high blood sugar doesn't seem that bad. After all, you can have it for years without even knowing it. The problem is the havoc it wreaks on your eyes, kidneys, nerves, heart, arteries and feet. Controlling your blood sugar is the critical first step to keeping diabetes-related complications at bay. But other simple strategies, such as taking a daily aspirin, having regular eye check-ups and wearing comfortable shoes, can go a long way towards preserving your health and general wellbeing.

SEVEN

7

Looking ahead

To manage diabetes successfully, it helps to be a visionary – someone who can see how the actions that you take (or don't take) now will affect you in the future. That's because diabetes makes you look ahead. If you don't control your disease, you can count on serious health problems later on. But if you take charge today, you can minimize – and even prevent – complications tomorrow.

For many people with diabetes, long-term complications have already set in. Even though it can take as long as 10 to 15 years for serious damage to occur, cases of Type 2 often develop silently over long periods, and many newly diagnosed people find that they already have related health problems.

Whatever your current situation, it's never too late to take steps that will keep you healthier in the days, months and years ahead. And if you have the benefit of an early diagnosis, the chances are good that you can avoid the worst effects of diabetes, which include:

▶ higher cardiovascular risks
▶ kidney disease
▶ eye disease
▶ nerve disease
▶ foot damage
▶ related complications, such as sexual dysfunction, gastrointestinal problems and infections.

Why complications?

It seems strange that one disease can cause so many other problems throughout the body. After all, kidney disease by itself doesn't cause heart disease, and eye damage doesn't promote nerve damage. Why do these seemingly unrelated problems appear together when you have diabetes? The answer is that they're not unrelated but linked by high blood sugar.

You know from handling sweet foods in your own kitchen that when sugar is more concentrated, it becomes stickier. The same is true in your blood. Excess glucose can stick to cells in the blood, making it more difficult for red blood cells to deliver oxygen or white blood cells to fight infection. Sticky glucose can also affect the flow of blood, impeding circulation to areas such as the feet and organs such as the kidneys and eyes. When glucose clings to fatty substances in the blood, they may be more likely to adhere to blood-vessel walls, gumming them up and leading to clogging that may cause a heart attack or a stroke.

Because high blood sugar is the common culprit in diabetes complications, the single most important thing you can do to reduce your risks for all of them is to control your blood sugar as well as possible. Recent studies show what a difference good glucose control can make.

▶ People with Type 1 diabetes who maintain tight blood-sugar control can cut their overall risk of complications by half, according to the US Diabetes Control and Complications Trial, or DCCT (1993). In that study, good blood-sugar control reduced risk of eye disease by 76 per cent, nerve damage by 60 per cent and kidney damage by 35 to 56 per cent.

▶ People with Type 2 diabetes who bring blood sugar down gain a 35 per cent reduction in risk of complications with every percentage-point drop in their haemoglobin A1c test results, according to the 20-year United Kingdom Prospective Diabetes Study (1998). The UKPDS highlighted the importance of tightly controlling both blood pressure and blood glucose levels to reduce long-term complications of Type 2 diabetes. The risk of heart disease is reduced by 56 per cent, stroke by 44 per cent, and both kidney disease and eye disease by up to 33 per cent.

▶ People with impaired glucose tolerance who improved their blood-sugar profile by losing weight with diet and exercise cut their risk of ever developing diabetes (and its complications) by 58 per cent, according to the US Diabetes Prevention Program (2002).

This mounting evidence prompts the question – why suffer from complications at all when it may be in your power not to?

Cutting cardiovascular risks

Cardiovascular disease and diabetes often appear together. Although it is not entirely clear how the two diseases affect each other, the most pertinent facts are clear enough: if you have diabetes, you are two to

WHAT THE STUDIES SHOW

People with diabetes are at a much greater risk from heart disease and strokes. In the UK one of the highest risk groups are women aged 40–59 with diabetes, who are up to eight times more likely to die from cardiovascular disease. The risk for men is five-fold. But Diabetes UK and the British Heart Foundation say that the problem is compounded by the fact that many people are unaware of the risk, and so are doing nothing to protect themselves.

four times more likely than the general population to have heart disease. In fact, cardiovascular disease (which includes stroke and coronary heart disease) will ultimately kill 80 per cent of people with diabetes.

By the time they are diagnosed with Type 2 diabetes more than 50 per cent of people will have evidence of cardiovascular disease (an umbrella term that refers to both the heart and the blood vessels), the greatest cause of morbidity and premature death in people with diabetes. Although people with diabetes represent about 3 per cent of the population, they account for between 10 and 15 per cent of those admitted to hospital with a heart attack and 20 per cent of those who die from them. Heart attack is just one of several problems to watch out for when you have cardiovascular disease. Most of them come down to two basic conditions, both of which you can take steps to control.

Assessing atherosclerosis

In a healthy person, a strong heart sends blood through the body via a network of smooth, elastic blood vessels. But problems arise when blood vessels become stiff, narrowed or clogged – a condition known as atherosclerosis. The condition can occur in a number of ways related to diabetes. High blood sugar can slow blood circulation and promote clot formation. Being overweight (especially if you carry fat mostly in the abdomen) and having high levels of such blood fats as cholesterol and triglycerides (common in people with diabetes) can lead to obstructions in blood vessels. Depending on where they occur, these slowdowns in blood flow can trigger a variety of problems.

▶ When arteries that feed the heart become obstructed, the heart can't pump as efficiently as it should. Initially, this can cause chest pain from angina, a condition in which heart tissue is damaged from lack of nutrients. If a coronary artery becomes completely blocked, the result is a heart attack.

▶ If blood flow slows down in the arteries that feed the brain, lack of oxygen can cause what is known as cerebrovascular disease, in which areas of the brain become impaired. Often, the condition starts with temporary loss of brain function which can produce symptoms such as slurred speech, weakness and numbness. A total blockage can cause a stroke.

▶ When blood flow to the arteries feeding the legs is

impeded, a condition known as peripheral vascular disease develops. A partial blockage can cause temporary pain (called claudication) in the thighs, calves or buttocks. A total blockage can cause gangrene, although this rarely happens, because blood to the legs can usually bypass the clog using other arteries. Nonetheless, poor leg circulation, often combined with nerve damage, can lead to serious problems in the feet.

High blood pressure havoc

High blood pressure can build up silently, just as diabetes can, and the two diseases often develop in tandem. If you have diabetes, you're twice as likely as the average person to have high blood pressure, a condition that affects almost four in every five people in the UK with Type 2 diabetes. Controlling high blood pressure is critical if you have diabetes because the damage it causes contributes not only to atherosclerosis but also to kidney and eye disease. All told, it has a role in 35 to 75 per cent of all complications associated with diabetes.

You need a certain amount of blood pressure (the force that blood exerts against artery walls) for good circulation. But too much pressure gradually weakens the heart by making it work harder and damages the lining of blood-vessel walls, making it easier for atherosclerosis to set in. High blood pressure can also weaken arteries in the brain and cause them to balloon, a condition called an aneurysm. The bursting of an aneurysm is potentially fatal.

Diabetes UK recommends that you keep your blood pressure down to 140/80mm Hg if you have diabetes – lower than that is even better.

> ## THE RACE FACTOR
> **Already at higher risk of diabetes, South Asians in the UK have a 50 per cent greater risk than the general population of dying prematurely from coronary heart disease (CHD). One-third of premature deaths in South Asian men and one-fifth in women are from CHD.**
>
> It seems that heart disease prevention messages are failing to make an impact. The British Heart Foundation states that 42 per cent of Bangladeshi men are smokers, compared to 29 per cent of the general population; Bangladeshi and Pakistani communities eat the least fruit and vegetables of all ethnic groups; and only 18 per cent of Bangladeshi men and 7 per cent of women meet the recommended physical activity levels (30 minutes of brisk walking, cycling or swimming five times a week).

Preventing cardiovascular disease

Some of the steps you're already taking to control diabetes can also work wonders for heart and vascular problems. But you and your doctor may want to try other options as well – including drugs that attack a number of diabetes-related problems at once. Here are some of the most important steps to consider:

⮑ **Keep up the good work** With regular exercise and a healthy diet, your your risk of cardiovascular complications should drop. Eating more carbohydrates and fibre and less saturated fat can reduce cholesterol in the blood and help you to lose excess weight – a major contributor to high blood pressure. Exercise strengthens the heart, keeps blood vessels supple, and appears to lower blood pressure even if you're not shedding pounds.

Collateral damage

Over time, poorly controlled diabetes can wreak havoc throughout the body. But keeping your blood sugar in line will significantly reduce your risks. What's more, there are additional steps you can take to minimize collateral damage.

SITE	DAMAGE	PREVENTION
Blood vessels	High blood sugar slows circulation, promotes high levels of such blood fats as cholesterol, and encourages the formation of blood clots. Potential result: blockages that can cause heart attack and stroke.	■ Lower blood pressure with diet and exercise. ■ Stop smoking. ■ Take aspirin. ■ Consider ACE inhibitors. ■ Eat heart-healthy foods such as fish, tea and antioxidant-rich fruits and vegetables.
Kidneys	Blood sugar gums up delicate capillaries that filter wastes. Kidneys work harder but less efficiently, gradually losing function and ultimately failing.	■ Have regular tests for signs of damage. ■ Bring down high blood pressure. ■ Drink cranberry juice to discourage urinary tract infections. ■ Consider eating less protein.
Eyes	High blood sugar weakens small blood vessels and makes them rupture. New blood vessels proliferate out of control, causing eye damage that can lead to vision loss or blindness.	■ Get regular checkups from an ophthalmologist. ■ Take steps to lower your blood pressure. ■ Consider laser surgery if necessary.
Nerves	Blood sugar may block nerve signals or interfere with normal nourishment of nerves. The range of effects can include pain, lack of sensation in the body's peripheries, muscle weakness, and loss of control over automatic functions such as heartbeat, digestion and sexual response.	■ Report symptoms to your doctor immediately. ■ Get more nerve-friendly B vitamins in such foods as potatoes, fish and meat. ■ Try over-the-counter analgesics for pain. ■ Change your diet to make digestion easier. ■ Ask about antidepressants to counter pain, and other drugs to treat specific symptoms.
Feet	A combination of poor circulation and nerve damage can make feet prone to injuries that heal slowly and can quickly become infected.	■ Wear good shoes everywhere. ■ Inspect feet daily. ■ Keep feet clean and dry. ■ Change socks frequently. ■ Tell your doctor about any changes.

○ **But go a little further** You may need to adjust your diet by eating less salt. According to the British Heart Foundation and the Food Standards Agency, there is a strong link between high salt intake and high blood pressure. Most of us eat too much salt. The Department of Health recommends that an adult's total salt intake should be no more than 6g per day, and a child's no more than 4g, but the average person's diet incorporates at least 9g per day. Only about a quarter of our salt intake comes from salt that we add to food. The rest is already in the processed foods we eat, which contain surprising amounts. For example, the main source of dietary salt in the UK comes from bread and cereals. Read the labels and avoid foods with a high salt content (see box on how to cut down your salt intake on page 97).

○ **Don't smoke** There are many reasons to give up smoking, but start with the fact that smoking doubles your risk of a heart attack. In fact, smoking speeds up or exacerbates almost every process that contributes to cardiovascular disease. It reduces blood flow by making arteries stiffer and narrower, raises blood pressure, contributes to the formation of plaques that can lead to blockages, makes it easier for blood to clot around obstructions and worsens pain from peripheral vascular disease.

○ **Ask about aspirin** This anti-inflammatory has proved highly effective in the battle against cardiovascular disease. As well as relieving pain, aspirin makes the clot-forming particles in blood (platelets) less able to stick together. One recent review in the UK of aspirin found that in patients with heart disease, regular daily aspirin reduces the risks of non-fatal heart attacks by one-third. Fatal heart attacks and stroke are reduced by one-sixth in patients with coronary heart disease. An estimated 7,000 deaths a year in the UK could be prevented by prescribing aspirin to patients with cardiovascular disease. A recent study found that there is potential benefit from a daily 75mg of aspirin for people with no evidence of heart disease but who have a risk factor for heart disease, such as high blood pressure.

The British Heart Foundation recommends taking between 75 and 150mg daily. But you should check with your doctor if aspirin is appropriate for you. Many people find that it irritates or causes bleeding in the stomach, although taking coated

WHAT THE STUDIES SHOW

Until recently, doctors assumed that aspirin protected against heart attack solely by thinning the blood. Now research published by the American Heart Association has found that the reason people originally took aspirin – to reduce inflammation (a contributor to pain) – plays a role as well. In this small study, people who took aspirin suffered less blood-vessel inflammation from a vaccine than people who didn't take aspirin. For this reason alone, blood flow in the arteries eight hours later was better in the aspirin takers, while blood flow in those who didn't take it was worse.

tablets that dissolve in the small intestine may help to avoid these problems. You should avoid aspirin if you have a stomach ulcer or liver disease. And talk to your doctor about how aspirin affects the performance of other medications you may be taking – including blood thinners and drugs for hypertension.

⬆ **Check your ACE in the hole** You can choose from an array of drugs that fight high blood pressure, but one class of medications appears to have special benefits to people with diabetes. Called ACE (angiotensin-converting enzyme) inhibitors, they work by blocking a process in which one hormone turns into another that constricts blood vessels. ACE inhibitors are popular for bringing down blood pressure because, compared with other blood-pressure drugs, they have few side effects other than causing a persistent dry cough in some patients. (Newer drugs called angiotensin II receptor blockers eliminate that problem.) Research shows that ACE inhibitors lower the risk of cardiovascular problems in people with diabetes even if they don't have high blood pressure. Furthermore, a study published in the *New England Journal of Medicine* in 2000 found that people taking the ACE inhibitor ramipril were 30 per cent less likely to develop diabetes, suggesting that the drug improves insulin sensitivity.

SHOULD YOU TAKE WEIGHT-LOSS DRUGS?

Slimming down has the double benefit of reducing your risk of cardiovascular disease and controlling high blood sugar, which makes weight-loss drugs sound like an appealing option for people with diabetes.

While it is not possible to lose pounds simply by taking a pill (you still have to exercise and eat a low-fat diet), two weight-loss drugs can help if diet and exercise aren't enough. A recent German study even found that one of them, orlistat (Xenical), lowered blood sugar after eating, reducing the need for glucose-controlling medication.

Still, doctors advise approaching diet pills with caution. Orlistat, which works by blocking fat absorption in the intestines, can cause a range of unpleasant gastrointestinal side effects, including having to defecate more often, fecal incontinence and oily stools. The other common weight-loss drug, an appetite suppressant called sibutramine (Reductil), often causes headaches, dry mouth and constipation. More important, it raises blood pressure in some people and should not be used if you have hypertension. Consult your doctor to see if weight-loss drugs are appropriate for you.

⊃ **Seek help from statins** People with diabetes often have high blood cholesterol, a risk factor for heart attacks. But many of them are not reaping the benefit of cholesterol-lowering drugs called statins. Two recent studies in the UK show overwhelmingly that the use of statins significantly cuts the risk of heart attacks and strokes in people with diabetes. One study, funded by the Medical Research Council and the British Heart Foundation, showed that the use of statins cuts the risk of heart attacks, stroke or coronary artery bypass grafts by one-third in patients with diabetes. The second study, of people with Type 2 diabetes, showed that in the group taking atorvastatin the number of cardiovascular events (such as heart attacks and strokes) was reduced by 37 per cent; acute coronary events (such as heart attack) were reduced by 36 per cent, and the number of strokes was reduced by 48 per cent.

Heeding the Warning Signs

Cardiovascular emergencies can sneak up on you suddenly, but there is often time to react effectively if you pay attention to warning signals. Call your doctor immediately if you experience any of the following symptoms:

AILMENT	SYMPTOMS
Heart attack	■ Tightness or pain in your chest ■ Pain or discomfort that radiates from the chest to the neck, shoulders or arms, especially on the left side where your heart is ■ Dizziness, lightheadedness, sweating, nausea or shortness of breath (Don't assume these are signs of hypoglycaemia if you're also experiencing pain.)
Stroke	■ Weakness or numbness of the face, arm or leg, especially on one side of the body ■ Difficulty speaking or understanding others ■ Mental confusion ■ Vision problems ■ Difficulty walking or keeping your balance ■ Severe headache
Aneurysm	■ Severe headache, back pain or abdominal pain that won't go away ■ Dizziness ■ Blurred vision ■ Nosebleeds

Diabetes UK believes that doctors should consider all of their patients with Type 2 diabetes for statin therapy even though it may not be suitable for everyone. Pharmacists can now (since July 2004) sell simvastatin over the counter, but people with diabetes should take them only after consultation with their doctor to ensure the most appropriate treatment.

⊃ **Turn to tea** Certain foods appear to have an especially powerful protective effect against cardiovascular damage. One of these is tea, which numerous studies have linked with better heart health. One recent study found that heavy tea drinkers (who averaged two or more cups a day) had a 44 per cent lower death rate after a heart attack than people who didn't drink tea; moderate tea drinkers had a 28 per cent lower death rate. Tea's protective effect is thought to come from its wealth of flavonoids, antioxidant compounds found in both black and green tea that appear to prevent cholesterol from clogging arteries, discourage blood from clotting and keep blood vessels supple.

⮕ **Eat more fish** Another food with potent heart-protecting power is fish – or, more specifically, oils they contain known as omega-3 fatty acids. These oils can make blood less prone to clotting, lower triglyceride levels and reduce blood-vessel inflammation, which can promote plaque build-up. Fish that are particularly rich in omega-3s include cold-water varieties such as salmon, trout, mackerel, sardines and fresh tuna.

The Food Standards Agency issued new guidelines on oily fish consumption in June 2004. There has been some concern about the build-up of toxins – and particularly dioxins in fish stocks as a result of industrial pollution. But the FSA for the first time recommended maximum levels at which the health benefits of preventing heart disease clearly outweigh the possible risk from dioxins. Men, boys and women past child-bearing age can eat up to four portions of oily fish a week. Women of child-bearing age, and particularly pregnant and breastfeeding women, and girls, can eat up to two portions a week. Long-standing public health advice continues to be that you should eat at least two portions of fish a week, one of which is oily, because there is good evidence that eating oily fish reduces the risk of death from heart disease. On average, people in the UK eat only one-third of a portion of oily fish a week, and seven out of ten people eat none at all.

⮕ **Include antioxidant-rich foods** Antioxidant nutrients such as vitamins C and E counteract a process called oxidation, in which unstable molecules produced by the body's use of oxygen damage healthy tissue. Among their benefits, antioxidants make cholesterol less likely to stick to artery walls. Vitamin C is found in such foods as citrus fruits, red and green peppers, broccoli and tomatoes. Peanuts, sunflower seeds, wheat germ and vegetable oils are sources of vitamin E.

⮕ **Don't forget folic acid** This B vitamin has been shown to lower levels of homocysteine, a substance linked to cardiovascular disease risk. Excellent dietary sources of folic acid are leafy green vegetables such as cabbage and broccoli, offal, whole grains and fortified cereals.

Caring for your kidneys

The first thing to appreciate about your kidneys is that you have two of them, nestled on either side of your spine towards the back of your torso just above your waist. Two is really more than you need – people can survive with only one (assuming it's healthy). But it's a sign of how important the kidneys are that the body comes with a pair of them.

The kidneys are the body's sewage plant, where blood flows to be filtered through a complex of tiny blood vessels called capillaries. Cleansed blood is sent back into circulation while wastes and toxins are taken out and sent to the bladder for excretion in urine. The kidneys are hardworking and efficient, and they tend to keep quiet even when their job becomes difficult – which is what happens when persistent blood-sugar overloads foul the delicate capillaries and structures that filter your blood.

The blood-cleansing kidney

The kidneys produce and eliminate urine through a complex system of some 2 million tiny filters called nephrons. At the top of each nephron, in the Bowman's capsule, is the glomerulus, a microscopic cluster of capillaries. Blood flows at high pressure through the glomerulus, where urea, toxins and other wastes are filtered out and ultimately expelled through the urine. The purified fluid is returned to the blood via the renal vein. Over time, high blood sugar destroys the nephrons.

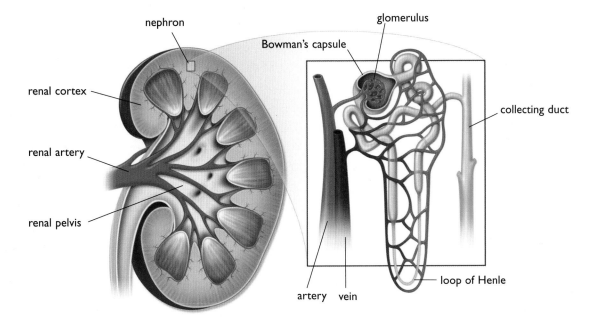

nephron · renal cortex · renal artery · renal pelvis · glomerulus · Bowman's capsule · collecting duct · loop of Henle · artery · vein

It takes years of blood-sugar abuse to wreck the kidneys, but once the kidneys are damaged, there's no repairing them. Total loss of renal function ultimately requires dialysis, in which you are hooked up to a blood-cleansing machine for 2 to 4 hours a few times a week. Another option is a kidney transplant.

The kidney-disease countdown

Diabetes is the leading cause of kidney failure in the UK, where about one-third of people with diabetes develop kidney disease. Yet the results of the UK Prospective Diabetes Study make it clear that you can avoid kidney disease, especially if you're alert to what happens as it progresses – and you act early. Uncontrolled kidney damage is likely to move ahead in several stages.

▶ First, the kidneys start filtering waste faster in an attempt to clear blood of excess sugar, boosting what is known as the glomerular filtration rate, or GFR. Some of the structures inside the kidneys start to enlarge, intruding on space normally used by blood-filtering capillaries, making them less efficient and causing the kidneys to work harder.

▶ After a year or so, the kidneys start becoming less able to filter waste or keep nutrients that should stay in the body from being expelled. Small amounts of a protein known as albumin may become detectable in the urine, a condition known as microalbuminuria.

▶ As the kidneys become more damaged, you lose more albumin, whose job is to keep water within the bloodstream. Water builds up in the body's tissues, causing such classic symptoms of kidney disease as puffiness around the eyes and swelling of the hands and feet. At the same time, the liver starts to pump out cholesterol and other fats involved in manufacturing albumin, boosting your cardiovascular risks. If you have Type 2 diabetes, you could still ward off kidney failure at this stage (known as nephrotic syndrome), but it may be too late if you have Type 1.

▶ The last two stages are in the realm of kidney failure, in which the body becomes increasingly unable to filter waste. In the first stage of kidney failure, called renal insufficiency, treatment may still help, but as damage increases you enter end-stage renal failure, when even good blood-sugar control is unlikely to stave off the need to have dialysis or a kidney transplant. In the UK, about 1,000 people a year have to go on to dialysis because of their diabetes.

How to combat kidney complications

Closely controlling blood sugar is the single most important way to keep kidney disease at bay. But managing high blood pressure, which can narrow arteries leading to the kidneys and damage the delicate blood vessels inside them, also plays a major role. That means there are plenty of steps you can take to reduce your risk or slow the progress of kidney disease. Some of these also reduce your chances of developing other complications.

➲ **Test regularly** Hallmark symptoms, such as swelling, fatigue and pain in the lower back, don't usually show up until a lot of kidney tissue has already been damaged – perhaps as much as 80 per cent. But it's possible to detect the early signs of kidney disease well before that with tests. One of the most sensitive is a test for microalbuminuria, which Diabetes UK recommends you have at least once a year. Your doctor may also suggest a test of your creatinine clearance rate. Creatinine is a waste product of muscles that a healthy kidney will clear from the blood but a damaged one will leave behind in detectable amounts.

➲ **Treat high blood pressure** Taking ACE inhibitors to control hypertension benefits the kidneys by relieving pressure that can damage delicate filtering structures and keeping blood vessels flexible. In fact, some studies find that taking ACE inhibitors reduces deaths from diabetic kidney disease by half. Even in people who don't have high blood pressure but have signs of kidney damage, research suggests that ACE inhibitors help. Anything else you do to bring down blood pressure – especially not smoking – will also benefit your kidneys.

➲ **Protect against infection** Feeling a burning sensation when you urinate, having to urinate frequently, and cloudy or bloody urine are signs of a urinary tract infection (UTI), which should be treated with antibiotics. UTIs are common in people with diabetes, partly because damage to nerves that control the bladder can keep you from voiding properly, leaving waste to fester in the body. That affects the kidneys, which can

DID YOU KNOW

Although people with diabetes are up to 20 times more likely to go blind than those who do not have diabetes, treatment can prevent blindness in 90 per cent of those at risk if applied early and adequately. Blindness is more prevalent among people with Type 1 diabetes. Twenty years after diagnosis, almost all people with Type 1 and 60 per cent of people with Type 2 diabetes will have some form of retinopathy.

be further damaged by the ravages of bacteria. Besides being alert for symptoms, make cranberry juice a regular part of your diet. Studies have found that it helps to prevent UTIs, possibly by making it more difficult for bacteria to adhere to tissue inside the urinary tract.

➲ **Check your medication** A wide range of prescription and over-the-counter drugs can cause kidney problems in susceptible people. Among them are aspirin and ibuprofen. Prescription drugs that can aggravate kidney damage include certain antibiotics and lithium. Whenever you get a new prescription ask your doctor if there are any warnings about taking it if you have kidney disease.

Be wise with your eyes

The eyes as well as the kidneys are nourished by small blood vessels that can easily be damaged when you have diabetes. Left alone, the damage can lead to vision loss, and diabetes remains the leading cause of blindness in adults. However, most eye problems can be treated if caught early – and it may be possible to avoid them altogether.

Again, close blood-sugar control makes a big difference. In the UK Prospective Diabetes Study, risk reduction from good blood-glucose and blood-pressure control was 33 per cent. But you should never be complacent about possible eye damage, especially because you typically won't notice it in its earliest stages.

Most eye damage from diabetes takes place in the retina, the light-sensitive area at the back of the eye that registers visual signals and sends them to the brain through the optic nerve. High blood sugar (especially when combined with high blood pressure) can weaken small blood vessels that supply the eyes with oxygen and nutrients, causing them to puff up and rupture like balloons – a condition known as nonproliferative retinopathy. In some cases leakage and lack of nourishment can directly damage the retina and make your vision blurry, but you may not notice anything at all.

If the damage progresses, a more severe condition called proliferative retinopathy may develop, in which more blood vessels start to sprout in the retina to make up for blood delivery lost through burst vessels. This only compounds the problem by leading to more ruptures. These can block light to the retina and cause haemorrhages and pressure inside the eyes, which contributes to scar tissue that can eventually cause the retina to start tearing away from the eye. Retinopathy can also cause macular oedema. In this condition, the central area of the retina (the macula), which allows you to see sharp detail and colour, swells, causing loss of fine vision.

Watch for symptoms

The key to keeping your sight clear is to be alert for symptoms that point to a problem.

➲ **Look out for changes** It's easy to dismiss subtle changes in your vision as minor annoyances, but when you have diabetes, you can't assume that you need a new spectacles prescription or that your eyes are simply getting 'old'. Granted, those may be possibilities – and high or low fluctuations in blood sugar can sometimes affect your vision temporarily.

How diabetes affects the eyes

Lining the interior of the eye is the retina, a delicate 10-layer membrane packed with nerve fibres and photoreceptors. Diabetic retinopathy occurs when uncontrolled high blood sugar damages or blocks the tiny blood vessels (capillaries) throughout the retina, cutting off the blood supply to small patches of retinal tissue. The damaged blood vessels also tend to leak, producing swelling within the retina. As retinal damage progresses, new blood vessels sprout, and vision may become increasingly blurred. About 25 per cent of people with diabetes have some degree of retinopathy.

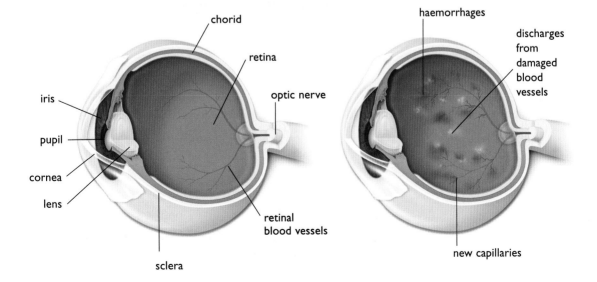

chorid
retina
optic nerve
iris
pupil
cornea
lens
retinal blood vessels
sclera

haemorrhages
discharges from damaged blood vessels
new capillaries

You should see your doctor or an ophthalmologist immediately if you have any of the symptoms listed below:

▶ Your eyesight seems blurry.

▶ You experience double vision.

▶ Your vision becomes distorted or straight lines, such as telephone poles, look warped.

▶ Spots or lines seem to float in front of your eyes.

▶ Your field of vision seems narrower.

▶ You have more difficulty seeing clearly in dim light.

▶ It seems as though a veil has been drawn over your field of vision.

▶ You feel pressure or pain in your eyes.

▶ You have trouble perceiving colours, especially blue and yellow, or making distinctions between similar colours.

➲ **Have regular checks** You may not be able to see or feel the earliest signs of retinopathy, but a doctor can easily identify them during an eye examination. Be sure to have regular vision checks by an ophthalmologist, who will give you a comprehensive exam that includes dilating your pupils to look directly at the retina. The National Service Framework for Diabetes has given priority to screening for retinopathy. By the year 2006 at least 80 per cent of people with diabetes are to be offered screening for the early detection and treatment of diabetic retinopathy, rising to 100 per cent by the end of 2007. The British Medical Association recommends screening upon diagnosis and annually thereafter.

➲ **Get help for hypertension** Easing your blood pressure can reduce your risk of retinopathy or slow its progression. Ask your doctor if, in addition to changing your diet, getting more exercise and not smoking, you should take medication.

➲ **Evaluate your exercise** Once you learn you have retinopathy, ask your doctor to take another look at your exercise programme. Certain forms of exercise can be jarring to the delicate structures within the eye or may increase the amount of pressure inside the eye and thus lead to more retinal bleeding.

➲ **Consider surgery** The best way to prevent further damage from retinopathy may be to fix the harm that has already been done. Using a type of laser surgery called photocoagulation, an ophthalmologist aims a thin beam of laser light at the retina to destroy ruptured blood vessels, seal areas that are leaking and prevent new vessels from forming. In some cases, laser surgery can slow the rate of vision loss by 90 per cent or more. Another form of surgery, cryotherapy, destroys abnormal blood vessels by freezing them with a probe – a technique especially useful in areas a laser can't reach or for people who still have proliferative retinopathy after laser surgery. In a third operation, called a vitrectomy, the eye's jelly-like core (vitreous humour) is taken out so that doctors can remove scar tissue from inside the eye and repair the retina if it has started to detach.

Nipping nerve damage in the bud

Nerve damage may be one of the most far-reaching complications of diabetes because the nervous system controls or contributes to everything from your sense of touch (and pain) to muscle movement, digestion and sexual function. Fortunately, you probably have time to prevent nerve damage, which usually develops after you have had diabetes for 10 to 15 years. Doctors don't fully understand how diabetes causes nerve damage, but likely possibilities are that high blood sugar upsets the balance of chemicals that allow nerves to transmit electrical impulses, deprives nerves of oxygen by impeding circulation, and damages the nerves' protective coating (the myelin sheath). Fortunately, diabetes does not seem to affect the brain and spinal cord – the components of the central nervous system. But the rest of the body's nerves, which carry electrical impulses through an intricate network of 'wires', are vulnerable to diabetes-related signal slowdowns, miscommunication or interruptions.

> ## TESTS OF NERVES
>
> While it's up to you to sound the neuropathy alarm, if you suspect you have nerve damage, your doctor can confirm and fine-tune the diagnosis with subtle tests. In one, the doctor may hold a tuning fork against body parts, such as your foot, to find out whether you can detect its vibration. Similarly, he or she may touch you with a hair-like fine wire to gauge your response to delicate stimuli or apply heat or cold to make sure that you could tell if you were being harmed by, say, scalding bathwater. If any of these tests indicate that you have nerve damage, your doctor will probably send you to a neurologist to learn the extent of the damage.

The three major types of nerve damage, or neuropathy, can each affect the body in many ways. If you develop neuropathy, your doctor will determine which kind it is mostly by your symptoms and where they occur.

Polyneuropathy: on the fringes The most common type of nerve damage affects multiple nerves throughout the body (*poly* means 'many'), but it mainly hits the long nerves of the peripheral nervous system that run through the arms and legs. This kind of nerve damage is often called distal symmetric neuropathy because it strikes areas away from the central nervous system (*distal* refers to distance from the centre) and tends to cause symptoms on both sides of the body (symmetric). Polyneuropathy generally does not affect movement; but it disrupts sensation, often causing pain, cramps or tingling in the hands or feet and, later, numbness.

Focal neuropathy: in the spotlight Far less common, focal neuropathy concentrates on a single nerve, or set of nerves, and often affects only one area of the body – which is why it is sometimes called mononeuropathy (*mono* means 'one'). Unlike polyneuropathy, which tends to develop gradually over time, it pops up suddenly, often causing numbness or pain, or weakness in the muscles, depending on which nerves are affected. Although it can crop up anywhere, focal neuropathy often causes Bell's palsy, in which nerves lose control over muscles in the face, causing your features to droop. Focal neuropathy can make your eyes cross if it affects muscles that control eye movement, and it can cause carpal tunnel syndrome, in which compressed nerves in the wrist produce pain or weakness in the hand and forearm.

Autonomic neuropathy: control issues The autonomic nervous system governs the body functions such as heartbeat, digestion, sweating and bladder control, which you don't normally think about much unless nerves are damaged. Problems that can result from autonomic neuropathy include:

▶ Cardiovascular glitches, such as irregular heartbeat and a condition called orthostatic hypotension, in which your blood pressure fails to adjust quickly when you stand up, making you feel faint or dizzy. Deadened nerves can also fail to pick up pain from a heart attack.

▶ Gastroparesis, a condition in which gastrointestinal tract muscles become slow and inefficient. Sluggish digestion causes nausea, vomiting, bloating, diarrhoea, constipation and appetite loss, and it also makes blood-sugar patterns more difficult to predict and counter with insulin.

▶ Poor bladder function, in which nerves may have trouble telling when the bladder is full and don't empty the bladder completely when you void. One result is higher risk of urinary tract infections, which in turn can accelerate kidney damage.

▶ Sexual dysfunction, in which men find it difficult to get or maintain an erection and women experience vaginal dryness or tepid sexual response. Usually, however, sex drive remains unaffected in both sexes.

▶ Dulled response to nervous symptoms of hypoglycaemia, such as shakiness, sweating and anxiety, a dangerous condition known as hypoglycaemia unawares.

▶ Profuse sweating without undue exertion and poor regulation of body temperature.

Keeping symptoms in check

In the case of nerve damage, closely controlling blood sugar – your top priority – can reduce your risk by as much as 60 per cent. Once neuropathy develops, treatments vary depending on how the nerve damage is affecting your body. These are some steps you can take to minimize damage and discomfort.

➲ **Get in touch with your feelings** As with most diabetes complications, the sooner you pick up on nerve damage, the more you can do to prevent it from escalating. Don't dismiss sensations or difficulties that disappear. In many cases, symptoms come and go or swing from mild to severe. Tell your doctor immediately if you experience any of the following:

▶ Tingling, numbness, burning or prickly pain in your arms, legs, hands or feet. Stay alert as the sensations can be very subtle at first. Try to be especially aware of unusual sensations in the feet, which are often affected first, or at night, when symptoms are usually worse.

▶ Sensitivity to touch – even the light brushing of your sheets against you when you're in bed.

▶ Leg cramps that may come and go, especially at night.

▶ Difficulty sensing the position of your feet or toes, or a sense that you can't keep your balance.

▶ Calluses or sores on your feet.

➲ **Adjust your diet** Ask your dietitian about dietary changes that might help to keep some symptoms of neuropathy in check. If you have gastroparesis, try eating smaller, more frequent meals or consuming softer foods to ease digestion. Ask if you should eat less fibre, which is good for blood-sugar control for the same reason that it may be bad for gastroparesis: it slows digestion. If you feel lightheaded when you stand, eating more salt may help to stabilize your blood pressure. Check with your doctor first though, especially if you may also be at risk for hypertension.

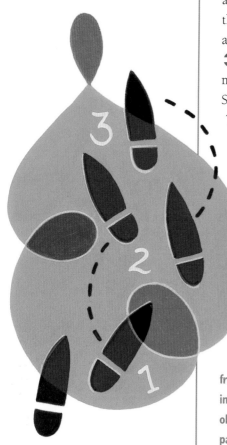

⮑ **Boost your B vitamins** In some cases, neuropathy is fostered by a deficiency in the vitamins B_6 and B_{12}, both of which are involved in the function of the nervous system. Vitamin B_6 is contained in avocados, bananas, poultry, pork, potatoes and fish such as tuna, while B_{12} is found in chicken, beef and a wide variety of seafood, including oysters, sardines and other fish. Ask your dietitian or doctor if you should take supplements.

⮑ **Supplement your nerve health** See page 200 to learn about alpha-lipoic acid, an antioxidant supplement that can help to protect the nerves and ease the pain of neuropathy.

⮑ **Reach for relief** Try to temper the pain of polyneuropathy with over-the-counter pain relievers – especially aspirin, which carries the bonus of cardiovascular benefits. (If you already take small doses of aspirin daily, ask your doctor how to adjust the amount.) You may also find relief from topical creams containing capsaicin, a compound found in chilli peppers that alleviates pain by interfering with signals that nerve cells send to the brain. When using these creams, be careful to keep them away from the eyes and other sensitive areas.

⮑ **Ask about medication** Drugs are available to help control many of the specific conditions that can result from neuropathy. Sildenafil (Viagra) for sexual dysfunction is just one example. There are also drugs that help you empty your bladder, ward off episodes of low blood pressure, and treat gastroparesis. You might also benefit from taking a tricyclic antidepressant, such as amitryptyline, nortriptyline or trazodone, which have been found to take the edge off neuropathy pain. Give these drugs time to work: it often takes several weeks for them to become effective. Your doctor might also recommend an anticonvulsant drug, such as phenytoin, carbamazepine (Tegretol), or gabapentin (Neurontin), which can reduce pain from nerve damage.

Sidestepping foot problems

Feet can take a beating when you have diabetes. Poor circulation from damaged blood vessels slows healing and makes feet prone to infection, while nerve damage can dull sensation and leave you oblivious to injuries that can quickly get out of control. Fortunately, paying a little extra attention to your feet can go a long way toward keeping them healthy.

In the grand scheme of things, foot problems seem almost comically mundane. But you can't dismiss broken skin, corns, calluses, bunions, ingrown toenails and other problems as minor irritations when you have diabetes. Left untreated for long, such conditions can put you at risk of losing a foot – or even a leg – to gangrene (tissue death). In the UK 90,000 people with diabetes (5 per cent) develop a foot ulcer in any one year. and 15 per cent of foot ulcers result in amputation.

It all begins with some form of injury that abrades or breaks the skin, the protective barrier that keeps germs out of your body. Perhaps your shoes don't quite fit or you stepped on a stone. Once the damaged area becomes infected, healing may prove difficult, especially if you keep walking on it or are unaware of it, and an open sore, or ulcer, can quickly develop. This is serious – and a reason to call your doctor. Infection from uncontrolled ulcers can burrow deeper into your skin and eventually reach the bone, putting the entire foot or leg at risk. When you have had diabetes for a long time, feet may also become vulnerable to a condition called Charcot's foot, in which numbness and poor reflexes from neuropathy cause missteps that over time destroy joints in the foot.

Here are some of the most important steps you can take to prevent foot problems before they start and avoid minor annoyances becoming a major problem.

Always wear shoes Think of your shoes as bodyguards for the feet, protecting them from blows, scrapes or sharp objects, as well as keeping them warm and dry. To maximize this protection avoid going barefoot (even on the beach, where sand can cause abrasions and debris can puncture the skin) or wearing open shoes, such as flip-flops, sandals or clogs. Don't even take your shoes off when you're indoors, where something as minor as stubbing your toe on the coffee table can lead to a foot ulcer.

Do a daily check Examine your feet once a day, perhaps at bedtime, going over them with your eyes and your hands. Tell your doctor if you find evidence of any problems. Besides blisters, cuts, bruises, cracking, peeling or other obvious signs of damage, look for areas that are paler or redder, which could indicate persistent pressure from shoes. Feel for areas of coldness, which could be a sign of poor circulation, or warmness, which might indicate an infection, along with redness or swelling. If you have difficulty seeing the soles of your feet, place a mirror on the floor and look at the reflection. If you have poor vision, ask a partner or friend to inspect your feet for you.

➲ **Wash and dry** Keep your feet clean by washing them every day with lukewarm water and soap. (Avoid hot water, which, if you have neuropathy, may scald you without your knowing it.) Avoid soaking your feet, though, which will soften skin and make you more vulnerable to infection. Dry feet by blotting (not rubbing), and be sure to dry between the toes to discourage fungal infections. Use a moisturizing cream to prevent dryness and cracking, but don't put it between your toes, where it may encourage skin to wear away.

Take-charge tips

Finding shoes that fit is important for everybody, but doubly so for people with diabetes. Your chiropodist can help if you have difficulty finding the right footwear, but you should be able to buy comfortable shoes off the rack if you heed these tips.

➲ **Follow three fit factors** Don't settle for any shoe that doesn't meet all three criteria for a good fit:

The tip of the shoe should extend about the width of your thumb beyond your longest toe.

The ball of your foot should fit comfortably – without cramping the toes – into the widest part of the shoe.

The heel should fit snugly without slipping when you walk.

➲ **Measure every time** Don't just tell the sales assistant your shoe size – ask for your foot to be measured. Changes in weight, blood circulation and foot structure can alter the size or shape of your foot.

➲ **Try on both shoes** It's likely that one of your feet is slightly larger than the other, so make sure shoes fit both feet. If necessary, buy for your larger foot and see your chiropodist about padding the other shoe.

➲ **Don't assume it will stretch** Shoes may mould better to your feet the longer you wear them, but don't let a sales assistant tell you the basic fit will improve with time. The shoe should fit – now.

➲ **Buy late in the day** Feet swell by as much as 5 per cent over the course of the day, so shopping later in the day will ensure that feet aren't cramped when you put new shoes on in the morning.

➲ **Ask about returns** If you have lost sensation in your feet, you can't trust how shoes feel in the store. Bring them home and wear them around the house for half an hour, then check your feet. If you see areas of redness, which indicate pressure from a poor fit, take the shoes back.

➲ **Clip with care** Keep your toenails neatly trimmed, cutting them straight across to prevent ingrown nails and filing rough edges to avoid damaging adjacent toes. Some doctors advise against using nail clippers as you could accidentally cut the skin next to the nail. As an alternative, use a file or an emery board to shave nails down (go no shorter than the ends of your toes).

➲ **Get a clean start** Begin each day by putting on a fresh pair of socks made of a breathable material such as cotton, cotton blend or wool, which wicks moisture away from skin and helps to keep your feet dry. Make sure your socks fit well, and don't wear socks with seams that will rub your feet, potentially causing pressure sores. If your feet tend to sweat a lot, change your socks throughout the day as needed.

➲ **Wear good shoes** Footwear should provide both comfort and protection. Leather uppers are best because they conform to the shape of your foot and breathe so that feet perspire less. Opt for low heels for stability and soles made of crepe or foam rubber for cushioning. It's a good idea to have at least two pairs of shoes that you wear regularly so you can alternate from one day to the next, giving shoes time to air between each wearing. Never wear new shoes for more than a few hours at a time. When you put on your shoes, shake them out and feel inside to make sure there's no debris that could cause pressure or irritation.

➲ **Consult your doctor**. A foot exam should be a routine part of every visit to the doctor, just like taking your blood pressure. Feet should be checked at least once a year – more often if you have signs of neuropathy or poor circulation or you've already had foot ulcers. (Bring your most-worn pair of shoes to the appointment so your doctor can check wear patterns.) But don't wait for your annual check-up if you notice any changes in your feet. Call your doctor if you develop an infection or sore, your foot is punctured by a sharp object, a toe becomes red and tender, or you notice any change in sensation, such as numbness, pain or tingling. Do not use acid treatments or over-the-counter wart or corn removers, and never try to perform do-it-yourself surgery to treat warts, corns, calluses or ingrown toenails.

Alternative therapies

You're following a healthy diet, watching your weight, getting exercise, and possibly taking drugs or insulin for your diabetes. Can anything else help? Maybe. Certain herbs and other supplements show promise for bringing down blood sugar and protecting the eyes, nerves, kidneys and heart. Other alternative therapies, such as biofeedback and acupuncture, may help to reduce stress and relieve nerve pain. Should you try them? Weigh the research evidence, consider any potential side effects, consult your doctor, then make the decision for yourself.

EIGHT

8

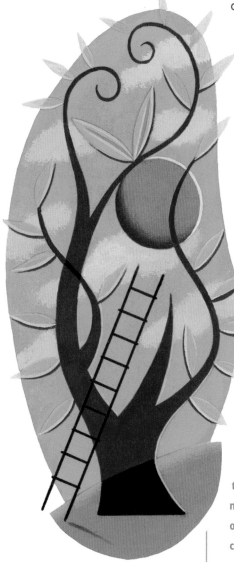

Drugs and alternative therapies

The wonders of modern medicine have given us such powerful drugs as Glucophage, to keep blood sugar in check, and statins, to lower the risk of heart-related complications. But what about the world of not-so-modern medicine? For thousands of years healers relied on natural therapies, many of them herb-based, to treat conditions such as diabetes. Can any of them help you?

More and more patients – and even many doctors – are starting to ask that question as interest in so-called alternative medicine continues to grow. A report published in 2000 for the Department of Health estimated there were over 60,000 practitioners of complementary and alternative medicine in the UK, and in addition up to 20,000 statutory health professionals who regularly practise some form of complementary medicine. An Office for National Statistics survey in 2001 found that one in ten people had used complementary therapy in the previous 12 months. While a recent study of GPs found that half of all practices offered access to some form of complementary medicine, and almost one-third provided it in-house.

What is alternative medicine?

In many ways, what you define as 'alternative' depends on your culture. Many alternative therapies come from Eastern regions, such as Asia and India, where healing traditions tend to be less scientific than they are in the West. But not all Western countries view medicine the same way, either. Germany, for example, has a long history of incorporating herbal therapies into conventional medicine and conducting research into their benefits. In the UK, herbal supplements, while growing in popularity, are less a part of mainstream medicine because they are not studied as vigorously as drugs are, nor are they subject to the same licensing controls as orthodox medicine.

In the UK non-orthodox treatments are often referred to as 'CAM' – for complementary and alternative medicine. 'Complementary' emphasizes the fact that alternative therapies may sometimes be useful as an adjunct to orthodox medical care but should never be seen as a substitute – as many alternative practitioners will be the first to tell you. In fact, you should ask your doctor about any supplement or alternative treatment you want to try, or at least inform your medical team what you are taking. Many alternative treatments, especially herbs, can interfere with other medications and may affect how your doctor advises you to treat your diabetes. The Integrated Healthcare Network, founded with support from the Department of Health, is an online information network for people seeking to combine complementary therapies with mainstream NHS healthcare services within the UK (www.ihn.org.uk).

How to judge alternative therapies

One way to summarize the difference between alternative and conventional medicine is that the former is more art and the latter is more science. That balance is beginning to shift as more research is done into the potential benefits of alternative therapies (although very little research is carried out in the UK). But one of the main drawbacks of CAM is that, in many cases, the scientific evidence that a therapy works is sketchy, and safety risks are often not well understood.

That does not mean that alternative medicine is worthless or dangerous. But it does give you reason to approach it with an open mind – including a healthy openness to scepticism. Marketing and promotional material, including that published in books and on websites, makes supplements and other products sound good. But you can't put a lot of stock in the ways manufacturers typically get their point across:

Unquestioning faith In many cases, labels and advertising will simply state what a product is used for as if there is no doubt that it will work.

Vague research In other cases, 'research' or 'a study' are cited with no further details about who conducted them.

Testimonials A favourite 'proof' that a therapy works is to quote somebody (preferably a celebrity) who says it was good for him or her. But from a scientific perspective, anecdotes are the least convincing form of evidence.

History The fact that a therapy has been used for hundreds or even thousands of years is often held out as evidence of effectiveness, but tradition is not necessarily proof.

?
DID YOU KNOW

The word *drug* comes from the French term *drogue*, meaning 'herb' – an indication that herbal remedies are not as far removed from conventional medicines as you might think. In addition to aspirin, many mainstream drugs have been developed from substances found in plants, including morphine and quinine.

The standards for studies

Why is the research thin on alternative remedies? Partly, it's a matter of money. No one can patent a natural product such as a herb, and pharmaceutical companies, which fund much of the research into conventional medicines, generally aren't willing to sink development money into products on which they have no exclusive claim.

So how can you tell if an alternative treatment will work for you? The only real answer – as is true for many drugs as well – is to try it and see, if your doctor approves. But before you do so, gather as much information about the therapy as you can and consider the research that has been done on it.

When evaluating research, you can get a sense of its value by looking at the criteria that researchers themselves use. In the world of medical science, the best studies are those that are:

Big Your diabetes isn't identical to the next person's, so if you and someone else both take the same supplement, you can expect slightly different results. In many cases, even the best conventional drugs don't work for some people. In other cases, a person's health may improve for reasons unconnected with the treatment being tested. Reliable findings therefore depend to some degree on conducting tests on as many people as possible. Most studies of alternative therapies, however, are small.

Human Scientists often start with laboratory tests to determine a substance's chemical properties and effects. These experiments can't reliably predict what will happen in the human body. Animal tests are more informative, and most telling are tests done on people.

Controlled The least reliable experiments are those in which people are simply given the therapy and asked if it makes them feel better. In many cases, people will say yes even when the treatment is known to have no medical benefit – a phenomenon known as the placebo effect. Better experiments are controlled, meaning that one group of people gets the real treatment while a second group gets an inactive alternative so that results can be compared and the possible impact of the placebo effect can be factored in.

Double-blind To guard further against the placebo effect, it's best that study subjects don't know which treatment they are getting. To make quite sure that subjects are kept in the dark –

that they won't get an inkling from the researchers, through body language or other subtle clues, of whether they're getting the real medicine or not – the people administering the treatments should not know who is getting what, either.

Peer-reviewed At the top of the heap are studies that not only meet all the above criteria but also have been assessed as valid by other experts in the field before being published in what is known as a peer-reviewed journal.

The natural medicine cabinet

Some of the most popular alternative therapies for combating diabetes or its complications are herbal and plant-based supplements, available from health-food stores and many pharmacies and supermarkets. Do they work? For the most part, the jury is still out, but research so far suggests that a few may hold real promise.

Whether to use herbal remedies is a decision you should make with the help of your doctor. You need to approach them, with caution. Don't assume that 'herbal' means 'safe', because, in most cases, thorough research on long-term effects has not been done. The fact is, many medicinal herbs do have effects on the body – which is reason for both hope and concern. The information given below is not an endorsement of these therapies, but it can start you thinking about whether certain supplements may be useful to you. The European directive on traditional herbal medicine products, setting out clear standards for the safety and quality of over-the-counter traditional herbal medicines, is due to be implemented in 2005.

Glucose control

The major goal of herbal therapies for diabetes is the same as for drugs and insulin: to bring down high blood sugar. But it's important to remember that herbal therapies are complementary. Even if they work, you should never take them as a substitute for your insulin or regular medication, though they might be useful in lowering the doses you require.

It's extremely important that you monitor your blood sugar closely if you take these remedies, for two reasons. First, you

WHAT THE STUDIES SHOW

A 2002 University of Michigan study of 145 people who had recently been hospitalized for heart attack or angina found that 74 per cent had used some form of complementary or alternative medicine in the previous six months – typically, herbal or nutritional supplements. About one-third were taking supplements that could thin their blood or interact with heart drugs they were taking. Most patients told their doctors what they had been taking – but 25 per cent did not.

won't know how effective they are unless you measure their impact on your glucose. Second, if they are able to bring blood sugar down, you need to be on the alert for an increased possibility of hypoglycaemia. Among the herbs that show the most promise for lowering blood sugar are:

Gymnema Known botanically as *Gymnema sylvestre,* this plant is native to Africa and India, where its Hindi name translates as 'sugar destroyer'. The name aptly describes what it does to the sense of taste. Placed on the tongue, it impairs the ability to distinguish sweetness and bitterness – perhaps one reason it has been used to treat diabetes in India for over 2,000 years.

Although herbalists generally regard gymnema as the most powerful herb for blood-sugar control, it has not been studied in experiments that are both controlled and double-blind. Nonetheless, the research that has been done suggests that the herb has promise. In one of the best controlled (but not blind) studies conducted in the USA, insulin requirements were cut in half for 27 people with Type 1 diabetes who took a 400mg extract of gymnema for 6 to 30 months, while the insulin needs of the control group did not change.

It is thought that gymnema might work by boosting the activity of enzymes that help cells to use glucose or by stimulating insulin-producing beta cells in the pancreas. Safety studies have not been done (be especially cautious if you're pregnant or nursing or have liver or kidney disease), but the herb is not known to cause serious side effects.

Fenugreek Better known nowadays as a spice from the Mediterranean and Near East than as a medicine, fenugreek has nevertheless been put to a variety of uses over the centuries. For example, records dating back to 1500 BC indicate that it was used to induce childbirth in ancient Egypt. In Europe, the German Commission E, which regulates herbal medicine, has approved it for use in an inflammation-fighting poultice.

Numerous animal trials and a few small studies conducted with a total of about 100 people have suggested that fenugreek seeds can lower blood glucose. In one of the largest (but not double-blind) studies, 60 people with Type 2 diabetes who took 25g of fenugreek daily showed significant improvement in their overall blood-sugar control, post-eating glucose levels, urine glucose and cholesterol levels.

The reason for these benefits may not be all that mysterious. Fenugreek is a legume – a relative of chickpeas, lentils, peanuts, and green peas – and is rich in fibre, which naturally slows digestion and the absorption of glucose. But laboratory research also indicates that fenugreek contains an amino acid shown to boost the release of insulin.

Don't take fenugreek supplements if you are pregnant or have liver or kidney disease, and don't ingest it within 2 hours of taking an oral diabetes medication because it may interfere with the body's absorption of the drug. Also be cautious if you are taking blood thinners, with which fenugreek may interact.

Bitter melon Also known as bitter gourd, balsam pear, karella or (scientifically) *Momordica charantia,* bitter melon is a dietary staple in Asia and India. Actually a vegetable, it has long been a folk remedy for diabetes in the East, and a number of studies in people (none of them double-blind) suggest that it may indeed have some benefits. In one uncontrolled study of 18 people who had recently been diagnosed with Type 2 diabetes, 73 per cent of those who drank about a half cup of bitter-melon juice (which lives up to its unpalatable name) saw significant drops in blood-sugar levels. In another study, five people who took 15g of bitter melon in powdered form (available in capsules) brought their blood sugar down by 25 per cent in three weeks.

Bitter melon is thought to help cells use glucose through such active ingredients as plant insulin, which is chemically similar to the insulin from cows that is often used to treat Type 1 diabetes. Other substances in bitter melon are thought to block sugar absorption in the intestine.

In addition to having a terrible taste, bitter melon can cause side effects such as gastrointestinal distress and headaches, and it should not be taken during pregnancy.

Ginseng In Chinese, *gin* means 'man' and *seng* means 'essence' – perhaps not only because the ginseng root's shape sometimes resembles a human figure but also because the root supposedly can treat just about everything. In fact, ginseng's genus name, Panax, comes from two Greek words for 'cure' and 'all'. Ginseng is said to have whole-body effects that make it broadly

useful for building resistance to disease, recovering from illness, combating the physical effects of stress and even promoting longer life (not to mention boosting your sex drive).

Can you take seriously something that sounds too good to be true? Some of the research into ginseng's effects on diabetes, while far from conclusive, is unusually strong and has appeared in respected peer-reviewed journals. In one University of Illinois study, published in a 2002 issue of the journal *Diabetes,* over-weight mice with Type 2 diabetes who were injected with an extract of Asian ginseng normalized their blood sugar, dropped 10 per cent of their body weight, and lowered their cholesterol by about one-third.

A University of Toronto study published in the *Annals of Internal Medicine* two years earlier found that ten people who took 3g of American ginseng 40 minutes before eating reduced their post-meal glucose levels by about 20 per cent compared with a control group. An earlier study reported in *Diabetes Care* found that taking ginseng lowered haemoglobin A1c numbers in people with Type 2 diabetes.

It is not clear how ginseng works, but slowing carbohydrate absorption, boosting glucose uptake and improving insulin secretion have all been suggested. So has the idea that ginseng, which can cause excitability, simply makes people more active. Possible side effects include headache, increased blood pressure and insomnia. Ginseng can interfere with certain heart drugs and the blood thinner warfarin.

Other potential blood-sugar busters

A number of other plant-based supplements have been suggested as blood-sugar busters, based on preliminary research that is even thinner than that for the supplements discussed above. Among these potential prospects are:

Bilberry Related to the blueberry and grown in Europe and Canada, bilberry is a folk remedy for diabetes, although no human studies have been done on its blood-sugar effects. In animals, it has been shown to lower blood glucose by 26 per cent and triglycerides by 39 per cent, potentially making it even more beneficial if you have heart disease. The safety of the extract has not been established (high doses may interact with blood thinners), but it is quite safe to eat as a fruit.

Prickly pear Also known as nopal, this cactus is a Mexican folk remedy for diabetes and has been studied in a number of small, uncontrolled trials. In two of them, people with Type 2 diabetes who consumed 500g of nopal (a sizable amount, equal to about a pound) saw their blood sugar drop significantly within a few hours. One suspected mode of action is prickly pear's high fibre content. Perhaps not surprisingly, possible side effects include gastrointestinal distress.

Pterocarpus marsupium The bark of this tree from India contains a compound, called epicatechin, that some studies have found improves the function of insulin-producing beta cells in the pancreas. In one study from India of 97 people with Type 2 diabetes, 69 per cent of those taking 2 to 4g of the herb daily achieved good glucose control within 12 weeks.

Nerves: a touchy subject

Some natural remedies for people with diabetes do not lower blood sugar, but may prove useful for reducing the impact of certain complications, such as neuropathy. That's hard to prove, because nerve damage occurs slowly, over years, while studies of natural remedies tend to be short-term. But at least two supplements seem to show some promise in negating neuropathy.

Alpha-lipoic acid Sometimes called ALA for short, alpha-lipoic acid is a powerful antioxidant that works to protect cells against the damaging effects of molecules known as free radicals. These chemical scourges are thought to contribute to neuropathy brought on by diabetes, and numerous studies suggest that ALA can stave off damage to nerves caused by free radicals. It may also reduce harmful swelling of nerves by blocking an enzyme that causes a glucose by-product (sorbitol) to build up inside nerve cells.

The body produces small amounts of ALA on its own, and you get a certain amount from such foods as meat and spinach. But neither of these sources provides enough to exert a therapeutic effect – especially since people with diabetes may be prone to low levels of ALA.

What are the effects of ALA? A number of high-quality studies around the world have addressed that question, and the answers, while not yet conclusive, are intriguing. For example, a Mayo Clinic study has shown that three months of ALA

? DID YOU KNOW

Ginseng is traditionally consumed in teas. Look for tea bags containing the powdered root. Such teas are sometimes labelled 'red ginseng'. This ginseng has been steamed and dried, a process that turns it red. 'White' ginseng is simply the dried root.

supplementation significantly improved the ability of nerves to conduct signals in people with diabetes. And a university study of more than 300 people with diabetes in Germany found that patients taking 600mg of ALA for three weeks experienced less pain and other symptoms of polyneuropathy.

Yet results have been mixed in some of the largest trials, done in Germany in a series of studies called ALADIN (Alpha-Lipoic Acid in Diabetic Neuropathy). In one double-blind trial involving 328 people with Type 2 diabetes, those who received daily ALA injections for three weeks felt significantly less pain from neuropathy than those receiving a placebo. But a larger follow-up study found little difference in symptoms between people treated with ALA injections and pills for nine months and those not receiving the real medication.

Beyond the issue of effectiveness is the question of safety. The safety of ALA has not been formally established, but the substance has been used to treat diabetes in Germany for more than 30 years without reports of serious side effects. Still, animal studies suggest that it is toxic to rats deficient in thiamin, so some natural therapists suggest taking a supplement of this B vitamin when using ALA.

Gamma-linolenic acid Although the name sounds similar to ALA, gamma linolenic acid (GLA) is an essential fatty acid whose most concentrated source in nature is the oil from a wild flower called evening primrose (so called because its yellow petals open at dusk). Normally, the body makes all the GLA it needs from other types of fat, but some research indicates that this process may be impaired in people with diabetes, suggesting that supplements may be a good idea. You need GLA because the body converts it to prostaglandins – hormone-like substances that regulate a variety of functions, including inflammation, dilation of blood vessels and hormone activity. Getting more GLA is thought to help to prevent neuropathy partly by boosting the flow of nutrients and oxygen to nerves.

At least one good-size, controlled, double-blind, peer-reviewed study backs up such claims. This investigation, which involved 111 people with neuropathy, found that those who took 480mg of GLA daily scored significantly better on 13 out of 16 tests for nerve damage after a year than people who received a placebo. Another double-blind study, although much smaller

(22 people), produced similar results with a smaller dose of GLA, contained in about 4g of evening primrose oil.

Because evening primrose oil has been studied as a treatment for a variety of problems (including eczema and rheumatoid arthritis) and is widely used in Europe, it has a fairly long safety record and is not known to cause serious side effects. However, small numbers of people may experience headache or gastrointestinal distress.

Natural eye protection

Can natural therapies protect eyes from the weakening and bursting of blood vessels that occur with retinopathy? Certain supplements may be helpful, although the evidence for them is not as strong as for some of the therapies recommended for other aspects of diabetes.

L-carnitine L-carnitine is a type of amino acid – small units of organic material that link together to form proteins. A form of L-carnitine called acetyl-L-carnitine, or ALC, is known to have a potent antioxidant effect and has been proposed as a treatment for both diabetic retinopathy and diabetic nerve disease. Dietary sources of L-carnitine are high-protein foods, such as beef and lamb, along with dairy products, but at least one European study suggests that people with diabetes may be naturally deficient in the amino acid.

Will L-carnitine prevent eye damage? Most of the evidence that hints at a benefit comes from animal research. One study, published in the journal *Diabetes*, found that rats given ALC reversed abnormal results on a test that measures retinal function, while rats in a control group showed no improvement. Similar results were produced in a Japanese study using another form of L-carnitine, called propionyl-L-carnitine.

Other studies have suggested that acetyl-L-carnitine may help to protect the heart by reducing the risk of angina, in addition to lowering blood sugar and reducing pain from intermittent claudication in the legs. It is also used to treat conditions unrelated to diabetes, such as muscular dystrophy. Wide use of L-carnitine has not revealed any problems with toxicity, but its safety has not been well studied.

Bilberry In addition to its reputed ability to lower blood sugar, bilberry is used to treat a variety of eye problems, including diabetic retinopathy. Evidence that bilberry improves vision is partly anecdotal. For example, during World War II, Royal Air Force bomber pilots claimed that they could see better on night raids after eating bilberry jam. But there's reason to believe that its benefits might be real. In one study, 31 patients were treated with bilberry extract daily for four weeks. Use of the extract fortified the capillaries and reduced haemorrhaging in the eyes, especially in the case of diabetic retinopathy. Bilberry is rich in flavonoids – vitamin-like antioxidant plant substances, some of which are known to strengthen tiny blood vessels such as those that nourish the retina. The fruit is particularly packed with flavonoids known as anthocyanosides, which have been shown both to make blood vessels less leaky and fragile and to shore up connective tissue such as that of the retina.

How much should you take?

Even though they may have medicinal effects, natural supplements are not prescribed like drugs, which have dosage guidelines based on research into effectiveness and safety. Yet in many (but not all) cases, studies suggest therapeutic supplement doses that, as far as is known, are non-toxic. You should check with your doctor for advice on dosages that might be right for you, but the following are typical.

SUPPLEMENT	DOSAGE	ADVICE
Vitamin B complex	One tablet each morning with food	Look for a B-50 complex with 50mcg vitamin B_{12} and biotin, 400mcg folic acid and 50mg other B vitamins
Chromium	200mcg once a day with food	May alter insulin requirements: consult your doctor
Magnesium	200mg twice a day	Do not take if you have kidney disease
Zinc	25mg a day	Buy a supplement that includes 2mg copper
Gymnema sylvestre	200mg extract twice a day	May alter insulin requirements: consult your doctor
Fish oils	2tsp to supply 2g of omega-3 fatty acids a day	Consult doctor if you take anticoagulant drugs
Antioxidants	1000mg vitamin C, 400 IU vitamin E, 150mg alpha-lipoic acid each morning	Consult your doctor before you take alpha-lipoic acid as it may affect blood sugar
Bilberry	160mg extract twice a day	Standardised to contain 25% anthocyanosides
Taurine	500mg L-taurine twice a day on an empty stomach	If using for over a month add mixed amino acids

One small, controlled, double-blind study of 14 people with retinal damage from diabetes or high blood pressure found that bilberry produced significant improvements in blood vessels in the eye. But little other controlled research has been done to show how well bilberry works. Still, it may be worth trying, with the approval of your doctor or dietitian. Bilberry supplements generally are not known to have ill effects, and the fruit is certainly safe – as are other foods containing anthocyanosides, such as blueberries, blackberries and grapes.

Help for the heart and kidneys

Complications of diabetes are often interrelated, and that is certainly true of heart and kidney disease. For example, kidney disease can raise blood levels of cholesterol and triglycerides, which not only boosts your risk of cardiovascular disease but also further accelerates kidney damage. A number of supplements may be able to break this vicious cycle.

OPCs If you pay attention to scientific names, you might guess that OPC supplements – short for oligomeric proanthocyanidin complexes (also sometimes referred to as PCOs) – share common ground with the flavonoids in bilberry. The two, in fact, are closely related and seem to have similar effects. OPCs, found primarily in grapeseed extract, are powerful antioxidants and appear to strengthen blood-vessel walls, making them less leaky – important for protecting the delicate capillaries that filter wastes in the kidneys.

Little controlled research has been done to show how well OPCs might protect the kidneys. In one study from France (where grapeseed extract was first popularized), people with diabetes or high blood pressure who took 150mg of OPCs daily decreased the leakiness and fragility of blood vessels in the kidneys. These results are preliminary. However, in tests on OPC safety it has come up clean, apart from occasional allergic reactions and mild gastrointestinal problems. There is one caveat: high doses may interfere with blood thinners, such as warfarin (Coumadin) or aspirin.

Garlic The ancient Greeks said that this pungent herb could clear the arteries – and modern research suggests that that may be only the beginning. Dozens of studies since the 1980s have looked at garlic's effects on a variety of cardiovascular risks and,

while not always consistent, results have generally been positive. Fortunately, capsule form used in many studies won't give you garlic breath.

Many of these studies, when taken together, suggest that garlic can lower cholesterol by 9 to 12 per cent, bring down blood pressure by 5 to 10 per cent, prevent blood from clotting around artery obstructions, make blood vessels more pliable, and lower your overall risk of heart attack. The research is not perfect. For example, in one study where garlic was shown to be just as effective as a prescription cholesterol-lowering medication, participants all made changes in their diets that could have affected the results. Yet the balance of evidence suggests that garlic has real benefits for the heart and blood vessels.

Garlic may thin the blood, so check with your doctor before taking garlic supplements if you're also taking aspirin or other blood-thinning drugs or other supplements with blood-thinning effects, such as ginkgo or high doses of vitamin E.

L-carnitine In addition to its possible benefits for the eyes, this amino acid has been shown in controlled studies to reduce death rates in people who have had a heart attack, relieve symptoms of intermittent claudication in the legs and improve heart function in people with angina. In one study, for example, people who took 4g of L-carnitine a day after experiencing a heart attack had a death rate of 1.2 per cent over the course of a year, while those who took a dummy pill had a death rate of 12.5 per cent. The people taking the L-carnitine also had healthier blood pressure, lipid profiles and heart rates. Paradoxically, the best dietary sources of L-carnitine – namely beef, lamb and dairy products – are not necessarily the most heart-healthy foods.

Gamma-linolenic acid (GLA) Although primarily used to treat diabetic neuropathy, GLA (typically from evening primrose oil) may also help the heart. In one five-year study of 102 people newly diagnosed with diabetes, those whose diets were enriched with linolenic acid (a precursor to GLA) developed fewer cardiovascular problems and suffered less heart damage compared to a control group.

The nutritional pharmacy

Certain vitamins and minerals may help to control blood sugar and reduce the risk of complications. These nutrients are best derived from food sources – but should you get more of them from supplements? Here are three you might consider.

(1) **Biotin** An adult body needs between 0.01mg and 0.2mg of this B vitamin a day from foods such as egg yolks, liver, corn and cauliflower for normal metabolism (including the breakdown of carbohydrates, fat and protein from food). But preliminary studies suggest that between 8mg and 16mg a day may lower blood sugar. In one study, Type 2 diabetes

BUYER BEWARE

The current regulatory arrangement for unlicensed herbal remedies does not set quality or safety standards, or require consumer information about the safe use of products. A new European Directive on Traditional Herbal Medicinal Productions should help to ensure that the public have access to properly researched, adequately labelled herbal goods and reduce instances of problems such as products with contaminants and cheap substitute ingredients.

In the meantime, bear in mind the following advice from the Medical and Healthcare productions regulatory agency when buying herbal products.

■ Remember that herbal remedies are medicines which are likely to have an effect on the body and should be used with care.

■ If you think you may have had an adverse reaction to a herbal remedy you should tell your doctor.

■ Some herbal remedies may interact with other medicines making them more or less effective. You should always tell your doctor or pharmacist if you are taking herbal remedies with prescription drugs.

■ Treat with caution any suggestion that a herbal remedy is '100 per cent safe' or is safe because it is 'natural'. Many 'natural' ingredients can be poisonous to humans or at least have a harmful effect on certain individuals. Take all medicines with care.

■ Any herbalist or supplier of herbal remedies should be willing and able to provide written information, in English, listing the ingredients of the product they are supplying.

■ If you are due to have a surgical procedure, tell the doctor about any herbal remedy you are taking.

■ Anyone with a previous or existing liver problem or other serious health complaint should always consult their doctor before taking a herbal remedy.

patients who took 9mg of biotin daily for one month lowered their fasting blood-glucose levels by an average of 45 per cent. Biotin seems to work by boosting insulin sensitivity and helping the body to use glucose. It may also help to protect against nerve damage. According to the Food Standards Agency, taking 0.9mg or less of biotin supplements a day is unlikely to cause any harm. The maximum dose in supplements sold in the UK is 2mg. Anecdotal reports suggest that typical daily doses of 10mg have no adverse effect.

(2) **Chromium** The adult daily requirement for the trace mineral chromium is 0.025mg. Chromium is thought to influence the way insulin behaves in the body, so it may affect the energy we get from food. Some studies find that taking supplements in amounts upwards of 500 micro-grammes brings down blood sugar, although other studies find no benefit. Should you take it? The Food Standards Agency says that a daily intake of up to 10mg of chromium from food and supplements is unlikely to cause any harm. There is insufficient evidence of what the effect might be of an intake of more than 10mg each day.

(3) **Magnesium** This mineral lends a hand to many chemical processes in the body, and it may help cells to use insulin. Deficiencies (common in people with diabetes) may promote eye damage. The daily requirement is 300mg for men and 270mg for women. The Food Standards Agency advises that up to 400mg a day of magnesium from supplements is unlikely to cause any harm.

Exploring other therapies

Taking a supplement feels like taking a conventional drug because they both come in pill and capsule form. But other types of alternative therapies may seem less familiar. For instance, there are mind-body approaches, techniques linked with Eastern ideas about energy flow, and other unconventional or scientifically unproven ideas.

Do these therapies work? Each should be judged on its own merit, but it seems clear from research that there is more to achieving healing and health than causing chemical changes with drugs or fixing the body with surgery. Even conventional medicine – by controlling for a placebo effect, in which thinking you'll get better can seem to make it happen – tacitly acknowledges that the mind and body are closely entwined. Theories that stress and other mental states can affect the immune system, once large- ly dismissed, are now widely accepted as studies continue to reveal connections between the nervous and the immune systems.

That does not mean that every therapy without a plausible explanation is valid and waiting for science to catch up. But some therapies do seem to offer promise. Although they may require an investment in time or money, they probably pose few risks. Here are three which may be worth trying.

Biofeedback: the mind-body loop

Doctors long assumed that automatic functions such as breath- ing, heartbeat and body-temperature regulation were beyond our control. In fact, that's one reason the nervous system was classified as having two distinct parts – the voluntary one, in which conscious thoughts, say, make your fingers wiggle, and the autonomic one, in which the body, on its own, for instance, makes your heart pump faster when you are in danger or stressed. The two systems were thought to be completely independent of each other Biofeedback, however, has shown that these systems, like the superpowers during the Cold War, have hidden communication links that allow the two to influence each other. With biofeedback, you are hooked up to a computerized machine that monitors body functions, such as sweating or brain activity. With training, you can learn to recognize your body's responses to stress and other states and exert conscious control over them.

Biofeedback became available in the UK in the mid-1990s. It is still not common and is fairly expensive. Although little research has been carried out in the UK, research at the National Institutes of Health has found biofeedback to be helpful for more than 100 different conditions, and numerous studies suggest that it may help in fighting diabetes and its complications. For exam- ple, one study published in the USA in *Diabetes Care* found that people using biofeedback were able to boost skin temperature in their toes by increasing blood flow by 22 per cent. Other studies in people with diabetes have shown that biofeedback can help to reduce stress and lower blood pressure, and (perhaps as a result) may help to stabilize blood sugar.

To take advantage of biofeedback, you will need to learn control techniques from a trained practitioner, but once you have mastered them, you can practise biofeedback at home.

Acupuncture: therapy with a point

According to traditional Chinese medicine, the real reason you develop diseases such as diabetes is that you suffer imbalances in the flow of life energy, or chi, through your body. Chi is thought to run through an invisible system of meridians, or energy pathways, that can be influenced by the insertion of extremely thin needles at specific sites known as acupoints.

In the West, such needle treatments, called acupuncture, have been dismissed as quackery, at least in part because the meridian system does not correspond to any known part of the anatomy. But acupuncture has gained a certain credence in Western medicine – it's not unusual to find practitioners who have medical degrees – because studies suggest that it may actually ease certain conditions, particularly nausea and pain. (The treatment itself can feel irritating but generally doesn't hurt.)

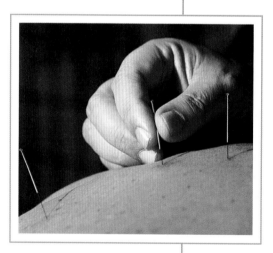

Much of the research into acupuncture's effects on diabetes comes from China, where the therapy is more widely accepted – which some doctors view as cause for scepticism. Still, in one review of several Chinese studies published by a researcher at a university in Beijing, acupuncture appeared to reduce blood-sugar levels by about half, on average. It was also seen to improve symptoms of complications such as neuropathy and heart disease. A study at Manchester Royal Infirmary found that 77 per cent of Type 2 patients with chronic pain from neuropathy showed significant improvement in their primary and secondary symptoms through acupuncture. In the follow-up period, 67 per cent were able to stop or significantly reduce their medications.

If you are considering trying acupuncture, expect to need up to 25 treatments over two to three months to see an effect. Find a suitably qualified and experienced practitioner through the British Acupuncture Council which has information about suitably trained practitioners on its website www.acupuncture.org.uk or call 020 8735 0400.

Magnets: an attractive option?

The idea that magnets can influence health is not new. It was popular in the early 20th century, but magnet therapies were discredited because of a lack of evidence that they worked. Recently, though, the idea has again been gathering adherents. Treatments range from holding magnets next to afflicted areas of the body to lying on magnetic mattresses.

In the case of diabetes, magnets are not thought to stabilize blood sugar, but there is some evidence that they may be useful in relieving pain from neuropathy, especially in extremities such as the feet. In one US study in which 19 people with neuro pathy (10 of whom had diabetic neuropathy) wore magnetic insoles in their shoes for four months, 90 per cent of those with diabetes reported dramatic reduction in foot pain.

Theories that magnets might help to promote health are not as wacky as they might seem. Tiny amounts of magnetic energy are involved in a vast range of biochemical processes in the body, from cell division and energy exchange right down to the subtle forces that hold the body's atoms together. It's thought that magnets may have therapeutic effects by drawing blood (which contains iron-rich haemoglobin) into areas that need more oxygen and nutrients, affecting the flow of ions that help blood-vessel walls relax, or stimulating the nervous system.

IS THE FORCE WITH YOU?

According to traditional Chinese medicine, good health depends on a balance of yin and yang – the positive and negative aspects of the universal life force known as chi, which flows through 14 meridians in the body. Is there anything to it?

Some research suggests that the traditional acupoints along the meridians differ slightly from the surrounding skin in electrical and magnetic properties while also containing dense concentrations of blood vessels and nerves. Laboratory tests on animals suggest that acupuncture releases endorphins and other chemical messengers that may help relieve pain.

Living well with diabetes

Diabetes is not simply a physical disorder; like any chronic condition, it also poses an ongoing emotional challenge. At various points, you're likely to experience anger, frustration and possibly even depression. You may also feel burned out from dealing with the condition day in, day out. Learning how to cope is essential. You'll also need to know how to handle diabetes when you're ill or when you're travelling. Just remember that diabetes doesn't need to get you down – or slow you down.

NINE

9

Focus on quality of life

Diabetes is a chronic condition – something you have to live with for the rest of your life. It even requires daily attention, which can seem burdensome. But always remember that, while you shouldn't deny the challenges of diabetes, there's no reason why every aspect of an enjoyable life can't be as rewarding for you as it is for anybody else.

Quality of life is an important element in diabetes care. In fact, you could argue that it's the point of everything you do to manage your condition – from eating healthily and walking regularly to checking your feet at night and taking daily doses of aspirin. The better you take care of yourself, the less likely you are to experience the complications that account for most of the suffering that goes with diabetes. When it comes to blood sugar, better control equals a better life.

This isn't mere cheerleading. In an attempt to shed light on how to live well with diabetes, researchers have studied quality-of-life issues in people with the disease. One study, published in the Journal of the American Medical Association, compared quality of life in people with diabetes who had good blood-sugar control with peers who did not. Those with good control had milder symptoms, felt better, and were more likely to feel mentally sharp than the other group. As a result, they tended to be more productive and less restricted in every aspect of life.

But living well with diabetes goes beyond blood sugar control. It also means managing your emotions (a significant part of dealing with diabetes) and contending with a raft of practical issues from day to day.

The feelings factor

'How are you feeling?' There are two ways to interpret that question. One is how you're feeling physically, which people tend to think of first. The other – equally important – is how you're feeling emotionally. Indeed, a growing body of research shows that mental and physical health are intertwined. If you're out of sorts emotionally, your physical health may follow. Studies find, for example, that people who suffer such negative emotions as anger, depression and anxiety tend to have higher rates of heart disease and weaker immune-system response than people with a more positive outlook – important considerations for people with diabetes. That doesn't mean you should worry about ruining your health if you're already feeling bad. But paying attention to your emotional well-being can help you to improve it.

Why diabetes can be a downer

Anybody with diabetes will probably agree that having a chronic disease makes your life more difficult than that of someone who is disease-free (or, at least, difficult in different ways). Yet it's interesting to note that, according to one recent study of people with chronic conditions (including diabetes, liver infection and gastrointestinal disease), those with diabetes tended to do better on the quality-of-life front. This study found that the daily chores of dealing with diabetes – including testing and taking drugs or insulin – doesn't bother people as much as might be expected. The real battle, it turns out, is with emotional, psychological and social issues. It is easy to see why this potentially life-threatening disease can take a toll.

It never goes away Diabetes is for life. Although it is possible to delay or ward off the most debilitating consequences, the knowledge that you're engaged in a never-ending battle can make you feel weary and defeated.

It's often hidden Diabetes is considered a silent, invisible disease in two respects. First, even while it is progressing you may not feel any symptoms, which can foster a deceptive sense that you don't really have a disease. As a result, you may find it tempting to stray from your diet, exercise or treatment plans. (Or you may have the unnerving sense that no matter what you do, diabetes is secretly eating away at your health.) The other hidden aspect of diabetes is that it is not obvious to others. On the surface, everything about you may seem 'normal', while underneath you realize that you're different from those around you in a fundamental way. This can make you feel socially awkward, especially in settings where food is being served.

It's inconsistent It would be easier if diabetes followed a predictable course that was the same for everyone, but it doesn't. For one thing, your diabetes is different from the next

?

DID YOU KNOW

A connection between diabetes and emotions was noticed at least as far back as the 17th century, when British physician Thomas Willis theorized that an emotional state he called 'profound sorrow' caused diabetes. For more than two centuries the idea persisted that diabetes might have psychological origins. Today's view is that while negative emotions may make diabetes more difficult to cope with or accelerate the disease process, they are more likely to be a consequence of the illness than a cause.

person's (based on your diabetes type, blood-sugar levels, pancreatic function, insulin resistance and other factors). But your own case of diabetes may also be subject to seemingly erratic changes. For example, blood sugar can move up and down in response to a wide variety of influences, from illness to physical activity (not to mention drug and insulin treatments), and it can be difficult to predict when glucose might plummet and cause a hypoglycaemic episode.

Coping with your emotions

Life is often an emotional roller coaster without the added burden of diabetes, so you don't always need to hold your disease responsible for your ups and downs. In fact, doing so may make you feel more helpless and out of control (and prevent you from solving problems not related to diabetes). But it is useful to recognize when diabetes does fan the flames of feeling – and address the emotions head-on.

The first step is to recognize that mood swings are a natural phenomenon with diabetes – even apart from the emotional challenges of managing the disease. Variations in your blood-sugar levels can affect mood directly. Low glucose levels can make you nervous, irritable and anxious, while high blood sugar can make you feel fatigued and down in the dumps. So the steps you take to control your blood sugar can have an emotional payoff as well. But you can also expect to contend with negative feelings that have nothing to do with blood sugar but everything to do with having diabetes.

Managing depression

Everybody feels low at least some of the time, and common sense suggests that having a chronic disease is ample reason to be depressed. In fact, people with diabetes may be as much as four times more likely than the rest of the population to suffer from the blues, and they may also suffer from depression for longer. All of which suggests that depression is normal if you have diabetes. But you don't have to – and shouldn't – accept low moods as inevitable or beyond your control.

● **Be alert to symptoms** Look at the criteria for clinical depression (see 'Diagnosing Depression', opposite) and see a doctor if you qualify. Your problem may have a physiological cause that can be remedied by, say, adjusting your diabetes medication or taking you off drugs that can have depressant side effects (including some blood-pressure medications and anti-histamines). Otherwise, your doctor can prescribe antidepressant medications that fine-tune levels of certain chemicals in the brain. SSRIs (selective serotonin reuptake inhibitors) are likely candidates as they are effective and generally have fewer side effects than other antidepressants, although in some people they can cause such side effects as nervousness, insomnia, lack of appetite and dulled sexual response. Drugs in this class include fluoxetine (Prozac), paroxetine (Seroxat) and sertraline (Lustral).

➲ **Talk it out** Sharing your feelings is one of the most effective ways of taking an emotional burden off your shoulders – which is why counselling is a mainstay of treatment for depression. Start by asking a friend or loved one if you can talk about what you're going through. Assure the person that he or she doesn't have to try to solve your problems but that an open ear might do you some good.

➲ **Socialize more** Simply being with other people in a social setting or a group such as a community club, volunteer organization, or religious congregation can take your mind off your troubles, brighten your mood and make you feel less alone.

➲ **Stick with the programme** Don't let your low mood derail your self-care programme, especially when it comes to regular exercise. In fact, physical activity has been shown to lift mild or moderate depression.

!

CAUTION

Depression doesn't only affect you emotionally. People who feel chronically blue also tend to have higher blood pressure and are more prone to heart disease than other people predisposed to it. Just as important, feeling low can make you less motivated to take good care of yourself, which puts your blood-sugar control – and your overall health – at risk.

DIAGNOSING DEPRESSION

Doctors distinguish between run-of-the-mill lows that come and go in response to events in your life and the clinging cloudiness of clinical depression, which can persist for weeks on end without letting up. If you are clinically depressed, medications may help. You may be clinically depressed if five or more of the following are true for at least two consecutive weeks.

- You feel sad, empty, anxious or irritable virtually all the time.

- You take little pleasure or interest in most, if not all, of your daily activities.

- You lack energy.

- Your normal appetite changes or you have lost or gained a significant amount of weight.

- You feel agitated or sluggish in your responses.

- You feel worthless or guilty.

- You have trouble sleeping – or you sleep more than usual.

- You have difficulty concentrating or making simple decisions.

- You often find yourself thinking about dying or suicide.

⊃ **Don't drink** Because it is a depressant, alcohol won't drown your sorrows, it will only aggravate them. Drinking in excess, of course, will also add empty calories to your diet and possibly erode your self-discipline.

Attacking anger

Most people go through a predictable cycle of emotions after they're first diagnosed with diabetes, typically starting with a this-can't-be-true sense of denial that eventually gives way to anger when you realize that you're in it for the long haul. You may feel that your body (or nature or God) has betrayed you, that your life has been turned upside down in ways you can't control, or that you don't deserve something like this and it just isn't fair.

These are normal responses that may make you irritable for weeks and even months at the outset. As you gradually accept your diabetes and settle into a self-care routine, your anger may subside.

But it's also possible that anger will persist, especially if you find yourself frustrated by your disease. For example, your best efforts at glucose control may not be producing the results you want. You may resent the intrusion diabetes has made on your daily routine or feel irritated by having to change your eating or activity patterns.

Frustration is a part of dealing with diabetes, but unchecked anger isn't good for your relationships, your mental health or your body. As with depression, anger is linked with higher rates of heart disease. It can seem a difficult emotion to control, but if you're alert to it and prepared to contend with flare-ups, you can get the upper hand. Here's how.

⊃ **Take responsibility** Making progress towards peace means working towards an attitude of acceptance – of the diabetes itself and of the emotional toll it takes. Diabetes can be frustrating, and it can make you angry. Those are realities, and it's okay to recognize them as such. This allows you to take a step back and see a bigger picture in which your emotions aren't overwhelming and out of control but rather predictable responses for which you can begin to take responsibility. Part of this responsibility involves understanding where your anger is coming from, and not unfairly blaming other people or circumstances. If you stay calmer, those around you will as well, and you'll likely find less fuel to fire your outbursts.

⟳ **Look for patterns** Try to predict when you're most likely to experience feelings of annoyance, frustration or rage. Is it waiting in long checkout queues with slow cashiers? Does a particular person tend to get under your skin? Do certain topics of conversation make you angry? If you are not aware of what triggers your anger, try writing down what's happening every time you become enraged to see if patterns start to emerge. Knowing your triggers can give you a greater sense of control. And, of course, it can help you to avoid them.

⟳ **Ignore the bait** One exercise some experts suggest is to think of yourself as a fish being baited by a hook. On the hook is a trigger for your anger. Do you take the bait or recognize it for what it is and pass it by? Consciously choosing not to bite allows you to take control of your anger by refusing to let another person or situation determine your feelings.

⟳ **Change your mental channel** Sometimes, even when you approach anger rationally, you still feel peeved. In such instances, try shifting your thoughts. If you're fuming while stuck in traffic, turn on the radio or listen to an audio book. Mentally replay last night's football game or crime drama. Repeat a quietening phrase such as 'Calm down' or a favourite prayer.

Seeking an anxiety antidote

If you're feeling depressed, you are likely to be experiencing anxiety as well – the two emotions often occur in tandem. But even if you're not battling the blues, having diabetes can give you plenty of cause for worry. For starters, there's the fear that progressing complications may impair your quality of life in the future. Even if you're doing a good job of monitoring and managing your diabetes, the unseen and unfelt nature of the disease can foster a nagging sense of dread.

Worrying about your diabetes is normal and, to some extent, even healthy because it helps to motivate you to follow your treatment plan. But anxiety can sometimes acquire a life of its

STOP ANGER IN ITS TRACKS

According to behavioural-medicine experts at Duke University in the USA, you can soothe your anger by asking yourself four questions about what is provoking you:

■ Is this important?

■ Is my reaction appropriate?

■ Can I change the situation?

■ If I can, is it worth taking action?

If you answer 'no' to any of these questions, the only rational choice is to cool down. While anger is not always rational, forcing yourself into an objective frame of mind can often be calming in itself.

own and can become counterproductive and unhealthy. If your fears are more intense than they need to be, crop up frequently, or persist even when circumstances no longer justify them, they can distract you from the better things in life, undermine your ability to manage your disease and paralyse more positive thinking. To release yourself from the grip of fear:

⮑ **See your doctor** Remember that nervousness and such symptoms as rapid heartbeat are signs of hypoglycaemia as well as anxiety, so your first step is to have your doctor evaluate your recent blood-sugar history. In some cases, a bout of anxiety might simply require an adjustment in your insulin or medication. If that is not the problem, your GP can refer you to a mental-health professional who may treat your anxiety with drugs or refer you for counselling.

⮑ **Talk back to yourself** Anxiety can blind you to positive emotions and cause you to focus only on negatives and potential catastrophes. You might fear that a slight slip from your blood-sugar goals is the first step down the road to vision loss or that if you take time to exercise, you'll never get all your work done and you'll be fired. Pay attention to what therapists call automatic thoughts, which set the tone for your mental state. If they tend to be negative ('This will never work' or 'I can't handle it'), try to be as objective as possible and ask yourself if evidence supports your thinking or whether you might be wrong. Refer back to challenges you have successfully met for proof that things can also work out for the better.

⮑ **Keep a notepad by your bed** Worries have a way of intruding on your thoughts in the middle of the night. If anxiety keeps you awake, keep a pad and pen by your bed so you can jot down what's bothering you. Write down the specific steps you can take to resolve your concerns; this provides a reassuring sense that you have tackled the problem. Getting better quality sleep will make you more refreshed and energetic in the morning, and this can help you to keep your anxieties in perspective.

Putting stress in its place

Too much stress is not good for anyone, but it may be especially bad for people with diabetes. It can prevent you from effectively managing your condition by thwarting your intentions to follow a healthy diet, keep up with your exercise programme, and remember to do regular finger-prick checks. Worse still, there is considerable evidence that stress makes blood sugar rise.

One reason for this is that when you're tense or under pressure hormones – particularly cortisol and epinephrine – pump glucose into blood from storage sites in the liver so the body has more energy available to meet a challenge. So-called stress hormones can have other harmful effects as well. One recent study found that stress inhibits the ability of blood vessels to expand, which might make it a factor in heart attacks.

The best way to deal with stress is to avoid whatever is making you tense. But since that's not always possible, you can benefit from taking other steps.

⮕ **Invest in relationships** Numerous studies find that surrounding yourself with family and friends buffers the strain of stress better than almost anything else. So-called social support leaves you feeling less isolated while bolstering your sense of control, which alone can make life seem less daunting. But treat those whose support you must rely on with the consideration you expect from them. When speaking with loved ones (especially a spouse), avoid put-downs and negative language; studies have found that sniping can produce a marked increase in stress hormones.

⮕ **Follow your faith** For many people, religious belief can help to put the trials and tribulations of life in a reassuringly larger perspective. Or – if faith doesn't come easily to you – it may provide an opportunity to receive social support through communal worship, along with a comforting sanctuary from life's storms.

DOES STRESS CAUSE DIABETES?

FACT Stress triggers the release of hormones such as cortisol.

FACT Stress hormones raise blood sugar levels.

FACT Stress may encourage fat to accumulate in the belly.

FACT High blood sugar and belly fat contribute to insulin resistance and, eventually, to diabetes.

Conclusion: stress causes diabetes.

Is it true? It's a controversial notion, and the answer is not yet clear. In a recent Dutch study published in *Diabetes Care*, researchers who surveyed more than 2,200 people with no history of diabetes found that those who reported the most major life stresses were more likely to have undiagnosed diabetes. Yet stress from some significant sources (notably work) did not seem to affect diabetes rates, calling the stress effect into question.

⮑ **Express yourself** People who write down their thoughts and feelings in a journal tend to feel less stress and may even be better able to resist illness. Just be sure to write down honestly what's bothering you. In one recent study, those who let loose on the page and were able to express and evaluate their concerns and anxieties had measurable improvements in immune function. In contrast, those who repressed their thoughts and feelings saw declines.

TEN TIPS FOR STRESS RELIEF

Stress often results from feeling overwhelmed by day-to-day responsibilities and problems. A simple solution is to list everything you need to do in order of genuine importance, noting what you can delegate, defer or strike off. You will end up with a realistic and manageable set of tasks. The Stress Management Society also recommends the following for stress relief.

1 STEER CLEAR OF STIMULANTS

Avoid turning to nicotine, alcohol or caffeine as a means of alleviating stress: they are stimulants, and have the opposite of the desired effect.

2 TAKE REGULAR PHYSICAL EXERCISE

Physical exercise is one of the best antidotes to stress. It reduces levels of adrenaline produced by pressure or anger and triggers the release of endorphins – chemicals in the brain that make you feel happier, calmer and more clear-headed. This leads to a sense of well-being and relaxation and encourages good sleep.

3 DO A DAILY RELAXATION EXERCISE

Set aside a period each day for some form of stress-reduction technique, such as meditation, deep breathing or Tai chi. This will free your mind from the whirring associated with stress.

4 SLEEP WELL

Be sure to get enough sleep and rest to recharge your batteries (the number of hours varies between individuals). You won't need sleeping pills if you adopt a healthy lifestyle.

5 BE KIND TO YOURSELF

If you become ill, take the time that you need to recover. Don't force yourself to carry on regardless

6 AVOID INTERPERSONAL CONFLICTS

Agree with somebody whenever possible. Life should not be a constant battleground.

7 KNOW WHAT TO ACCEPT

Learn to accept what you cannot change. To do otherwise will only lead to unhappiness, cynicism and bitterness.

8 MANAGE YOUR TIME BETTER

Prioritize and delegate, take one thing at a time and beware of 'overdoing it'. Create time buffers to deal with unexpected demands or emergencies.

9 RECOGNIZE WHEN YOU ARE TIRED

Learn to acknowledge when you are tired and stop and take the time to recover.

10 LEARN HOW TO SAY 'NO'

Use this simple, highly effective skill to prevent too much pressure building up in the future.

Battling 'diabetes burnout'

Although dealing with diabetes round the clock week in week out can seem overwhelming at first, many people willingly adjust to a new lifestyle of dedicated self-care. Yet over time, a creeping sense of fatigue and frustration can set in – some experts call it 'diabetes burnout'. You may feel sick and tired of the never-ending diabetes grind. As a result, your all-important motivation may start to wane.

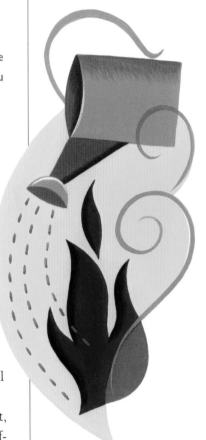

Although burnout won't directly cause physical changes in the body, feeling frustrated – often because you may sense that you're not making progress against your disease – can have a negative impact on your health. You may start to be less rigorous about your diet, exercise, drug regimen or self-monitoring programmes.

If diabetes care is wearing you down the first step is to talk to your doctor or counsellor. Your GP may be able to make adjustments in your treatment – fewer shots using different combinations of insulin, for example – to ease your burden. A counsellor may be able to suggest new ways of thinking that can boost your sense of purpose. But then you'll need to take steps on your own to fortify your resolve.

Check your goals At some point earlier in your treatment, you and your medical team established objectives for your self-care – blood-sugar targets, a healthy diet, and exercise goals. These were based on what you thought was possible then, but it may be time to review your list of objectives. Pretend you're starting again. Knowing now what you didn't know then, do you feel that your goals are reasonable? Being successful in meeting your objectives is a key to staying motivated.

Evaluate your progress Maybe you haven't made as much progress as you would like. But be objective about what you have accomplished. How has your blood-sugar control improved? How about your weight or your overall fitness? Have you managed to be disciplined about testing and taking medication? You may find that you've done better than you give yourself credit for. On the other hand, your frustration may be a good sign: it means you are motivated to do better.

Identify problem areas If you're like most people, you have probably been more effective with some elements of your self-care than with others. But don't allow your weakness or lack of progress in one area to colour the entire picture. Instead, try to isolate the aspects of your care with which you have the most trouble. Is it a challenge to control your appetite? Are you forgetting to take your medication or insulin? Is finding time for exercise a constant battle?

⤷ **Seek solutions** Once you have identified problem areas, you can start to focus on solutions. Why do you feel that a particular challenge is such a struggle? What could change to make it more manageable? For example, if following your diet is the issue, ask your dietitian to suggest changes in your diet that will

make it more appropriate for you and your personal preferences – it's not compulsory to eat foods you hate just because they are 'good for you'. Your dietitian may be able to suggest ways of making your pet hates more palatable or give you alternative foods with similar nutritional benefits. If you hate your workouts, try to find forms of exercise that combine fitness and fun – such as a dance class – which give you an enjoyable social focus as well. Or perhaps you need a goal to aim at – a walk or run for charity might motivate you to get out there more regularly.

⤷ **Enlist support** Remember, you're not in this battle alone. Talk to other people with diabetes for perspective, ideas and encouragement. Think about joining a diabetes support group (Diabetes UK has some 430 local voluntary groups across the country), or try to find an internet chat group that you're comfortable with. Enlist friends to join you for exercise sessions – it's much more fun to go to the gym, for a walk or on a bike ride when you have someone else to talk to – they'll probably be delighted to have someone else encouraging them to get fit. Keep friends posted on your progress as well. Knowing that someone else is following your case can help to spur you on.

⤷ **Keep your eyes on the prize** Try to stay focused on the quality of life you gain by controlling your diabetes rather than on the negatives – namely, the complications – that you avoid. It's a subtle distinction, but cringing in fear of consequences is generally a less effective motivator than striving for more joy, freedom and flexibility in your life.

How to think about diabetes

When you have diabetes, your attitudes are tugged in two seemingly opposite directions. You need to make good blood-sugar control a top priority, to the extent that your time and daily activities are organized around your self-care routine. On the other hand, you want to live as normal a life as possible. Should diabetes always be in the forefront of your mind, or should you try not to dwell on it?

These questions represent a spectrum with two unhealthy extremes at each end. One is denial (especially common in the early days of a diagnosis), in which you fail to realize or accept all the changes necessary to take charge of diabetes and ensure a high quality of life over the long term. The other is obsession, in which you desperately strive for perfection in every aspect of your treatment to the extent that you think about little else.

You need to incorporate a little of both extremes into your attitude towards diabetes. A degree of denial allows you to set aside gloomy thoughts of complications so that you can concentrate on enjoying your life today. And a certain amount of obsession encourages you to be diligent about your care. But taken too far, both outlooks can threaten your health – denial because it leads to poor glucose control; and obsession because your inevitable failure to achieve perfect control leads to disappointment and discouragement. Finding the right balance depends in part on the way you approach life as a whole.

↻ **Seek serenity** The adage that we should have the courage to change the things we can change, the serenity to accept the things we can't change and the wisdom to know the difference applies particularly well to diabetes. It's important to take responsibility for your disease and do everything in your power to manage it, but also to let go of the idea that you'll ever gain total control over diabetes – or any other aspect of your life.

↻ **Embrace ambiguity** If you wrestle with whether you should consider yourself ill as opposed to well, or in control versus at the mercy of your disease, step back and ask if you need to see everything as black or white. The path of wisdom may be simply to accept the situation's inherent ambiguities.

↻ **Know yourself** The real issue in how you think about diabetes may be how you think about yourself. Do you see yourself as a person with a disease or someone who is loving, creative, resourceful and appreciated by family, friends and community? The less you define yourself by your condition, the easier it will be to see the measures you take to control your diabetes as stepping stones to fulfilling your truly important roles in life.

Sex and diabetes

When you think about enjoying life and all its pleasures, great sex may be one of the first things to pop into your mind. The good news is that there is no reason why you can't have a full and satisfying sex life if you have diabetes. But you need to understand how your disease can affect different aspects of your sexuality and sexual function.

First, bear in mind that sexual intimacy can be physically vigorous, burning calories. That means that, like exercise, it may put you at risk of hypoglycaemia – inconvenient when making love, to say the least. To keep blood sugar stable, it is wise to take glucose readings before and after sex to gain an idea of how your body responds. Try having a sugary drink or a small snack beforehand or, with your doctor's approval, adjusting your insulin if you know that sexual intimacy is likely to be in the offing.

For women only

Sexuality is complex in women even without inter ference from a chronic disease, so it's no surprise that women generally experience more sexual side effects related to diabetes than men do. But the problems can be overcome. These are some of them.

Blood-sugar fluxes Many women notice that their blood sugar rises a few days before their monthly period begins. Researchers suspect (although not all agree) that fluxes in female sex hormones, such as oestrogen and progesterone, temporarily make cells more resistant to insulin. If you suspect that this is a problem for you:

▶ For several months, keep a log of when your period begins, then compare it to your daily blood-sugar records. If you find a distinct correlation between your glucose levels and your menstrual cycle, talk to your doctor about adjusting your insulin or medication dosage.

▶ Consider an alternative cause. Some doctors think that the reason blood sugar rises before your period is that the cravings and irritability of premenstrual syndrome make you eat more – or more erratically – thereby causing unusual peaks and troughs in blood-sugar levels. Try eating at regular intervals to keep blood sugar stable, and avoid alcohol and caffeine, which can affect mood.

▶ If you take oral contraceptives, ask your doctor which pill is the best for you. Monophasic oral contraceptives, containing fixed amounts of oestrogen and progestin, appear to keep blood-sugar levels more stable than triphasic and progesterone-only contraceptives.

Vaginal dryness Women with diabetes sometimes find that they lack natural lubrication during sexual arousal, although this problem is not limited to people with high blood sugar. To deal with it, try using water-based lubricants, available at any pharmacy. If the problem persists, check with your GP; you may have low oestrogen levels that can be boosted with topical oestrogen cream or hormone replacement therapy (HRT). Weigh the HRT option carefully, however. Although it may solve the lubrication problem, it may also raise the risk of other health problems.

Infections Excess sugar in the blood encourages the growth of fungal organisms and bacteria, making women with diabetes more prone to yeast infections and vaginitis. If you experience vaginal discharge or itching, see your doctor for an antifungal cream or antibiotics.

For men only

Sex can sometimes seem more straightforward for men, but the male sexual response is also a complex melding of mind and body involving numerous systems that can be affected by diabetes.

IF YOU'RE PREGNANT AND HAVE DIABETES

Having a baby when you have diabetes poses risks for you and for your child, but many women with diabetes get through pregnancy with no problems.

Before conceiving, you should have a thorough evaluation for complications of diabetes, such as retinopathy, kidney damage, nerve damage and high blood pressure – all of which can be made worse by pregnancy. To guard against complications and protect the health of the baby, be prepared to control your blood sugar even more tightly than before. Between 4 and 10 per cent of women with diabetes have babies with congenital abnormality, but studies show that this can be reduced to about 1 per cent if blood sugar control is very good during the first eight weeks of pregnancy.

Tight blood sugar control also prevents the baby from growing too large and causing delivery problems. If you have Type 1 diabetes, you will probably need more insulin injections and may want to switch to a pump. If you have Type 2, drugs are not advised, so you'll need to start or modify an insulin programme. Discuss with your dietitian a nutritious diet for you and your baby, and be sure to stay physically active throughout your pregnancy, both to control blood sugar and to condition your body for labour.

The major difficulty men may face is erectile dysfunction (also called impotence), the inability to achieve or maintain an erection – a problem that often occurs with age and is not limited to men with diabetes. In many cases, the cause is purely physical. When you have diabetes, poor circulation can prevent blood from properly engorging chambers in the penis, and nerve damage can interfere with signals involved with sexual response. (Fortunately, the nerves that enable orgasm are seldom impaired.) But depression and anxiety can also cause erectile dysfunction, and sexual difficulties may involve a combination of factors. Here are some steps you can take.

➲ **Check possible causes** Talk to your doctor about possible causes so you know how to treat the problem. It may be a simple matter of adjusting one of your medications. Many drugs, including some for high blood pressure, can interfere with sexual function. If that's not the issue, look for patterns. If erectile dysfunction happens on and off, strikes suddenly, or occurs in some circumstances but not others, the problem may have a psychological component. If you gradually and consistently lose function over time, there is more likely to be a physical cause.

➲ **Ask about Viagra** The drug sildenafil citrate (Viagra) induces erections lasting at least an hour in about 80 per cent of patients who take it. If side effects such as headache, low blood pressure and diarrhoea bother you, other medications are available, although they tend to be less effective. If you have heart trouble, you may not be able to take Viagra.

➲ **Go to extremes** If oral drugs don't work, try alprostadil (Caverject). Like Viagra, it relaxes smooth-muscle tissue in the penis to boost blood flow, but it is injected with a needle. Other injectable drugs (papaverine, phentolamine) are also available. Non-drug approaches include vacuum devices (which use a hand-pumped tube that fits over the penis to draw blood into the organ) and surgically implanted rods that can be bent or inflated by a man (or his partner) when he wants an erection.

Planning for when you're ill

Being ill is no fun for anyone, but it takes a special toll if you have diabetes because it can throw your blood sugar levels out severely and put you at risk for significant short-term complications. The best way to deal with illness is to make sure you are fully prepared for it before you're laid up. Discuss with your diabetes healthcare team a strategy that you can quickly put into action the next time a cold, the flu or some other illness strikes.

Illness is a form of stress that – like emotional stress – rouses the body's defences. One effect is that the liver steps up glucose production to provide more energy. At the same time, stress hormones are released that make cells more insulin resistant. The net result is that your blood sugar can rise dramatically when you are ill. The following serious problems may result.

▶ **Ketoacidosis** If there is not enough available insulin to move glucose into cells (mostly a problem with Type 1 diabetes), the body will start tapping its fat stores, releasing toxic ketones and putting you at risk of a coma.

▶ **Hyperosmolar nonketotic coma** When blood sugar levels in Type 2 patients become too high, the body tries to get rid of glucose through the urine, which can produce severe dehydration that can also lead to a coma.

To keep your blood sugar in check when you're ill and help yourself to feel better faster, follow these steps.

⟳ **Step up your monitoring** It's more important than ever to keep track of your blood-sugar levels, so you'll probably need to test yourself more often than usual – at least every 3 to 4 hours. If your blood sugar exceeds 15mmol/l, do a urine ketone test as well (ketone testing strips are available on prescription from your GP). If ketone results are positive – or if your blood sugar consistently hovers above 15mmol/l – call your doctor.

⟳ **Nourish yourself** Illness can ruin your appetite (especially if you have trouble keeping food down), but you need to eat enough to provide your body with the energy it needs. Ask your dietitian for advice on what you should eat when you're ill. Foods such as oatmeal, toast and soup offer good nutrition and are easy on the stomach. If you find meals unappetizing, try to eat small amounts frequently throughout the day.

⟳ **Drink plenty of fluids** This familiar advice is especially relevant when you have diabetes because water is drawn into excess glucose and excreted in the urine, which can cause dehydration. Aim to drink a cup of fluid (which includes soup broth) every half hour or so. If lack of appetite prevents you from eating enough food to meet your energy needs, sip sugared drinks like non-diet soda, fruit juices or sports beverages instead of water to ensure that your body gets at least some calories.

⮑ **Stay the drug course** Unless your doctor instructs you otherwise, it's important to keep taking your medications or giving yourself insulin even if you're not up to eating. In fact, your doctor may want you to take more insulin when you're feeling under the weather: the amounts will depend on your blood-sugar readings and how ill you are. Even if you have Type 2 diabetes and don't normally take insulin, it's wise to keep a vial of short-acting insulin on hand in case your doctor feels it's necessary when illness strikes.

⮑ **Beware of over-the-counter remedies** Some common over-the-counter medicines, such as decongestants with pseudo ephedrine, can raise blood sugar. Check with your doctor before taking any drug, herbal remedy or dietary supplement when you're ill.

⮑ **Be alert to danger** Know the signs of ketoacidosis (which include stomach pain, vomiting, chest pain, difficulty breathing, feelings of weakness, sleepiness, fruity-smelling breath, blurry vision) and of dehydration (extreme thirst, dry mouth, cracked lips, sunken eyes, mental confusion, dry skin). Call your doctor immediately if you experience symptoms of either condition.

Travelling with diabetes

Today, most of us consider travel a simple pleasure, and a right as well. We're ready to pack our bags and take off whenever the opportunity presents itself. Whether you need to travel regularly for work, enjoy taking short breaks in this country or a foreign city, or regularly venture abroad for a longer holiday, there's no reason why diabetes should prevent you from travelling. That is, provided that you take some reasonable precautions to ensure that while you're away your blood sugar stays under control.

It is important to plan ahead. Let your doctor know your itinerary. Depending on how long you'll be gone, your doctor may want to give you a thorough examination before you depart. And to ensure smooth sailing, heed the following advice.

◯ **Keep glucose goods close at hand** If you are travelling by plane, pack your medications, insulin, syringes, test strips, lancets, ketone strips and other supplies in your hand luggage so there's no chance of losing them. Consider bringing extra supplies in your checked-in luggage. Make sure all medications bear the original pharmacy prescription labels.

◯ **Pack a snack** Wherever you go, take a snack such as an apple, an energy bar, a banana, raisins or cheese and crackers in case your blood sugar starts to dip when you have no immediate access to other food. If you sample your snacks en route, replenish your supplies as soon as possible.

◯ **Anticipate airport security** With the increased security at airports these days, expect your supplies to get a thorough once-over. British Airways advice is that you should always telephone the airline in advance explaining your needs. The airline may wish to store your medication separately somewhere in the cabin. Be sure to carry a letter from your GP confirming your need to carry syringes, needles and medication, and make yourself known upon arrival at the check-in. These guidelines are subject to change, and individual airlines may have more stringent rules, so telephone in advance to check current policies.

◯ **Mind your meals** If you're flying or taking an extended trip by rail, call the carrier a few days before you depart and ask what special meals they have available for people with diabetes or heart disease (there may be more than one option to choose from). When en route, wait for meal service to begin before you take your pre-meal insulin to make sure you don't experience low blood sugar in the event that service is unexpectedly slowed or cancelled. When travelling by car, try to stick to your regular mealtime schedule to keep your blood sugar stable. If that is not possible, carry snacks with you and be alert for symptoms of low blood sugar, such as nervousness, sweating or crankiness. If you feel a hypoglycaemic episode coming on, pull over immediately and take a sugar pill or eat something. Wait at least 10 to 15 minutes for the feeling to pass before continuing your journey.

◯ **Get in the zone** Travelling across time zones can throw your normal insulin and meal schedule out of kilter, but you can compensate for the disruption if you're careful. When adding hours to your day by travelling west, you may need to take more insulin. When losing hours by travelling east, you may need less. Check with your doctor for specific recommendations. As for timing your injections and meals, keep your watch set to your home time as you travel to your destination, then switch your watch – and your schedule – to the local time the morning after you arrive.

⮑ **Organize for overseas** If you're planning to travel abroad, and will need to acquire additional insulin, be aware that in some countries the strength of insulin used is 40 or 80 units per ml (U40/U80) instead of the 100 units per ml (U100) available in the UK. If U100 syringes are used for U40 insulin the dosage will be too small. And if a U40 syringe is used for U100 insulin you will take too much insulin. Always match the strength of insulin on your bottle with the unit markings on your syringe.

Take-charge tips

Knowing what you should pack when you go travelling is always a challenge, but it's an even bigger challenge when you have diabetes. Follow this advice.

⮑ When it comes to supplies, such as drugs, insulin, test strips and lancets, the rule of thumb is: pack twice as much as you think you'll need. It's easier to carry extra than to get more on the road.

⮑ In case you do need to restock while you're away, ask your doctor to give you prescriptions for refills. It's also a good idea to ask for a printout of all your medications and a letter outlining the details of your condition so you'll have all the information you need to explain your history in case you need to see a doctor while on your travels.

⮑ Also ask your doctor to prescribe a glucagon kit, which contains an emergency dose of a hormone that someone with you can inject to make your liver pump out glucose if you have a hypoglycaemic emergency that leaves you unable to swallow or makes you lose consciousness.

⮑ If you don't already have one, get a medical ID bracelet or necklace that alerts people that you have diabetes and provides a number to call in an emergency.

EXERCISING AWAY FROM HOME

It's difficult to stay physically active when travelling – but not impossible. Try to keep your body in gear by planning ahead and seizing opportunities as they arise.

■ Make the most of the health and fitness facilities where you are staying. In many hotels, you should be able to use the swimming pool and gym free of charge or for payment of a small fee.

■ If your hotel doesn't have an on-site gym, ask if it provides access to a local health club. If the answer is no, ask which gyms are in the area and see if you can make arrangements on your own – or book a hotel that's more accommodating.

■ Pack comfortable clothes for impromptu walks or workouts, including T-shirts, shorts, socks and trainers or walking shoes. Don't forget your swimsuit in case the hotel has a pool.

■ Bring lightweight exercise gear that you can use in your hotel room, such as a skipping rope, elastic resistance bands (from sporting-goods shops) or an aerobics video.

■ If you're away on business, wear smart walking shoes rather than more formal shoes to encourage walking during breaks or before your first meeting.

■ If you are travelling for work, you may be able to enlist colleagues to help you to keep to your exercise programme – it will give you all a break from the business in hand as well.

■ Use airport delays as an opportunity for a brisk walk around the terminal. Avoid using travellators and walk the distance to your boarding gate.

■ Plan your holiday so there is plenty of scope for you to keep physically active. Stay somewhere where you can walk or jog daily. Or aim to book a holiday which specifically includes some form of enjoyable exercise such as a walking, cycling or sailing holiday.

Breakthroughs
of the future

A cure for diabetes is still out of reach — but not for long if progress continues at its current pace. Research is yielding fresh insights into the disease and its causes, and new drugs and surgeries are in the pipeline to treat it. An insulin inhaler is close at hand, as is a mechanical system that amounts to an artificial pancreas. And new discoveries in islet-cell transplants could eliminate the disease at the root level for a small number of people.

TEN

10

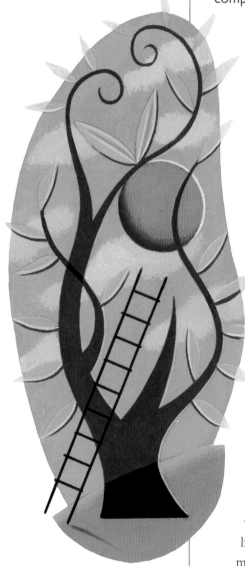

The pace of innovation

Imagine not having any treatments for diabetes: no insulin, no drugs to control blood sugar, no high-tech surgeries for complications in the eyes or kidneys – and little hope for a long or healthy life. That was the situation into which the World War II generation was born, but this book has shown how diabetes care has made great strides in a relatively short time. And today the pace of innovation is gathering speed.

As the incidence of diabetes has grown, understanding how the disease works and finding effective new treatments has taken on even greater urgency. As a result, researchers are continually making advances that mean the future of diabetes care looks brighter than ever before. While much about managing diabetes will remain in the hands of patients (particularly when it comes to diet and exercise), you can look forward to an array of new tools in years to come. To some extent, the future is already here. Consider some of the important advances that have taken place even within the past five years or so.

▶ New drugs, such as the alpha-glucosidase inhibitor Glucobay and fast-acting Novonorm, have been added to the line-up of glucose lowering agents.

▶ New types of insulin provide even more options for keeping blood sugar stable throughout the day and after meals. These include the new insulin glargine (Lantus), which stays evenly active for 24 hours, and rapid-acting lispro and insulin aspart, which start to work within 5 minutes of taking them.

▶ New glucose-monitoring methods such as the laser lancet allow you to test your blood sugar without pricking your finger. Particularly interesting is the GlucoWatch, a device you wear on your wrist that draws glucose through the skin using an electric current. The GlucoWatch analyses the sample, then calculates your blood-glucose level.

Building on the present

Few medical advances come out of the blue. Instead, they are built on previous groundbreaking work. Researchers are continually forging ahead with new insights and developments. The following is a selection of the kind of advances we can look forward to seeing in coming years.

New insulins 'For decades we didn't have a good basal insulin [such as insulin glargine],' says Professor Philip Home of the Department of Medicine at Newcastle University. 'Now we do. We will certainly see more of these insulins become available, if for no other reason than that pharmaceutical companies will seek to expand their share of this market.' That means more options for patients, along with competitive pressures that may help to keep down rising medication costs.

New monitoring methods Companies are working on a number of different ways to get blood-sugar readings without pricking your finger with a lancet – many by analysing interstitial fluid, a relatively clear liquid that surrounds cells and lies just below the surface of the skin. (Blood-glucose readings from interstitial fluid are not identical to readings from blood, but meters can translate the difference.) One system now undergoing clinical trials uses lasers to create microscopic holes in the skin that allow interstitial fluid to be siphoned out and drawn through a tube into a wearable meter. Another method in trial, called the SonoPrep Continuous Glucose Monitoring System, uses a low-frequency ultrasound device to disrupt the outer layer of the skin so that fluid can be taken up by a second device that is pressed to the skin. The real goal, however, is a blood-glucose test that is completely noninvasive. One promising approach (although it is not close to being marketed yet) is to shine a beam of light through the thin tissue of, say, an earlobe or a finger web and analyse the blood by measuring the light spectrum.

New standards for care Whatever advances in drugs or treatments for complications may be in the pipeline, the most important way to deal with diabetes will still be to control blood glucose as tightly as possible. As studies continue to shed light on how high blood sugar poses risks for diabetes, heart disease and complications, the medical community is moving to make standards of care more stringent. The World Health Organization (WHO) now recommends that the cut-off for a diagnosis of diabetes be lowered from a fasting plasma glucose level of 7.8mmol/l to 7.0mmol/l.

The future of insulin delivery

If you take insulin, finding any way besides injection to get it into your body is probably top of your wish list – and scientists are working hard to make it happen. That may sound like a tall order, considering that injections have been the only delivery system available in the more than 80 years that insulin has been used. Yet, although challenges remain, novel alternatives may be available before long.

Numerous methods (including eyedrops, rectal suppositories and wax pellets placed under the skin) have been tried unsuccessfully over the years, but researchers haven't yet run out of ideas. In fact, at least one promising no-needle system is in late-stage clinical trials and appears to be headed for approval in the USA. Here's what to watch out for.

An insulin inhaler Closest to being marketed is a powdered form of insulin that you breathe into the permeable tissues of the lungs with the help of an inhaler similar to an asthma inhaler. It's considered the single most viable alternative to injections because it is effective and has already been extensively studied in humans. In people with Type 1 diabetes, studies find, inhaled insulin controls blood sugar just as well as short-acting injections do, and it improved glucose control in Type 2 patients who previously only took oral medication. One concern is that some people using the inhaler in trials did more poorly in a test of lung function, and some developed a mild to moderate cough. 'The inhaler is very close, but research has been dragging as the Food and Drug Administration [FDA] looks more closely at how it affects the lungs,' says Professor Philip Home, Department of Medicine at Newcastle Univeristy. Additional tests are scheduled. Barring unforeseen safety problems, FDA approval could come soon.

Exploring oral insulin Researchers have been stymied for years in their attempts to develop insulin you can swallow because the hormone is naturally broken down during digestion before it reaches the bloodstream. However, a number of approaches in development may overcome this barrier. One method being explored in both the USA and Europe is to encase pills in a resin or plastic coating that breaks down only after the drug reaches the bloodstream. Another tactic is to avoid the gastrointestinal tract altogether by using a spray or patch that allows insulin to be absorbed through the cheek.

Using molecular messengers On the distant horizon of the coming decades is the prospect of loading insulin into designer molecules called nanoshells – tiny hollow spheres made of silica and coated with gold. On their injection into the body, a handheld infra-red laser would be used to heat the nanoshells, causing them to release small amounts of insulin. Theoretically, each nanoshell injection could provide needle-free insulin for months.

The disease frontier

Researchers still have much to learn about diabetes and how to prevent it. In Type 2 diabetes, for example, it is not clear how the body becomes insulin resistant or why obesity poses such great risks. In Type 1 diabetes, which can be only partly attributed to genes, the disease's environmental triggers remain a mystery.

Here are some ways in which researchers are trying to get at the roots of diabetes and thereby shed light on its prevention and treatment.

Looking AHEAD During the next decade, researchers at 16 centres funded by the National Institutes of Health in the USA will be conducting a study called Look AHEAD (Action for Health in Diabetes). The study will compare a programme of intensive lifestyle measures, such as diet and exercise specifically designed to achieve weight loss, with a less disciplined approach that provides general support and education, but not a weight-loss programme, for adults over the age of 45 with Type 2 diabetes. It will be the largest study ever to look at how weight loss affects death rates from cardiovascular problems in people with Type 2.

Boosting insulin power No matter how closely you control blood sugar with insulin, it is difficult to get perfect results. For example, blood sugar can still swing too high after meals and too low when you're not eating – and when control is good, you tend to gain weight. Enter amylin, a hormone that is released by

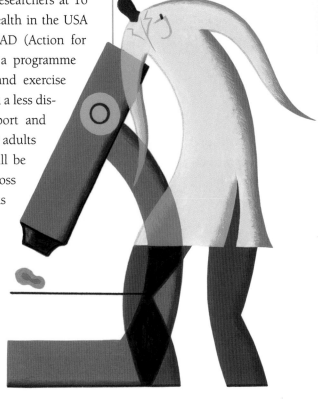

beta cells in the pancreas at the same time that insulin is secreted. People with Type 1 and Type 2 diabetes who require insulin are deficient in amylin. This has led researchers to try to stabilize blood sugar with a synthetic amylin replacement called pramlintide. It appears to work by suppressing secretion of another hormone (glucagon) that raises blood glucose and slows digestion by reducing movement of food from the stomach to the small intestine. Clinical trials have been encouraging. In a recent year-long study of 538 people with Type 2 diabetes, those who had pramlintide injections with meals dropped their haemoglobin A1c scores without changing their insulin dosage or experiencing hypoglycaemia – and they lost weight.

Making pre-emptive strikes Animal studies have suggested that taking insulin, either as injections or pills, twice a day might prevent Type 1 diabetes in people at risk of developing it. Two major trials called the Diabetes Prevention Trials are putting these ideas to the test in rearly 1,000 people in North America. Results so far suggest that the injections don't work. While disappointed, researchers haven't given up on the idea that exposing the body to supplemental insulin can train the immune system not to attack the pancreas. (Taking insulin pills in these experiments is not meant to lower blood glucose.) The second phase of the study is testing the insulin pills, which can be given at a much higher dose than the injections; results are due in 2005. Researchers are also looking into similar trials using modified insulin. 'Essentially, we're searching for a diabetes vaccine,' says Mark Peakman, Professor of Clinical Immunology at King's College, London, 'and there are lots of ideas about how this might be done.'

Unlocking secrets with drugs Many drugs are developed in 'backwards' fashion – that is, scientists don't always understand why they work, just that they do. But a drug's effectiveness may provide clues about the mechanisms of the disease itself. In the case of Type 2 diabetes, scientists are particularly studying

A DIABETES FORECAST

One encouraging finding from the Diabetes Prevention Trial-Type 1 (DPT-1) conducted in the USA is that the presence of certain types of molecules known as autoantibodies are closely linked with development of Type 1 diabetes. While antibodies are normally involved in protecting the body from infection as part of the immune system, certain types of antibodies appear to help the immune system mount an inappropriate attack on islet cell products in the pancreas, such as insulin. 'By looking at specific types of autoantibodies, we can now tell with greater precision whether someone is likely to develop Type 1 diabetes in the next three years,' says Mark Peakman, Professor of Clinical Immunology at Kings College, London.

thiazolidinediones, also called glitazones – drugs that help to lower blood glucose by making cells more sensitive to insulin. Diabetes UK says: 'Insulin resistance is a feature of an increased risk of developing Type 2 diabetes. Glitazones are interesting because they don't only have beneficial effects in one type of cell but work across the board in fat, liver and muscle cells – all places affected by diabetes.' Research into how glitazones work and achieve their effects will help in the development of even better drugs in the future.

Searching for triggers If the origins of Type 1 diabetes are only partly genetic, environmental factors must play a role too. But which factors? One theory is that exposure to cow's milk early in life may make children more susceptible to diabetes, possibly because of protein similarities between milk and pancreatic beta cells. An international study based in Europe called the Trial to Reduce Diabetes in the Genetically At-Risk (TRIGR) is testing this idea by following diabetes rates in children who are breastfed for the first six months of life versus those who are exposed earlier to cow's milk. Preliminary results suggest that risks are significantly lower for those who drink less cow's milk.

Finding culprit genes Research is progressing to find the genes responsible for causing diabetes, regulating functions such as insulin production, or contributing to complications. For example, an international team of researchers called the Type 1 Diabetes Genetics Consortium is collecting genetic data on families around the world and analysing it for clues about which genes might contribute to Type 1 diabetes. Similar work on Type 2 diabetes is taking place at the US National Institutes of Health, in the UK and in Europe. Meanwhile, a US study called GoKinD (Genetics of Kidneys in Diabetes) and a parallel study in the UK (Warren 3) are looking to find genes that play a role in diabetic nephropathy, or kidney damage, which appears to run in families.

Understanding the genetics of diabetes could have almost limitless practical payoffs in new drugs and therapies. For instance, researchers at the Joslin Diabetes Center, in Boston, USA, recently announced that they had isolated and cloned the third of three genes thought to be responsible for regulating insulin production by beta cells in the pancreas. The researchers now believe that they can use these genes to make cells other than beta cells manufacture insulin. It is possible that such genetically modified cells could then be implanted in people as beta-cell substitutes.

Pursuing peptides Protein fragments called peptides help to regulate a number of processes in the body that may contribute to Type 1 diabetes, and scientists are working to develop peptide-based therapies to treat the disease. One drug, called DiaPep277, seeks to fend off assaults on the pancreas by triggering the release of cytokines, hormones that regulate immune-system cells and appear to stop the progression of newly diagnosed Type 1 diabetes. In animal studies and preliminary trials in humans, DiaPep277 appeared to preserve insulin function without affecting the immune system's ability to protect the body from infection.

Stopping the destruction T-cells play a vital role in the body's defence against invaders and diseases, but when they turn against insulin-making beta cells in the pancreas (for reasons no one understands), they cause Type 1 diabetes. To fend them off, researchers treated 12 recently diagnosed Type 1 patients with an antibody thought to quell T-cell activity. The results were reported in *The New England Journal of Medicine* in May 2002. After only 14 days of treatment, nine of those receiving the antibody maintained or improved their insulin production after one year, compared with only two patients in a control group that did not receive the antibody. Most Type 1 patients have already lost 80 per cent of their beta cells at diagnosis. Scientists hope that tackling T-cells will help to preserve the remaining 20 per cent of insulin-producing capacity in newly diagnosed Type 1 patients – and provide a significant edge in their ability to control blood glucose.

Working on weight loss

Keeping your weight down is a critical factor in controlling Type 2 diabetes, but how the body regulates appetite, metabolism, fat accumulation and other factors is not well understood. As rates of obesity in the UK continue to climb along with rates of diabetes, it is time to take these conditions seriously. In the meantime, researchers are working to create new tools for managing weight gain.

The main principle of weight loss is simple: in order to lose pounds, you need to burn more calories than you take in. But many people find this difficult because the body seems programmed to keep weight constant. Much of the research into obesity seeks to understand how the body's internal controls work. Here are some recent insights.

Finding 'fat' genes What you do (or don't do) has a lot to do with how much you weigh, but it's also clear that being overweight runs in families. It is estimated that as much as 40 to 70 per cent of such traits as body mass and fat formation in the gut are determined by your genes. Now that the human genome has been mapped, scientists are trying to identify the genes – and there are likely to be many – that make individuals susceptible to weight control. One exciting development was the discovery of a genetic defect that curbed production of a recently identified appetite-regulating hormone called leptin. Now researchers are looking at clusters of genes on two different chromosomes that may predispose people to abdominal fat and insulin resistance. The hope is to determine how the relevant genes interact with each other and eventually to custom-design drugs that can reverse the effect an individual's genetic make-up has on weight increase.

Making the most of leptin Genetic defects may not be the most important influence on leptin. In fact, most obese people have ample amounts of the hormone but don't seem to be abe to benefit from its ability to signal when appetite is satisfied. Researchers are not sure why, but they may now have another piece of the puzzle. In an exciting development at Harvard's Beth Israel Deaconess Medical Center in the USA, scientists have identified a protein that appears to help regulate signals that allow leptin to work. The protein has two important effects: it makes laboratory mice stay slim, even when they are fed a high-fat diet, and it boosts insulin sensitivity. This makes the protein, known as PTP1B (protein tyrosine phosphatase 1B), a potentially powerful agent against both obesity and Type 2 diabetes. This research, funded by both the US National Institutes of Health and the American Diabetes Association, has not yet gone beyond animal testing, but it provides an intriguing basis for further study.

Suppressing the appetite Everyone dreams of a safe pill that would act as a switch to turn off appetite. It is unlikely that a single chemical agent will do the trick because the urge to eat is regulated by a complex biochemical process with many players.

Scientists at Imperial College, London, noticed that people feel less hungry after lunch. They found that this wasn't due to the food as such, or any filling of the stomach, but the release of

a special 'satiety hormone', known as PYY, from the gut. They were able to show that if you gave volunteers the same amount of PYY that a meal would release, the volunteers felt a lot less hungry solely due to the hormone. They have now set up a company called Thiakis, to try to exploit this.

Meanwhile, researchers are working to identify other players in the biochemical process with a view to helping dieters. One candidate described recently in the science journal *Nature* is a molecule called oleylethanolamide (OEA). Levels of OEA in the intestine increase when you eat. Scientists believe that the compound helps to trigger feelings of fullness that make you stop eating. In studies at the University of California, rats that were given OEA reduced their food intake and their weight. A chemically similar drug developed by a French company is now being tested on humans.

Another prospect is a compound called C75, which appears to curb appetite by affecting several brain chemicals at once. Obese lab rats injected with C75 ate less even after fasting, according to a study at Johns Hopkins University School of Medicine in the USA. Furthermore, the compound seems to increase metabolism to make animals burn more energy – meaning it may boost weight loss by both cutting and burning calories. Drug tests in humans are likely within three years.

Obesity and the brain If you remember the high-fashion emaciated look known as 'heroin chic', then you have a picture of what narcotics do besides blow your mind: they curb the appetite and make you lose weight. Wasting your mind and body is hardly a path to good health, but the link between weight loss and pleasure-producing chemicals in the brain has not been lost on scientists. Of particular interest is dopamine, a neurotransmitter produced when you satisfy urges such as those for sex and food. Brain researchers at Brookhaven National Laboratory in the USA have found that obese people have fewer sites, or receptors, on cells for dopamine to dock with than normal-weight people. The scientists speculate that overeating may be caused by a greater need for stimulation to produce satisfaction. The implication is that other activities that boost dopamine in the brain – such as exercise – can take the edge off cravings.

Other studies by the same researchers reveal another difference in obese people: areas of the brain that process sensual signals about food from the mouth, lips and tongue are more active than they are in people of normal weight. This raises the possibility that drugs that make food less palatable may help people to lose weight despite sensory hot spots in the brain.

Controlling complications

If you follow all the advice contained in this book, your prospects for avoiding future complications may be bright even without any further medical advances. In fact, the most important developments in preventing damage from diabetes continue to focus on understanding how tight control of blood glucose can reduce your risks. But researchers are also looking into ways to minimize the impact of diabetes on your health even if blood glucose does get out of hand.

Such advances are potentially significant because many people with diabetes – especially Type 2, which usually develops without symptoms over a long period of time – already have complications by the time they are diagnosed.

Eye protection

Vision loss leading to eventual blindness is one of the complications of diabetes that people fear the most. Good blood-glucose control will significantly reduce your risk of eye problems – by as much as 76 per cent. And medical advances should improve those odds even further. Here are some of the possibilities being explored to reduce diabetic eye damage.

Genes to fight blindness In addition to surgery and laser treatment for diabetic retinopathy (in which fragile blood vessels sprout in the eye and burst, causing damage to the retina) scientists may soon add gene therapy. Already, in experiments

By far the most common complication of diabetes is cardiovascular disease. People with diabetes have a two-to-four-fold increased risk of heart disease and stroke. However, these risks can be greatly reduced with currently available therapies. For example, in the UK a recent trial sponsored in part by the national charity Diabetes UK, the Collaborative Atorvastatin Diabetes Study (CARDS), showed that even among patients without high cholesterol, the use of the cholesterol-lowering drug atorvastatin reduced the risk of heart attack by more than one-third and almost halved the risk of stroke.

with mice, researchers at Johns Hopkins Wilmer Eye Institute in the USA have used gene therapy to reduce blood-vessel growth from a retinopathy-like condition by as much as 90 per cent. One of the genes the scientists used causes the body to manufacture endostatin, a substance that may inhibit abnormal blood-vessel growth in tumours. A second gene codes for PEDF (pigment epithelium-derived factor), a protein found naturally in the eye that promotes the survival of retinal cells. More research is needed to establish whether these approaches could help humans.

Help from ACE inhibitors Already used to bring down high blood pressure, ACE (angiotensin-converting enzyme) inhibitors have shown potential for improving insulin sensitivity and for preserving kidney function. Now research suggests that ACE inhibitors may improve circulation to the eyes. If taken before blood vessels proliferate due to retinopathy, the drugs may help reduce the risk of proliferation and haemorrhaging in the future.

A nervy proposition One way in which high glucose levels can lead to complications is that blood glucose converts to a substance called sorbitol, a modified form of glucose that is especially prone to building up in tissue. In the eyes, sorbitol contributes to clouding of vision, while in the nerves it traps water in cells, which can impair function by making nerves swell. Scientists have found that an enzyme called aldose reductase speeds the conversion of blood glucose to sorbitol, and pharmaceutical companies are working to develop drugs that block the enzyme's effects. So far, aldose reductase inhibitors have not impressed doctors, but research continues in the belief that more effective drugs can still be found.

Head-to-toe help

From the heart to the kidneys to the feet, here are the most promising advances currently in the pipeline for treating or preventing other complications of diabetes.

Double-duty drugs Like ACE inhibitors, another class of drugs that may have unforeseen benefits are thiazolidinediones, also called glitazones. In addition to making cells more sensitive to insulin and preventing damage to the kidneys and eyes due to high blood pressure, some studies indicate that glitazones may help to relax the endothelium, a layer of cells lining the blood vessels and cavities of the heart. If the effect is demonstrated in further studies, glitazones may prove to be useful in fighting cardiovascular complications while they lower blood glucose.

Grappling with growth hormone Studies suggest that naturally occurring growth hormone may help to trigger the onset of kidney damage from diabetes. In one study, for example, lab mice with diabetes whose cells were genetically programmed not to respond to growth hormone did not develop kidney disease, while other diabetic mice did. Now researchers are working to develop a class of drugs that – when the likelihood of serious disease warrants it – can block growth hormone's action by attaching themselves to a part of the cell normally reserved for the hormone. There is also evidence that so-called growth hormone antagonists may help to prevent diabetic eye disease.

Stopping tissue stiffening Another process that contributes to damage from complications is a stiffening of tissues due to advanced glycosylation end products, or AGEs – structures that form when sugars bind with the amino acids of proteins in a process sometimes likened to the toughening of meat when browned in cooking. AGEs appear to contribute to virtually every major complication of diabetes, including retinopathy, nerve damage, high blood pressure, foot ulcers and cardiovascular disease. Impeding their action has long been a research priority. While some chemical agents have shown promise, few have been found to be both effective and safe. But work on AGE inhibitors continues. Scientists are also looking at drugs that may be able to break up the links between proteins created by AGEs after they have formed.

Biological skin substitutes Poorly healing foot ulcers are the most common reason that people with diabetes have to go into hospital. One way to treat them has been skin-graft operations. But these require anaesthesia and can be hampered by poor healing, infection and scarring. But an emerging type of therapy can overcome these problems by using living skin equivalents known as biological skin substitutes. These biotechnology products contain the ingredients of skin

(such as collagen and other proteins) and can be fused with a person's own skin tissue to significantly speed healing. Some of them – for example, Regranex, which is made from yeast, and

Dermagraft, cultured in labs from neonatal skin cells – already approved for use in the UK.

Patching up the pancreas

Whether you have Type 1 or Type 2 diabetes, at least part of your problem is that you have a malfunctioning pancreas. Either it has stopped working altogether (Type 1) or it is no longer performing properly (Type 2). As Type 2 progresses, the condition of your pancreas – particularly the beta cells that make insulin – may even worsen. So why not replace the old, broken parts with new ones?

Pancreas transplants are not new, but nor are they a widely pre-scribed treatment. One problem is that the body rejects foreign tissues, which means patients must take drugs that suppress the immune system, potentially leading to unpleasant side effects. A second problem is that there are only around 800 donor pan-creases (obtained from cadavers) available in the UK each year and the number of candidates for transplants is far higher. Fortunately, there may soon be alternatives.

Islet cell transplants

There may be no reason to get rid of the entire pancreas – which produces digestive enzymes and hormones as well as insulin – if it's only the beleaguered beta cells that are in trouble. That is the idea behind islet cell transplants, in which doctors replace clumps, or islets, of cells – including beta cells – that are clustered throughout the pancreas.

The procedure was pioneered in animals in the 1970s and has since been made possible in humans. In fact, hundreds of people around the world have now received islet cell transplants. To begin with, the success rates were very poor, with the procedure working only about 8 per cent of the time. One reason for this was that immunosuppressant drugs used at that time appeared to be toxic to beta cells. However, there is new hope that this obstacle might have been overcome with an islet cell transplant procedure pioneered in Canada at the University of Alberta, Edmonton. The technique uses a combination of three new steroid-free drugs that appear to prevent rejection of transplanted islet cells and also halt immune-system attacks that cause Type 1 diabetes in the first place.

Early results of what is now called the Edmonton Protocol were electrifying. Researchers reported that some Type 1 patients in a small trial were able to stop using insulin for up to 14 months. The protocol has now been used successfully in more than 300 patients, with 85 per cent of them free of insulin treatment for more than a year – and many of those have reversed their diabetes for two or more years. 'This research has really spurred interest in this whole field,' says a spokesperson for Diabetes UK. New studies of the treatment are now being conducted at medical centres across the USA and in Europe.

Research is still in its early stages and much more work is required to improve the success rate of the procedure and develop ways of maintaining the transplanted islets over time. But as studies continue, researchers are hopeful that such powerful new approaches to restoring pancreatic function will eventually be more widely available.

THE SUPPLY-SIDE CHALLENGE

Even if techniques for islet cell transplants are refined, a significant barrier to making the procedure a mainstream treatment is the lack of donor pancreases from which cells can be extracted.

To resolve this dilemma, researchers are looking for ways to produce islet cells without having to rely on donor supplies. Studies are now looking at how islet cells multiply, in the hope that ways can be found to make them grow faster – work already being pioneered in animals. Researchers are also investigating the possibility of using cells from animals such as pigs, in humans.

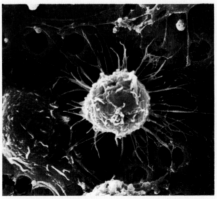

Perhaps the most significant (and controversial) area of research involves the use of embryonic stem cells – cells that have the capacity to become virtually any type of cell in the body. Laboratory studies have already shown that stem cells can be genetically manipulated to produce insulin, suggesting that they might make a viable source for transplants. Other options might be to use adult stem cells extracted from bone marrow or blood, which may hold promise for producing insulin, or to convert liver cells into insulin-making cells. Animal research also suggests that stem cells can be developed from unfertilized eggs instead of embryos; if it can be done in humans, this would circumvent the ethical issues surrounding the use of embryonic tissue.

An artificial pancreas

Even with all the progress being made on the transplant front, some researchers believe that a different approach is even closer to becoming a reality – developing a mechanical system that mimics the insulin-controlling functions of the pancreas. Such a system requires two basic parts: an internal monitor to keep track of blood-glucose levels and a dispensing device to respond automatically to glucose changes by releasing just the right amount of insulin to keep blood sugar stable.

The basic elements of such a system have already been invented. For example, Medtronic MiniMed has developed an implantable sensor, which will continuously monitor blood-glucose levels, and an implantable insulin pump. Both devices are currently being tested in clinical trials. When commercially available, the pump will communicate with the implantable sensor (or with an external sensor) using radio-frequency electro magnetic waves in order to release the exact amount of insulin needed at any given time.

Researchers are now working on ways to keep the devices functioning inside the body for long periods and communicating reliably with one another so that glucose levels and the system's insulin response are always closely matched. According to Diabetes UK: 'This technology is already feasible and, with more work, it could revolutionize the treatment of diabetes.' Some researchers believe that a combined implantable meter and pump system could be available within the next few years.

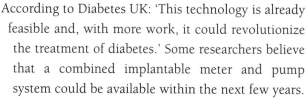

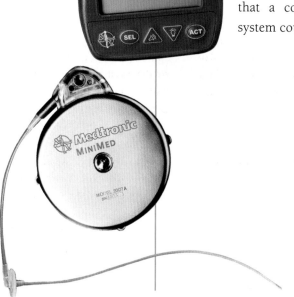

REAL-LIFE MEDICINE

FROM ISLET CELLS TO ICE CREAM

When she was diagnosed with Type 1 diabetes at 22, Mary Jenkins, from Maidstone, Kent, resigned herself to daily insulin injections and blood-sugar tests for the rest of her life. But she was determined to lead as normal a life as possible, and at 40 she even took up running. Now 60, she has completed more than 20 marathons, half-marathons, long-distance relays and cross-country runs.

But not long ago it looked as if repeated hypos might spell the end of her running days. 'My blood glucose kept dropping without any warning.' But the hypos weren't confined to when she was running. 'I'd be taking the dog for a walk and suddenly my legs would buckle under me.' Then one day she collapsed in the bushes returning from a run and had to be brought home.

Mary had been in regular contact with doctors at King's College, London, ever since she went there for her first insulin pen. When she told them about her hypos, she was put forward to become one of a small group to participate in the UK Islet Transplant Consortium's research programme. She underwent a rigorous selection procedure and an interview before a committee. Finally they said yes. At first, Mary was very hesitant about the procedure because of the risk of infection. 'But I knew the hypos weren't going to get any better, so I decided to go for it.' She then had to wait for a donated pancreas to become available. It can take months to get a match, but fortunately for Mary the call came after only six weeks.

Her husband drove her up to London in the early morning. At the hospital, Mary was made ready for the procedure. 'That takes a while, then they have to check that the cells they've extracted are suitable,' she explains. The procedure, in which islet cells were infused into her liver, took only half an hour, and Mary became one of the first two people in the UK to have this type of transplant.

The effect was almost immediate, and Mary was able to reduce her insulin injections straight away. After a second transplant of cells six months later, she had a few problems, particularly with anaemia, which were solved with iron infusions.

Mary's life is transformed. At the most, she now takes two units of fast-acting insulin occasionally and then four to five units at night. 'Before the operations I was taking 40 units,' she says. Best of all for Mary is that she can now run without worry. Recently she ran the Great North Run and set a new personal record. 'I feel so much better now, and it's great being able to run without having to snack all the way round.'

RECIPES

BREAKFAST 249
Scrambled eggs with smoked salmon and dill
Apple and blackberry brioches
Blueberry and cranberry granola
Banana and mango shake

APPETIZERS & SNACKS 251
Naan bread with lentil caviar
Ciabatta with garlic mushrooms
Quick bap pizzas
Dolcelatte and pear toasts

SALADS 253
Apple and fennel with blue cheese dressing
Tabbouleh with goat's cheese
Bacon and broad bean salad
Chicken Caesar salad

SOUPS 256
Teriyaki-style noodles with tofu
Potato and bacon chowder
Cauliflower cheese soup

MEATS 258
Hoisin beef stir-fry
Steak sandwich
Lamb steaks with rosemary
Aromatic spiced lamb cutlets
Pork chops in barbecue sauce
Seared pork with kumquats

POULTRY 262
Chicken and sweet potato hash
Chicken with apricots and cumin
Chicken livers sautéed with sage
Turkey escalopes with chestnut mushrooms
    and Madeira
Braised duck with crunchy Oriental salad
Chinese-style omelette

FISH AND SHELLFISH 266
Salmon with mango salsa
Anchovy and sesame-topped tuna
Chinese-style steamed plaice rolls
Malay-style braised fish
Stir-fried scallops and prawns
Classic grilled Dover sole

VEGETABLES 271
Speedy two-bean chilli
Penne primavera
Eggs with spicy peas and lentils
Moroccan-style pumpkin and butter beans
Chakchouka

PASTA, BEANS & GRAINS 274
Pasta with fresh sage, rocket and feta cheese
Stir-fried beef with fine noodles
Pasta with potato, beans and pesto
Sun-dried tomato and bean risotto
Couscous and flageolet niçoise

DESSERTS 277
Cherry brandy clafoutis
Summer fruit fool
Strawberry shortcake
Sultana lemon cheesecake

BREAKFAST

Scrambled eggs with smoked salmon and dill

Scramble eggs in a double saucepan or in a bowl over simmering water, then mix with crème fraîche, with deliciously creamy, low-calorie results.

Serves 4

6 eggs

3 tbsp semi-skimmed milk

6 plum tomatoes, halved

4 thick slices wholemeal bread

3 tbsp crème fraîche

75g (2½oz) sliced smoked salmon, cut into thin strips

1 tsp lemon juice

1 tbsp chopped fresh dill

salt and pepper, sprigs of fresh dill to garnish

1 Lightly beat the eggs together with the milk in a heatproof bowl or in the top of a double saucepan. Set over a saucepan containing barely simmering water – the base of the bowl or pan should just touch the water. Cook for 6–8 minutes or until the eggs begin to thicken, stirring frequently.

2 Preheat the grill to high. While the eggs are cooking, arrange the tomatoes cut side up on the rack of the grill pan, and sprinkle them with a little salt and pepper. Add the slices of bread to the rack. Grill for 4–5 minutes, turning the bread over halfway through, until the tomatoes are lightly browned and the bread is toasted on both sides.

3 Add the crème fraîche to the eggs, and season to taste with salt and pepper. Cook for a further 1 minute, stirring constantly, until the mixture is softly scrambled. Sprinkle the smoked salmon with the lemon juice, then add this to the eggs together with the chopped dill. Immediately remove the mixture from the heat.

4 Divide the smoked salmon scramble among the toast. Garnish each with a sprig of dill. Add 3 grilled tomato halves to each plate and serve.

NUTRITION PER SERVING:
kcal 363, **protein** 22g, **fat** 21g (of which saturated fat 9g), **carbohydrate** 24g (of which sugars 6g), **fibre** 4g

Apple and blackberry brioches

An irresistible start to the day – toasted brioche slices topped with caramelized apple rings and fresh blackberries, with a hint of cinnamon.

Serves 4

25g (1oz) butter

4 apples

½ tsp ground cinnamon

4 individual brioches

200g (7oz) fresh blackberries

4 tsp demerara sugar

1 Preheat the grill. Line the grill pan with foil, put the butter on top and set it under the grill to melt. Meanwhile, core the apples and slice each one into 6 rings, discarding the top and bottom pieces. Dip the apple rings in the melted butter to coat both sides, then lay them out in a single layer on the foil and sprinkle with the cinnamon.

2 Grill the apple rings for about 4 minutes or until they are starting to brown, turning them over once. Remove the apples on their foil from the grill pan and set aside.

3 Slice each brioche horizontally into 3 and spread out the slices in the grill pan. Toast lightly on both sides. Place 2 apple rings on top of each toasted brioche slice, add a few blackberries and sprinkle with the sugar. Put back under the grill and warm the berries for 2–3 minutes, then serve.

NUTRITION PER SERVING:
kcal 280, **protein** 5g, **fat** 10g (of which saturated fat 6g), **carbohydrate** 44g (of which sugars 31g), **fibre** 4g

Blueberry and cranberry granola

A delicious toasted muesli, this is made from a mix of grains, nuts, seeds and colourful berries. Stirring maple syrup and orange juice into the mix helps to keep the oil content down.

Makes 500g (1lb 2oz)

225g (8oz) rolled oats
45g (1½oz) wheatgerm
55g (2oz) millet flakes
1 tbsp sesame seeds
2 tbsp sunflower seeds
2 tbsp slivered almonds
50g (1¾oz) dried blueberries
50g (1¾oz) dried cranberries
15g (½oz) soft brown or demerara sugar
2 tbsp maple syrup
2 tbsp sunflower oil
2 tbsp orange juice

1 Preheat the oven to 160°C (325°F, gas mark 3). In a large bowl, combine the oats, wheatgerm, millet flakes, sesame and sunflower seeds, almonds, dried berries and suger. Stir until well mixed.

2 Put the maple syrup, oil and orange juice in a small jug and whisk together. Pour this mixture slowly into the dry ingredients, stirring to ensure that the liquid is evenly distributed and coats everything lightly.

3 Spread the mixture out evenly in a non-stick roasting tin. Bake for 30–40 minutes or until slightly crisp and lightly browned. Stir the mixture every 10 minutes to encourage even browning.

4 Remove from the oven and leave to cool. Store in an airtight container for up to 2 weeks. Serve with yoghurt, milk or fruit juice.

NUTRITION PER SERVING:
kcal 250, **protein** 7g, **fat** 11g (of which saturated fat 0.8g), **carbohydrate** 32g (of which sugars 7g), **fibre** 4g

Banana and mango shake

A thick banana shake with a tropical touch, it is packed with nourishment and very easy to prepare.

Serves 2

½ ripe mango
1 small ripe banana, sliced
150ml (5fl oz) semi-skimmed milk
120ml (4fl oz) orange juice
2 tsp lime juice
1 tsp caster sugar
2 heaped tbsp vanilla frozen yoghurt
sprigs of fresh lemon balm to decorate (optional)

1 Peel the skin from the mango and cut the flesh away from the stone. Chop the flesh roughly. Put into a blender with the banana.

2 Add the milk, orange juice, lime juice, sugar and frozen yoghurt and blend on maximum speed for about 30 seconds or until mixed and frothy.

3 Pour into glasses and serve immediately, decorated with sprigs of lemon balm, if you like.

NUTRITION PER SERVING:
kcal 150, **protein** 5g, **fat** 2g (of which saturated fat 1g), **carbohydrate** 30g (of which sugars 29g), **fibre** 1g

Naan bread with lentil caviar

Yoghurt spiced with garlic and mint, then mixed with raw vegetables and high-protein lentils, is delicious on warmed naan bread.

Serves 4

LENTIL 'CAVIAR'
340g (12oz) plain low-fat yoghurt
2 garlic cloves, chopped
1 can green lentils, about 300g, drained
½ cucumber, finely chopped
½ green pepper, seeded and cut into fine dice
1 ripe tomato, finely chopped
1 tbsp chopped fresh mint
¼ tsp ground cumin, or to taste
large pinch of curry powder
juice of ½ lemon
2 tbsp extra virgin olive oil
salt and cayenne pepper
TO SERVE
4 individual plain naans, cut into wedges
leaves from 3–4 sprigs of fresh mint
3 tbsp fresh coriander leaves
few rocket leaves
2 carrots, grated
2 tbsp chutney of choice or lime pickle

1 Preheat the grill. Mix together all the ingredients for the lentil 'caviar' and season with salt and cayenne pepper to taste.

2 Sprinkle the naans with water, then place under the grill and toast for 1 minute on each side. Transfer them to individual plates.

3 Spoon the lentil 'caviar' over the warm breads, dividing it equally among them. Sprinkle with the fresh mint, coriander and rocket leaves and the grated carrots. Serve at once, with the chutney or lime pickle on the side.

NUTRITION PER SERVING:
kcal 420, **protein** 17g, **fat** 14g (of which saturated fat 1g), **carbohydrate** 60g (of which sugars 20g), **fibre** 6g

Ciabatta with garlic mushrooms

Garlic mushrooms make a delightful starter but many recipes use generous quantities of butter. This version is deliciously buttery without being over-indulgent.

Serves 4

1 part-baked ciabatta loaf
1 tbsp extra virgin olive oil
30g (1oz) unsalted butter
2 garlic cloves, crushed
450g (1lb) button mushrooms, halved
1 tbsp wholegrain mustard
dash of Worcestershire sauce
30g (1oz) Parmesan cheese shavings
salt and pepper
sprigs of fresh flat-leaf parsley to garnish

1 Preheat the oven to 200°C (400°F, gas mark 6). Cut the ciabatta diagonally into eight 2.5 cm (1 in) thick slices – they should be long and oval in shape. Place the slices of bread on a baking sheet and brush them lightly with oil. Bake the bread for 8–12 minutes or until crisp and golden.

2 Meanwhile, melt the butter in a frying pan. When the butter starts to sizzle, add the garlic and cook for 1 minute. Add the mushrooms and cook over a moderately high heat, stirring occasionally, for 4–5 minutes or until the mushrooms are lightly cooked.

3 Stir in the mustard. Reduce the heat slightly and add the Worcestershire sauce and seasoning to taste. Cook for a further 1 minute, then remove the pan from the heat.

4 Place 2 slices of ciabatta bread on each plate. Spoon the mushrooms and their cooking juices over the bread. Scatter on the Parmesan shavings and garnish with sprigs of parsley. Serve immediately.

NUTRITION PER SERVING:
kcal 290, **protein** 11g, **fat** 14g (of which saturated fat 6g), **carbohydrate** 34g (of which sugars 2g), **fibre** 2g

Quick bap pizzas

The sweetness of the passata and yellow pepper contrasts deliciously with the savoury wholemeal baps, making this a tasty starter for healthy appetites.

Makes 4 pizzas

1 large courgette, thinly sliced
1 yellow pepper, seeded and thinly sliced
1 tbsp extra virgin olive oil
2 large wholemeal baps, split open in half
120ml (4fl oz) passata with onion and garlic
handful of fresh oregano leaves
200g (7oz) mozzarella cheese, sliced
salt and pepper

1 Preheat the grill to the hottest setting. Line the grill pan with a piece of foil. Put the courgette and pepper slices on the foil, sprinkle with the olive oil and toss together. Spread out the vegetables, then grill them for about 5 minutes or until they begin to soften.

2 Add the baps, laying them on top of the vegetables, crust sides uppermost, and toast lightly on the crust side. Remove the baps. Turn the vegetables and continue grilling them while you add the topping to the baps.

3 Spread the untoasted cut side of each bap with passata, allowing it to soak into the bread. Add a

few oregano leaves to each one, then arrange the grilled vegetables on top, sprinkling them with seasoning to taste. Lay the slices of mozzarella cheese over the vegetables.

4 Put the bap pizzas back in the grill pan. Cook under the hot grill for 3–5 minutes or until the cheese melts and begins to brown. Serve immediately, while piping hot.

NUTRITION PER PIZZA:
kcal 325, **protein** 20g, **fat** 15g (of which saturated fat 7g), **carbohydrate** 30g (of which sugars 7g), **fibre** 5g

Dolcelatte and pear toasts

Slices of fresh juicy pear, tasty blue cheese and pecan nuts on toasted bread make a lovely flavour combination in this starter.

Serves 4

2 ripe pears, preferably red-skinned
lemon juice
200g (7oz) wedge of Dolcelatte cheese
30g (1oz) pecan nuts
8 large slices of baguette, about 2cm (¾in) thick
4 tbsp mango chutney
30g (1oz) watercress sprigs
30g (1oz) rocket
pepper
cherry tomatoes to serve

1 Preheat the grill. Core and quarter or slice the pears, then toss with a squeeze of lemon juice to prevent the pears from discolouring. Cut the cheese down the length of the wedge to make 8 thin, triangular slices.

2 Lightly toast the pecan nuts under the grill, watching carefully to make sure they don't burn, then roughly chop them. Set aside. Spread out the bread slices on the grill pan and toast lightly on both sides.

3 Spread the mango chutney on the toasted bread and top with the watercress and rocket. Arrange a slice of cheese and a quarter of the pears on each piece of toast and scatter over the pecan nuts. Season with pepper. Serve at once, with halved cherry tomatoes.

NUTRITION PER SERVING:
kcal 440, **protein** 18g, **fat** 24g (of which saturated fat 12g), **carbohydrate** 38g (of which sugars 16g), **fibre** 5g

Apple and fennel with blue cheese dressing

This tasty salad is perfect for the winter when salad leaves and tomatoes are not at their best.

Serves 4

30g (1oz) shelled hazelnuts
1 large bulb of fennel, thinly sliced
1 large head of chicory, cut across into shreds
2 red-skinned dessert apples
100g (3½oz) radicchio leaves
2 tbsp snipped fresh chives
BLUE CHEESE DRESSING
55g (2oz) blue cheese, such as Danish Blue, crumbled
2 tbsp tepid water
6 tbsp plain low-fat bio yoghurt
pepper

1 To make the dressing, put the blue cheese in a bowl with the water and mash to a smooth paste using the back of a spoon. Stir in the yoghurt to make a thick, fairly smooth dressing. Season to taste with pepper. Set aside.

2 Heat a small non-stick frying pan over a high heat. Add the hazelnuts and toast for about 2 minutes or until they smell nutty, stirring frequently. Immediately tip onto a clean tea-towel and rub to remove the papery outer skins. Coarsely chop the nuts.

3 Add the fennel and chicory to the dressing and stir to combine. Core the apples and cut into very thin slices, then add to the salad. Toss gently, making sure the apples are coated in dressing. Fold in the hazelnuts.

4 Arrange the radicchio leaves on 4 plates. Top with the salad and sprinkle with the chives. Serve at once.

NUTRITION PER SERVING:
kcal 141, **protein** 5g, **fat** 10g (of which saturated fat 3g), **carbohydrate** 10g (of which sugars 8g), **fibre** 4g

Tabbouleh with goat's cheese

Tabbouleh is a classic Middle Eastern salad made with bulghur wheat.

Serves 4

280g (10oz) bulghur wheat
1 yellow pepper, seeded and chopped
20 cherry tomatoes, quartered
1 small red onion, finely chopped
10cm (4in) piece of cucumber, seeded and chopped
1 large carrot, grated
5 tbsp chopped parsley
2 tbsp chopped fresh coriander
2 tbsp chopped fresh mint
1 small fresh red chilli, seeded and finely chopped
(optional)
200g (7oz) rindless soft goat's cheese, crumbled
salt and pepper
LEMON AND CUMIN DRESSING
¼ tsp ground cumin
1 small garlic clove, very finely chopped
1 tbsp lemon juice
3 tbsp extra virgin olive oil
TO SERVE
lettuce leaves
12 radishes, sliced

1 Put the bulghur wheat in a mixing bowl, pour over enough boiling water to cover and stir well. Leave to soak for 15–20 minutes.

2 Meanwhile, make the dressing. Whisk together the cumin, garlic and lemon juice in a small bowl, then whisk in the olive oil.

3 Drain the bulghur wheat in a sieve, pressing out excess water, then return it to the bowl. Add the pepper, tomatoes, onion, cucumber, carrot, parsley, coriander and mint, plus the chilli, if using. Pour the dressing over the top and season with salt and pepper to taste. Fold gently to mix well.

4 Arrange the lettuce leaves on 4 plates or a serving platter. Pile the bulghur salad on the leaves and sprinkle the goat's cheese over the top. Garnish with the radishes and serve.

NUTRITION PER SERVING:
kcal 473, **protein** 16g, **fat** 18g (of which saturated fat 7g), **carbohydrate** 64g (of which sugars 10g), **fibre** 3g

Bacon and broad bean salad

This delicious warm salad is packed with strong flavours and makes a fabulous supper or lunch served with chunks of crusty bread or a side dish of new potatoes.

Serves 4

1 tbsp sunflower oil
200g (7oz) lean smoked back bacon, rinded and snipped into large pieces
1 large red pepper, seeded and cut into strips
2 red onions, cut into wedges
2 slices of bread
400g (14oz) frozen broad beans, thawed
2 small firm heads of radicchio, cut into wedges
chopped fresh flat-leaf parsley to garnish (optional)
DEVILLED DRESSING
4 tbsp mayonnaise
2 tsp Worcestershire sauce
1 tbsp Dijon mustard
generous pinch of caster sugar
3–4 tbsp milk
salt and pepper

1 Preheat the grill if not using a toaster for the bread. Make the dressing by mixing together the mayonnaise, Worcestershire sauce, Dijon mustard and sugar. Add enough milk to make a drizzling consistency. Season with salt and pepper to taste, and set aside.

2 Heat the sunflower oil in a large saucepan. Add the bacon, red pepper and onions, and fry over a high heat for 4 minutes, stirring, until the onions have softened.

3 Meanwhile, toast the bread in a toaster or under the grill. Cut it into cubes. Set aside.

4 Stir the broad beans into the bacon mixture and add 1 tbsp water. Heat until sizzling, then cover the pan and leave to cook for 4 minutes.

5 Arrange the wedges of radicchio on top of the bean and bacon mixture. Cover again and cook for 3 minutes or until the radicchio has wilted, but still holds its shape.

6 Spoon the salad into shallow bowls and drizzle over the dressing. Scatter the toasted bread cubes over the top, sprinkle with chopped flat-leaf parsley and serve.

NUTRITION PER SERVING:
kcal 350, **protein** 19g, **fat** 20g (of which saturated fat 4g), **carbohydrate** 24g (of which sugars 9g), **fibre** 8g

Chicken Caesar salad

A variation on the classic Caesar salad, this includes chunks of tender chicken, green beans and tasty anchovy croutons, all tossed in a light creamy dressing.

Serves 4

200g (7oz) thin green beans
1–2 cos lettuces, about 450g (1lb) in total,
 torn into bite-sized pieces
1 small head chicory, sliced crossways
4 celery sticks, sliced
400g (14oz) cooked skinless boneless chicken breasts
 (fillets), cut into chunks
1 egg
1 can anchovy fillets, about 50g
1 garlic clove, crushed
12 thin slices of French bread, 100g (3½oz) in total
30g (1oz) Parmesan cheese, finely pared into
 shavings or grated
CAESAR DRESSING
1 tsp Dijon mustard
3 tbsp extra virgin olive oil
2 tsp sherry vinegar or wine vinegar
2 tbsp plain low-fat yoghurt
large pinch of caster sugar
½ tsp Worcestershire sauce
pepper

1 Preheat the oven to 200°C (400°F, gas mark 6). Cook the beans in a saucepan of boiling water for 3 minutes or until just tender. Drain and refresh under cold running water. Halve the beans and put into a large salad bowl. Add the lettuce, chicory, celery and chicken. Set aside in the fridge.

2 Put the egg in a saucepan, cover with cold water and bring to the boil. Reduce the heat and simmer for 10 minutes.

3 Meanwhile, tip the anchovies into a bowl with the oil from the can (about 1 tablespoon). Add the garlic and mash with a fork to a paste. Spread thinly over one side of each slice of French bread. Arrange on a baking sheet and bake for about 10 minutes or until the croutons are crisp and golden. Cool slightly, then break into pieces.

4 While the croutons are baking, make the Caesar dressing. Whisk together the mustard, olive oil, vinegar, yoghurt, sugar, Worcestershire sauce and

pepper to taste. Cool the hard-boiled egg under cold running water, then peel and chop. Stir into the dressing.

5 Drizzle half of the dressing over the chilled salad and toss to coat everything evenly. Add the croutons and toss again. Drizzle over the remaining dressing and scatter the Parmesan on top. Serve at once.

NUTRITION PER SERVING:
kcal 382, **protein** 37g, **fat** 23g (of which saturated fat 4g), **carbohydrate** 20g (of which sugars 5g), **fibre** 4g

---

SOUPS

Teriyaki-style noodles with tofu

This rich, fresh-tasting Japanese-style broth, flavoured with vibrant herbs, ginger and garlic, peps up firm cubes of tofu and long strands of earthy buckwheat noodles.

Serves 2

150g (5½oz) soba (Japanese buckwheat noodles)
225g (8oz) mixed vegetables, such as asparagus tips, broccoli, carrots, cauliflower, green beans or mange-tout
100ml (3½fl oz) light soy sauce
300ml (10fl oz) vegetable stock
4 tbsp rice wine (sake or mirin) or dry sherry
280g (10oz) firm tofu, diced
2 spring onions, chopped
1 fresh red chilli, seeded and chopped
1 heaped tbsp chopped fresh mint
1 heaped tbsp chopped fresh coriander
1 large garlic clove, crushed
½ tsp grated fresh root ginger
2 tsp toasted sesame oil (optional)

1 Bring a large saucepan of water to the boil and cook the soba noodles for about 6 minutes, or according to the packet instructions, until al dente.

2 Meanwhile, cut all the mixed vegetables into bite-sized pieces. Add them to the simmering pasta for the final 3–4 minutes of cooking.

3 Drain the pasta and vegetables through a large colander. Place all remaining ingredients in the empty saucepan and return it to the heat. Heat until simmering, then reduce the heat to the minimum setting. Return the pasta and vegetables to the pan, and cook very briefly until they are reheated.

4 Serve in deep soup bowls, with a spoon to drink the tasty broth and a fork or chopsticks for picking up the solid ingredients.

NUTRITION PER SERVING:
kcal 495, **protein** 30g, **fat** 14.5g (of which saturated fat 1g), **carbohydrate** 65g (of which sugars 4.5g), **fibre** 5g

Potato and bacon chowder

Onions, potatoes, bacon and milk are turned into a hearty and satisfying soup, which is finished with spinach and parsnip.

Serves 4

1 litre (1¾pints) whole/creamy milk
1 tbsp extra virgin olive oil
55g (2oz) lean smoked back bacon, rinded and finely chopped

1 large onion, finely chopped

2 tbsp plain flour

400g (14oz) smooth thin-skinned potatoes, such as
    Desiree, scrubbed and finely diced

1 parsnip, about 150g (5½oz), grated

freshly grated nutmeg

115g (4oz) baby spinach leaves

salt and pepper

1 Bring the milk just to the boil in a saucepan. Meanwhile, in another large saucepan heat the oil over a moderately high heat. Add the bacon and onion and cook for 2 minutes, stirring frequently. Add the flour and stir to combine, then slowly add about one-quarter of the hot milk, stirring and scraping the bottom of the pan to mix in the flour. When the mixture thickens, stir in the remaining hot milk.

2 Add the potatoes and parsnip. Season with salt, pepper and nutmeg to taste and bring just to the boil, stirring occasionally. Adjust the heat so the soup bubbles gently. Half cover the pan and continue cooking for about 10 minutes or until the vegetables are nearly tender, stirring occasionally.

3 Stir in the spinach and continue cooking for 1–2 minutes or until the spinach has wilted. Taste the soup and adjust the seasoning, if necessary. Serve at once.

NUTRITION PER SERVING:
kcal 355, protein 15g, fat 14g (of which saturated fat 7g), carbohydrate 43g (of which sugars 17g), fibre 4g

Cauliflower cheese soup

A classic combination as a vegetable dish, cauliflower and Cheddar cheese are equally good partners in a soup.

Serves 4

15g (½oz) butter

1 onion, chopped

¼ tsp mustard powder

1 large cauliflower, about 900g (2lb),
    broken into small florets

600ml (1 pint) semi-skimmed milk

150ml (5fl oz) vegetable stock

1 bay leaf

2 tsp sunflower oil

100g (3½oz) mature Cheddar cheese, grated

salt and pepper

chopped fresh flat-leaf parsley to garnish

1 Melt the butter in a large saucepan. Add the onion and cook over a moderate heat for 3 minutes, stirring frequently, until soft. Sprinkle over the mustard and stir it in.

2 Reserve about 85g (3oz) of the cauliflower florets; add the rest to the saucepan together with the milk, stock and bay leaf. Bring to the boil, then reduce the heat. Cover and simmer for 10 minutes or until the cauliflower is tender.

3 Meanwhile, heat the oil in a non-stick frying pan. Break the reserved cauliflower into tiny florets and fry for 4–5 minutes or until lightly browned, stirring frequently. Set aside.

4 Remove the bay leaf from the soup. Purée in the pan with a hand-held blender, or in a blender or food processor. Season with salt and pepper to taste, then reheat until just bubbling.

5 Remove from the heat, add the grated cheese and stir until melted. Ladle into 4 warmed soup bowls and sprinkle with the sautéed cauliflower florets and parsley. Serve immediately.

NUTRITION PER SERVING:
kcal 303, protein 20g, fat 18g (of which saturated fat 10g), carbohydrate 17g (of which sugars 15g), fibre 5g

MEATS

1 sirloin steak, about 200g (7oz), trimmed of fat
     and cut into thin strips
85g (3oz) mange-tout, halved lengthways
4 spring onions, cut into chunky lengths
3 tbsp hoisin sauce
1 tbsp light soy sauce
1 tsp toasted sesame oil (optional)
shredded spring onion to garnish

1 Put the noodles in a bowl, cover with boiling water and leave to soak for 5 minutes, or according to the packet instructions.

2 Meanwhile, heat the sunflower oil in a wok or large frying pan, add the garlic and ginger, and cook very briefly to release their flavour. Toss in the red pepper and mushrooms, then stir-fry over a high heat for 2–3 minutes or until starting to soften.

3 Add the strips of steak, mange-tout and spring onions, and stir-fry for a further 1–2 minutes or until the meat just turns from pink to brown.

4 Mix in the hoisin and soy sauces and stir well until bubbling, then drizzle in the sesame oil, if using. Drain the noodles. Serve the stir-fry on the noodles, garnished with shredded spring onion.

NUTRITION PER SERVING:
kcal 620, **protein** 38g, **fat** 20g (of which saturated fat 5g), **carbohydrate** 76g (of which sugars 11g), **fibre** 6g

Steak sandwich

This bumper sandwich is made with half-size ciabatta loaves baked until crusty, then split and packed with quick-fried steak and healthy salad.

Serves 4

4 ready-to-bake half ciabatta loaves, about 150g
     (5½oz) each
12 thin slices flash-fry or sandwich steak, about
     340g (12oz) in total
2 tsp extra virgin olive oil
3 tbsp black olive paste (tapenade)
4 tomatoes, about 340g (12oz) in total, sliced
45g (1½oz) rocket leaves
juice of ½ lemon
salt and pepper

1 Preheat the oven to 200°C (400°F, gas mark 6). Bake the ciabatta for 8–10 minutes or according to the packet instructions. Remove the bread from the oven and keep warm.

Hoisin beef stir-fry

For a quick supper, try this colourful stir-fry of strips of tender steak with fresh ginger, mushrooms, red peppers and crisp mange-tout, served on a bed of egg noodles.

Serves 2

2 sheets medium Chinese egg noodles,
     about 170g (6oz) in total
1 tbsp sunflower oil
2 large garlic cloves, cut into shreds
1 tsp grated fresh root ginger
1 large red pepper, seeded and thinly sliced
125g (4½oz) baby button mushrooms, halved

2 Heat a ridged cast-iron grill pan or non-stick frying pan until hot. Season the steak with salt and pepper to taste. Brush the pan with the oil, then add the steak slices, in batches if necessary, and cook for 30 seconds on each side for rare, 1 minute on each side for medium to well-done.

3 Quickly split each loaf in half lengthways. Spread the bottom halves with the olive paste. Cover with sliced tomatoes and top with the steak.

4 Toss the rocket leaves with the lemon juice. Pile on top of the steak, then drizzle the pan juices over and top with the remaining bread halves. Serve with more rocket and sliced tomatoes.

NUTRITION PER SERVING:
kcal 500, **protein** 31g, **fat** 13g (of which saturated fat 4g), **carbohydrate** 66g (of which sugars 4g), **fibre** 4g

Lamb steaks with rosemary

Quick-cooking lamb steaks are coated with a rich-flavoured sauce made with red onions, rosemary and black olives, and served with a garlicky flageolet bean mash.

Serves 4

2 tbsp extra virgin olive oil
2 large red onions, thinly sliced
3 large garlic cloves, thinly shredded
6 sprigs of fresh rosemary, each about 2.5cm (1in) long, plus extra sprigs to garnish
4 lean lamb steaks, about 130g (4¾oz) each

1 tbsp balsamic vinegar
4 tbsp red wine
30g (1oz) stoned black olives, sliced
1 tsp sugar
200ml (7fl oz) vegetable stock
FLAGEOLET BEAN AND GARLIC MASH
1 tbsp extra virgin olive oil
3 garlic cloves
2 cans flageolet beans, (2 x 400g), drained and rinsed
5 tbsp vegetable stock
3 tbsp chopped parsley
salt and pepper

1 Heat the olive oil in a large frying pan, add the onions, garlic and rosemary, and cook over a moderate heat for about 10 minutes, stirring frequently, until the onions have softened and are starting to turn golden.

2 Meanwhile, make the flageolet bean and garlic mash. Heat the olive oil in a saucepan, add the peeled garlic cloves and cook over a very low heat for 4–5 minutes or until tender. Add the flageolet beans and vegetable stock, cover the pan and cook gently for 4–5 minutes to heat through. Mash until smooth, season to taste and stir in the parsley. Keep warm.

3 Push the onions to the side of the frying pan, and add the lamb steaks. Fry for 3–4 minutes on each side, depending on how well done you like your meat.

4 Lift the lamb steaks from the pan and place on warmed serving plates. Add the balsamic vinegar, wine, olives and sugar to the frying pan and cook over a high heat until the liquid has evaporated. Stir in the stock and bubble for 1 more minute, then pour the sauce over the lamb. Garnish with fresh sprigs of rosemary and serve with the flageolet bean mash.

NUTRITION PER SERVING:
kcal 500, **protein** 40g, **fat** 21g (of which saturated fat 6g), **carbohydrate** 38g (of which sugars 12g), **fibre** 12g

Aromatic spiced lamb cutlets

The ingredients in this Middle Eastern recipe offer a good range of nutrients, including lots of vitamins and minerals.

Serves 4

8 lamb best end of neck cutlets, about 400g (14oz)
    in total, trimmed of fat
1 tsp cumin seeds
1 tsp coriander seeds
juice of ½ lemon
2 garlic cloves, crushed
2 tbsp extra virgin olive oil
salt and pepper
sprigs of fresh mint to garnish
MINTED YOGHURT SAUCE
¼ cucumber
150g (5½oz) plain low-fat yoghurt
1 garlic clove, crushed
1 tsp bottled mint sauce
1 tbsp chopped fresh mint
APRICOT AND ALMOND COUSCOUS
280g (10oz) couscous
100g (3½oz) dried apricots, chopped
500ml (17fl oz) boiling vegetable stock
50g (1¾oz) whole blanched almonds, toasted
2 tbsp chopped fresh mint
2 tbsp chopped fresh coriander
juice of ½ lemon
2 tbsp extra virgin olive oil

1 Preheat the grill to high. Place the lamb cutlets in a shallow dish. Grind the cumin and coriander seeds briefly in a pestle and mortar to crack them, then mix with the lemon juice, garlic and oil, and season with salt and pepper to taste. Pour the mixture over the lamb cutlets, turn them over to coat both sides and set aside to marinate while you make the sauce.

2 Cut the cucumber in half lengthways and scoop out the seeds with a teaspoon. Grate the cucumber coarsely and drain off any excess water. Mix with the yoghurt, garlic, mint sauce and fresh mint. Set aside.

3 Place the lamb cutlets on the rack in the grill pan and grill for 10–12 minutes, turning once. The cutlets will be medium-rare; if you prefer them medium to well-done, cook for 12–14 minutes.

4 Meanwhile, put the couscous and apricots in a large bowl and pour over the boiling stock. Stir well, then cover with a plate and set aside to soak for 5 minutes.

5 Stir the almonds, chopped mint and coriander, lemon juice and oil into the couscous. Spoon the couscous onto plates, top each serving with 2 lamb cutlets and put a spoonful of the sauce on the side. Garnish with sprigs of fresh mint and serve immediately.

NUTRITION PER SERVING:
kcal 615, **protein** 39g, **fat** 30g (of which saturated fat 8g), **carbohydrate** 51g (of which sugars 15g), **fibre** 3g

Pork chops in barbecue sauce

A sweet and sour barbecue sauce is the perfect partner for simply cooked pork chops. With a fruit and pine nut pilaf and a mixed leaf salad, this makes a tempting and substantial supper.

Serves 4

1 tbsp sunflower oil
4 boneless pork loin chops, about 140g (5oz) each, trimmed of fat
100ml (3½fl oz) orange juice
4 tbsp clear honey
2 tbsp soy sauce
2 tbsp dry sherry
2 tbsp red wine vinegar
2 tbsp French mustard
2 tbsp tomato purée
salt and pepper
PINE NUT AND RAISIN PILAF
250g (8½oz) basmati rice
1 tbsp sunflower oil
1 onion, sliced
1 garlic clove, finely chopped
50g (1¾oz) pine nuts
50g (1¾oz) raisins
600ml (1 pint) vegetable stock

1 Heat the oil in a frying pan and add the chops. Fry for 5 minutes or until browned on both sides, turning them over once.

2 In a small bowl, blend together the orange juice, honey, soy sauce, sherry, vinegar, mustard and tomato purée. Pour over the chops, then leave to simmer for 15 minutes or until the chops are cooked through and tender, turning them once or twice.

3 Meanwhile, make the pilaf. Put the rice in a sieve and rinse under cold running water until the water is clear. Drain well. Heat the oil in a saucepan, add the onion and garlic and cook for 5 minutes or until softened and beginning to brown. Sprinkle in the pine nuts and raisins and cook, stirring, for 2–3 minutes or until the nuts turn golden brown.

4 Add the rice and stir well to mix. Pour in the stock and bring to the boil. Reduce the heat, cover and simmer for 10 minutes or until the rice is tender and all the stock has been absorbed. Season to taste.

5 To serve, spoon the pilaf onto warmed plates and arrange the chops in barbecue sauce alongside.

NUTRITION PER SERVING:
kcal 671, **protein** 40g, **fat** 19g (of which saturated fat 2g), **carbohydrate** 85g (of which sugars 33g), **fibre** 1g

Seared pork with kumquats

Here, thinly sliced pork fillet is quickly browned in a sizzling hot, ridged cast-iron grill pan, then simmered with tangy kumquats, honey, mustard, white wine and stock.

Serves 4

675g (1½lb) floury potatoes, peeled and cut into chunks
340g (12oz) green beans
1 tbsp extra virgin olive oil
400g (14oz) pork fillet (tenderloin), thinly sliced
1 small onion, thinly sliced
115g (4oz) kumquats
1 tbsp clear honey
1 tbsp Dijon mustard
150ml (5fl oz) dry white wine
150ml (5fl oz) vegetable stock
3 tbsp semi-skimmed milk
freshly grated nutmeg
salt and pepper
snipped fresh chives to garnish (optional)

1 Cook the potatoes in a saucepan of boiling water for 15 minutes or until tender. Steam the green beans in a steamer basket or colander over the potato pan for the last 5 minutes of the cooking time.

2 Meanwhile, heat the oil in a large ridged cast-iron grill pan. Add the slices of pork in batches and fry over a very high heat for 1 minute on each side or until browned. Lift the slices out of the pan and set aside.

3 Add the onion to the pan and fry over a high heat for 3 minutes, stirring. Reduce heat slightly, then return the pork to the pan and fry for 5 minutes.

4 Thinly slice the kumquats, skin and all. Add to the pan together with the honey and cook for 1 minute. Mix the mustard, wine and stock together, and pour the mixture into the pan. Season with salt and pepper to taste and simmer for 3 minutes.

5 Drain the potatoes and mash them with the milk. Season with salt, pepper and nutmeg. Spoon the mashed potato into the centre of 4 serving plates. Arrange the pork slices on top of the mash and pour over a little of the sauce. Add the kumquats and beans and pour over the remaining sauce. Garnish with chives, if using.

NUTRITION PER SERVING:
kcal 380, **protein** 26g, **fat** 11g (of which saturated fat 3g), **carbohydrate** 38g (of which sugars 12g), **fibre** 5g

---

POULTRY

Chicken and sweet potato hash

And not like ✗

This hash is a great dish to make with leftover roast chicken or turkey. Sweet potatoes add bright colour and sweetcorn gives a delightful crunchy texture.

Serves 4

300g (10½oz) potatoes, peeled
500g (1lb 2oz) orange-fleshed sweet potatoes, peeled
225g (8oz) leeks, sliced
2 tbsp sunflower oil
225g (8oz) cooked chicken meat, without skin, diced
170g (6oz) frozen sweetcorn, thawed and drained
8 sun-dried tomatoes packed in oil, drained
      and chopped
1 tsp paprika
salt

YOGHURT-GARLIC SAUCE
150g (5½oz) plain low-fat yoghurt
1 small garlic clove, crushed
½ tsp paprika

1 Cut the potatoes and sweet potatoes into small bite-sized chunks. Drop into a pan of boiling water, bring back to the boil and boil for 2 minutes. Add the leeks and cook for a further 1 minute. Drain well.

2 Heat the oil in a large non-stick frying pan and add the leeks and potatoes. Cook over a moderate heat, stirring frequently, for 3–4 minutes or until beginning to brown.

3 Add the chicken, sweetcorn, sun-dried tomatoes, paprika and salt to taste, and mix thoroughly. Continue cooking for 3–5 minutes, pressing down well to make a cake in the pan, and turning it over in chunks, until brown and crispy on both sides.

4 For the sauce, put the yoghurt, garlic and paprika in a bowl and stir to mix. Serve portions of hash topped with the yoghurt sauce.

NUTRITION PER SERVING:
kcal 460, **protein** 23g, **fat** 18g (of which saturated fat 3g), **carbohydrate** 56g (of which sugars 16g), **fibre** 6g

Chicken with apricots and cumin

Fresh apricots and fennel make good partners for chicken thighs, when spiced up with cumin.

Serves 4

2 tbsp sunflower oil
8 chicken thighs, about 450g (1lb) in total
1 onion, sliced
2 garlic cloves, chopped
2 tsp ground cumin
2 tsp ground coriander
300ml (10fl oz) chicken stock
3 carrots, halved crossways, then each half cut into
      6–8 thick fingers
1 bulb of fennel, halved lengthways, then cut
      crossways into slices
300g (10½oz) ripe but firm apricots,
      stoned and quartered
salt and pepper
chopped fennel leaves or herb fennel to garnish

1 Heat the oil in a large flameproof casserole and fry the chicken thighs for 5–10 minutes, turning occasionally, until golden brown all over. Remove from the pan. Add the onion and garlic to the casserole and fry for 5 minutes or until soft and golden.

2 Stir in all the spices and fry for 1 minute, then add the stock. Return the chicken to the casserole together with the carrots and fennel. Bring to the boil. Stir well, then cover and simmer gently for 30 minutes or until the chicken is tender. Remove the lid. If there is too much liquid, boil to reduce it slightly.

3 Add the apricots to the casserole and stir gently to mix. Simmer over a low heat for a further 5 minutes.

NUTRITION PER SERVING:
kcal 370, **protein** 26g, **fat** 24g (of which saturated fat 6g), **carbohydrate** 12g (of which sugars 11g), **fibre** 4g

Chicken livers sautéed with sage

The addition of a few well-chosen flavours, like the sage and balsamic vinegar used here, transform chicken livers into something rather special.

Serves 4

8 rounds French bread
2 tbsp extra virgin olive oil
15g (½oz) butter
1 small red onion, finely chopped
2 garlic cloves, chopped
400g (14oz) chicken livers
225g (8oz) small chestnut or button mushrooms, quartered
3 tbsp balsamic vinegar
2 tbsp shredded fresh sage
salt and pepper
small sprigs of fresh sage to garnish

1 Preheat the oven to 180°C (350°F, gas mark 4). Arrange the French bread on a baking tray. Using 1 tablespoon of the oil, lightly brush the slices of bread on the top side, then bake for 10 minutes or until golden brown.

2 Meanwhile, heat the remaining 1 tbsp of oil with the butter in a heavy-based frying pan. Add the onion and garlic, and sauté over a moderately high heat for 2–3 minutes or until softened.

3 Add the chicken livers and mushrooms, and cook, stirring constantly, to brown on all sides. As they cook, break up any large livers into bite-sized pieces, using the side of the spatula.

4 Add the balsamic vinegar, shredded sage and seasoning to taste. Reduce the heat a little and continue cooking for 5–10 minutes or until the livers are just cooked through.

5 Serve the chicken livers on top of the baked French bread rounds, garnished with sprigs of fresh sage.

NUTRITION PER SERVING:
kcal 315, **protein** 24g, **fat** 12.5g (of which saturated fat 4g), **carbohydrate** 29g (of which sugars 2g), **fibre** 1.5g

1 Put the turkey steaks between sheets of cling film and pound them to flatten to about 5mm (¼in) thickness. Mix the flour with some salt and pepper, and use to coat the escalopes, shaking off the excess.

2 Heat the oil and butter in a large frying pan. Add the turkey escalopes, in one layer, and fry for 2–3 minutes on each side. Transfer the turkey to a plate and keep warm.

3 Add the onion to the pan and soften gently for 2–3 minutes. Add the mushrooms and cook for a further 1 minute or until softened.

4 Stir in the Madeira and allow to bubble for about 2 minutes, then stir in the mustard, oregano and stock. Return the escalopes to the pan and simmer gently for 3–4 minutes.

5 Using a draining spoon, spoon the turkey and mushrooms onto a warm serving platter. Stir the crème fraîche into the sauce and warm through, then check the seasoning. Pour the sauce over the turkey, sprinkle with parsley and serve.

NUTRITION PER SERVING:
kcal 355, **protein** 43g, **fat** 13g (of which saturated fat 6g), **carbohydrate** 13g (of which sugars 2g), **fibre** 1.5g

Turkey escalopes with chestnut mushrooms and Madeira

Simmered with chestnut mushrooms and a creamy Madeira sauce, lean and tender turkey escalopes make a dish that is perfect for easy entertaining.

Serves 4

4 small skinless turkey breast steaks, about 115g (4oz) each
2 tbsp plain flour
1 tbsp sunflower oil
25g (scant 1oz) butter
1 small onion, finely chopped
250g (8½oz) chestnut mushrooms, sliced
4 tbsp Madeira
2 tsp wholegrain mustard
1 tbsp chopped fresh oregano or 1 tsp dried oregano
150ml (5fl oz) chicken or turkey stock
2 tbsp crème fraîche
salt and pepper
2 tbsp chopped parsley to garnish

Braised duck with crunchy Oriental salad

Braising duck breasts in red wine with garlic and ginger, plus a little redcurrant jelly for sweetness, produces moist, delicious meat.

Serves 4

3 boneless duck breasts, about 525g
    (1lb 3oz) in total
120ml (4fl oz) red wine
1 tbsp redcurrant jelly
1 tsp bottled chopped garlic in oil, drained
1 tsp bottled chopped root ginger in oil, drained
2 tbsp extra virgin olive oil
2 tsp balsamic or sherry vinegar
2 oranges
225g (8oz) red cabbage, finely shredded
¼ head of Chinese leaves, shredded
150g (5½oz) beansprouts
85g (3oz) watercress
1 can water chestnuts, about 220g,
    drained and sliced
salt and pepper

1 Preheat the oven to 220°C (425°F, gas mark 7). Remove all the skin and fat from the duck breasts. Place them in an ovenproof dish, pour over the wine and add the redcurrant jelly, garlic and ginger. Place the dish in the oven and cook the duck for 20–25 minutes or until tender.

2 Meanwhile, mix together the oil, vinegar and salt and pepper to taste in a large salad bowl. Cut the peel and pith from the oranges with a sharp knife and, holding each orange over the bowl to catch the juice, cut between the membrane to release the segments. Add them to the bowl. Add the red cabbage, Chinese leaves, beansprouts, watercress (reserving a few sprigs for garnishing) and water chestnuts. Toss well to coat everything with the dressing.

3 Remove the duck from the oven and transfer it to a warm plate. Pour the cooking liquid into a saucepan. Boil the liquid rapidly for 1–2 minutes to reduce slightly, while cutting the duck diagonally across the grain into neat slices. Pour the wine sauce over the salad and toss together. Pile the slices of duck on top, garnish with the reserved sprigs of watercress and serve.

NUTRITION PER SERVING:
kcal 334, **protein** 31g, **fat** 12g (of which saturated fat 3g), **carbohydrate** 20g (of which sugars 16g), **fibre** 4g

Chinese-style omelette

Combining fresh vegetables with bits of turkey or chicken is a great way to stretch a small amount of protein.

Serves 4

100g (3½oz) minced turkey
2 tsp soy sauce
2 tbsp sunflower oil
200g (7oz) Chinese leaves, cut into shreds
100g (3½oz) bean sprouts
30g (1oz) frozen peas, thawed with boiling water
    and drained
125g (4½oz) smoked turkey or chicken, in thin slices
100g (3½oz) canned water chestnuts, sliced
    or quartered
2 spring onions, thinly sliced
2 tbsp chopped fresh coriander
6 eggs
2 garlic cloves, finely chopped
2 tsp finely chopped fresh root ginger
2 tbsp dry sherry
TO FINISH
½ tsp toasted sesame oil
1½ tbsp Chinese bean sauce
1 tbsp balsamic vinegar
few drops of Chinese chilli sauce
fresh coriander leaves to garnish

Salmon with mango salsa

Here is a wonderful mixture of bright colours and zingy flavours, from the peppery salmon topping to the mustardy watercress and fragrant mango salsa with its surprise kick.

Serves 4

4 pieces of salmon fillet, 150g (5½oz) each
4 tsp mixed peppercorns (black, white, green and pink)
675g (1½lb) baby new potatoes, scrubbed, and halved if large
170g (6oz) watercress

MANGO SALSA

1 mango, about 400g (14oz)
3 spring onions, finely chopped
1–2 tsp pink peppercorns in brine, rinsed and roughly chopped
3 tbsp chopped fresh coriander
2 tbsp lime juice
2 tbsp extra virgin olive oil
Tabasco sauce to taste

1 Check the salmon fillets for any tiny pin bones and remove them with tweezers. Roughly crush the peppercorns in a pestle and mortar. Press them into the flesh side of the salmon. Set aside.

1 Preheat the grill to high. Mix the minced turkey with 1 teaspoon of the soy sauce, rubbing together with your fingers. Heat the oil in a heavy frying pan, about 26cm (10½in) in diameter and add the turkey, breaking it up with a spoon, and cook for 3–5 minutes or until it is lightly browned and crumbly. Add the Chinese leaves, bean sprouts, peas, smoked turkey or chicken, water chestnuts, spring onions and coriander, and stir-fry for 2–3 minutes.

2 Lightly beat the eggs with the garlic, ginger, sherry and remaining 1 teaspoon of soy sauce. Add to the pan, pouring the egg mixture evenly over the vegetables and turkey. Cook, stirring gently with a wooden spatula and lifting the sides of the omelette to let the uncooked egg mixture run onto the pan, until the omelette is set on the base. Slide the pan under the grill (keeping the handle away from the heat if it isn't ovenproof) and cook briefly to set the egg on top.

3 Meanwhile, mix together the sesame oil, bean sauce, balsamic vinegar and chilli sauce.

4 Cut the omelette into wedges and serve drizzled with the bean sauce mixture and garnished with a sprig of coriander.

NUTRITION PER SERVING:
kcal 300, **protein** 28g, **fat** 18g (of which saturated fat 4g), **carbohydrate** 5g (of which sugars 3g), **fibre** 1.5g

2 Put the potatoes in a saucepan, cover with boiling water and bring back to the boil. Reduce the heat and simmer for 10–12 minutes or until tender. At the same time, preheat a ridged grill pan.

3 Meanwhile, make the salsa. Stone and peel the mango, and dice the flesh. Put into a large bowl and mix in the spring onions, pink peppercorns, coriander, lime juice, olive oil and a good dash of Tabasco sauce.

4 Brush the grill pan with a little oil if necessary, then put the salmon fillets in, skin side down. Cook over a moderately high heat for 4 minutes. Turn them over and cook for another 4 minutes or until the fish is cooked. Drain the potatoes.

5 Arrange the watercress and new potatoes on 4 serving plates. Place the salmon on top and serve with the mango salsa.

NUTRITION PER SERVING:
kcal 500, **protein** 32g, **fat** 24g (of which saturated fat 5g), **carbohydrate** 41g (of which sugars 16g), **fibre** 5g

Anchovy and sesame-topped tuna

Peppers, tomatoes and a touch of chilli make a zesty topping for quickly prepared tuna steaks, which are baked with a crisp topping.

Serves 4

1½ tbsp extra virgin olive oil
1 large onion, thinly sliced
1 large red pepper, seeded and thinly sliced
1 large yellow pepper, seeded and thinly sliced
2 garlic cloves, finely chopped
1 can chopped tomatoes, about 400g
1 tbsp tomato purée
1 bay leaf
½ tsp chilli purée
2 large tuna steaks, 2cm (¾in) thick, 550g (1¼lb)
Anchovy and sesame topping
55g (2oz) fresh wholemeal breadcrumbs
1 garlic clove
4 anchovy fillets, drained
10g (¼oz) parsley
2 tbsp sesame seeds
2 tsp extra virgin olive oil
salt and pepper

1 Preheat the oven to 200°C (400°F, gas mark 6). Heat the oil in a frying pan or wide saucepan over a moderate heat and add the onion, peppers and garlic. Cover and cook, stirring frequently, for 3–4 minutes or until the onion has softened. Stir in the tomatoes and their juice, the tomato purée, bay leaf and chilli purée. Cover again and cook, stirring frequently, for about 7 minutes or until the peppers are just tender.

2 Meanwhile, make the topping. Combine all the ingredients in a blender or food processor and process until finely chopped. Alternatively, chop together the breadcrumbs, garlic, anchovies and parsley, put in a bowl and mix in the sesame seeds and oil with a fork until well combined.

3 Turn the pepper mixture into an ovenproof dish large enough to hold the fish in one layer. Season the tuna steaks and cut each one in half. Lay the four pieces in the dish and spoon over the topping to cover them evenly. Bake for 10 minutes or until the fish is just cooked. It will still be a little pink in the centre. If you prefer tuna more well done, cook for 1–2 minutes longer. Serve immediately.

NUTRITION PER SERVING:
kcal 384, **protein** 39g, **fat** 17g (of which saturated fat 3g), **carbohydrate** 21g (of which sugars 13g), **fibre** 5g

Chinese-style steamed plaice rolls

Here rolled up plaice fillets, flavoured with oyster sauce, ginger and spring onions, are set on a bed of the sea vegetable samphire and then steamed.

Serves 4

340g (12oz) mixed long-grain and wild rice
4 plaice fillets, about 600g (1lb 5oz) in total, skinned
2 tbsp oyster sauce
½ tsp caster sugar
3 garlic cloves, finely chopped
1 tsp finely chopped fresh root ginger
3 spring onions, thinly sliced
100g (3½oz) fresh samphire
1 carrot, shaved into strips using a vegetable peeler
1 tsp toasted sesame oil
1 tbsp chopped fresh coriander
sprigs of fresh coriander to garnish

1 Add the rice to a large saucepan of cold water and bring to the boil. Reduce the heat and simmer for about 15 minutes, or cook according to the packet instructions, until tender. Drain well.

2 While the rice is cooking, cut the fish fillets in half lengthways. Arrange the strips, skinned side upper-most, on a plate and spread over the oyster sauce. Sprinkle with the sugar, half of the garlic, half of the ginger and half of the spring onions. Roll up strips.

3 Place the samphire in a steamer and arrange the fish rolls on top. Sprinkle with the remaining chopped garlic and ginger, and add the carrot shavings. Cover and steam over a high heat for 5–6 minutes or until the fish will flake easily and the samphire is just tender.

4 Arrange the samphire and plaice rolls on plates with the carrot shavings. Drizzle with the sesame oil and sprinkle with the remaining spring onions and the chopped coriander. Garnish the rice with coriander sprigs, and serve.

NUTRITION PER SERVING:
kcal 455, **protein** 32g, **fat** 4g (of which saturated fat 0.5g), **carbohydrate** 78g (of which sugars 3g), **fibre** 1g

Malay-style braised fish

Gentle braising is an excellent cooking method for fish, keeping it moist and succulent. Spiced and simmered in coconut milk, the fish here is delicious with plain noodles or rice.

Serves 4

1 tbsp sunflower oil
4 spring onions, chopped
1 red chilli, seeded and thinly sliced
2 celery sticks, thinly sliced
1 red pepper, seeded and thinly sliced
1 garlic clove, crushed
½ tsp fennel seeds
2 tsp ground coriander
½ tsp ground cumin
¼ tsp turmeric
1 can chopped tomatoes, about 230g
120ml (4fl oz) coconut milk
300ml (10fl oz) fish stock, bought chilled or made
    with a stock cube
2 tbsp fish sauce or light soy sauce
1 can sliced bamboo shoots, about 220g, drained
675g (1½lb) thick skinless white fish fillet, such as cod,
    hake, haddock or hoki, cut into chunks
16 raw tiger prawns, peeled
juice of ½ lime
TO GARNISH
2 spring onions, chopped
1 tbsp chopped fresh coriander

1 Heat the oil in a large frying pan. Add the spring onions, chilli, celery and red pepper, and fry, stirring constantly, for 5 minutes or until the vegetables are slightly softened.

2 Stir in the garlic, fennel seeds, coriander, cumin and turmeric and cook for 1 minute. Add the tomatoes with their juice, the coconut milk, stock and fish sauce or soy sauce. Bring to the boil, then reduce the heat and cover the pan. Simmer for 5 minutes.

3 Stir in the bamboo shoots, white fish and prawns. Cover the pan again and simmer for 5–7 minutes or until the pieces of fish are just cooked and the prawns have turned pink. Stir in the lime juice.

4 Serve the braised fish at once, garnished with a sprinkle of chopped spring onions and fresh coriander.

NUTRITION PER SERVING:
kcal 330, **protein** 47g, **fat** 10g (of which saturated fat 5g), **carbohydrate** 7g (of which sugars 6 g), **fibre** 2.5g

Stir-fried scallops and prawns

For a fast and delicious treat, this Oriental seafood stir-fry is hard to beat. It requires very little oil and the seaweed and vegetables add lots of flavour and texture.

Serves 4

juice of 1 lemon or 1 lime
2 tsp clear honey
2 tbsp light soy sauce
4 medium-sized scallops,
    about 200g (7oz) in total, quartered
24 peeled raw tiger prawns,
    about 170g (6oz) in total
10g (¼oz) dried wakame seaweed
340g (12oz) fine Chinese egg noodles
1 tbsp stir-fry oil, or 2 tsp sunflower oil mixed with
    1 tsp toasted sesame oil
300g (10½oz) bean sprouts
150g (5½oz) pak choi, shredded
1½ tbsp pickled ginger

1 Mix together the lemon or lime juice, honey and 1 tablespoon of the soy sauce. Pour this marinade over the scallops and prawns and set aside to marinate for about 5 minutes.

2 Meanwhile, place the wakame in a bowl, cover with 300ml (10fl oz) cold water and leave for 8–10 minutes to rehydrate. Place the noodles in a large mixing bowl and pour in enough boiling water to cover them generously. Leave to soak for 4 minutes, or according to packet instructions, until tender. Drain when they are ready.

3 Drain the scallops and prawns, reserving the marinade, and pat dry with kitchen paper. Heat a wok or heavy-based frying pan until very hot, then add the oil and swirl to coat the wok or pan. Add the scallops and prawns and stir-fry for 2–3 minutes or until the prawns have turned pink and the scallops are opaque. Remove the scallops and prawns from the wok and set aside.

4 Add the bean sprouts, pak choy, reserved marinade, remaining tablespoon soy sauce and pickled ginger and stir-fry for 1–2 minutes.

5 Return the scallops and prawns to the wok with the well-drained wakame and stir-fry for 1 minute or until just heated through. Serve the stir-fry with the egg noodles.

NUTRITION PER SERVING:
kcal 492, **protein** 33g, **fat** 11g (of which saturated fat 3g), **carbohydrate** 70g (of which sugars 7g), **fibre** 5g

Classic grilled Dover sole

Few classy meals could be quicker and simpler. Dover sole – usually sold skinned and cleaned – is a real treat and its superb taste can be fully appreciated in this dish.

Serves 4

4 small Dover sole, about 225g (8oz) each
750g (1lb 10oz) baby new potatoes, scrubbed
1 large sprig of fresh mint
40g (1¼oz) unsalted butter
finely grated zest and juice of 1 large lemon
450g (1lb) baby leaf spinach
freshly grated nutmeg (optional)
salt and pepper
sprigs of fresh mint to garnish
lemon wedges to serve

1 Preheat the grill to high. Cut a piece of foil to fit the grill pan and lay the fish on top (depending on the size of the grill, you may have to cook the sole in 2 batches).

2 Put the potatoes in a saucepan, cover with boiling water and add the sprig of mint. Cook for about 15 minutes or until the potatoes are just tender.

3 Meanwhile, melt the butter in a small saucepan and mix in the lemon zest and juice. Season with salt and pepper. Brush the lemon butter over the fish and grill for 5–6 minutes or until the flesh close to the bone flakes easily when pierced with a knife. Carefully turn the fish over, brush again with the lemon butter and grill for a further 5–6 minutes.

4 While the fish is cooking, steam the spinach for 2–3 minutes or until just wilted. Season with salt, pepper and nutmeg to taste.

5 Drain the potatoes and put into a warmed serving dish. Add plenty of black pepper, toss gently and garnish with mint sprigs. Transfer the sole to warmed dinner plates and spoon over any cooking juices from the grill pan. Add lemon wedges and serve, with the potatoes and spinach.

NUTRITION PER SERVING:
kcal 412, **protein** 43g, **fat** 13g (of which saturated fat 6g), **carbohydrate** 32g (of which sugars 4g), **fibre** 4g

VEGETABLES

Speedy two-bean chilli

This non-meat chilli combines two varieties of beans with sweetcorn in a rich tomato sauce flavoured with herbs and fresh chilli.

Serves 4

2 tbsp extra virgin olive oil
1 large onion, halved and sliced
1 fresh red chilli, seeded and chopped
1 can chopped tomatoes, about 400g
1 tbsp chilli sauce
2 tbsp tomato ketchup
600ml (1 pint) hot vegetable stock
1 tbsp chopped parsley
1 tbsp chopped fresh oregano
1 can red kidney beans, about 400g,
     drained and rinsed
1 can cannellini beans, about 400g,
     drained and rinsed
200g (7oz) frozen sweetcorn
salt and pepper
TO SERVE
150g (5½oz) fromage frais
2 tbsp snipped fresh chives
fresh oregano leaves to garnish

1 Heat the oil in a large frying pan. Add the onion and chilli, and fry over a moderate heat for 5 minutes, stirring occasionally, until the onion is lightly browned.

2 Stir in the tomatoes with their juice, the chilli sauce, ketchup, stock, parsley and oregano, with seasoning to taste. Bring to the boil, then reduce the heat and simmer for 10 minutes, stirring occasionally.

3 Add the kidney and cannellini beans and the sweetcorn. Simmer for a further 10 minutes.

4 Meanwhile, mix the fromage frais with the snipped chives. Taste the chilli for seasoning and adjust if necessary. Serve the chilli sprinkled with the oregano leaves and offer the fromage frais mixture separately.

NUTRITION PER SERVING:
kcal 385, **protein** 20g, **fat** 10g (of which saturated fat 3g), **carbohydrate** 56g (of which sugars 16g), **fibre** 15g

Penne primavera

This classic Italian dish is intended to make the most of freshly picked young spring produce.

Serves 4

340g (12oz) penne or other pasta shapes
170g (6oz) young asparagus
170g (6oz) green beans, trimmed and cut into 3cm
     (1¼in) lengths
170g (6oz) shelled fresh peas
1 tbsp extra virgin olive oil
1 onion, chopped
1 garlic clove, chopped
85g (3oz) pancetta, chopped
115g (4oz) button mushrooms, chopped
1 tbsp plain flour
240ml (8fl oz) dry white wine
4 tbsp single cream
2 tbsp chopped mixed fresh herbs,
     such as parsley and thyme
salt and pepper

1 Cook the pasta in boiling water for 10–12 minutes, or according to the packet instructions, until al dente. Drain well.

2 While the pasta is cooking, cut the asparagus into 3.5cm (1½in) lengths, keeping the tips separate. Drop the pieces of asparagus stalk, the green beans and peas into a saucepan of boiling water. Bring back to the boil and cook for 5 minutes. Add the asparagus tips and cook for a further 2 minutes. Drain thoroughly.

3 Heat the oil in a saucepan. Add the onion and cook for 3–4 minutes or until softened. Add the garlic, pancetta and mushrooms, and continue to cook, stirring occasionally, for a further 2 minutes.

4 Stir in the flour, then gradually pour in the wine and bring to the boil, stirring. Simmer until the sauce is thickened. Stir in the cream and herbs with seasoning to taste. Add the vegetables to sauce and heat gently for 1–2 minutes, without boiling.

5 Divide the pasta among 4 serving bowls and spoon the sauce over the top. Serve immediately.

NUTRITION PER SERVING:
kcal 560, **protein** 20g, **fat** 17g (of which saturated fat 6g), carbohydrate 77g (of which sugars 5.5g), **fibre** 7g

Eggs with spicy peas and lentils

This simple, satisfying dish provides a wealth of vital vitamins and minerals and the right balance of essential protein and fibre.

Serves 4

1 tbsp sunflower oil
1 onion, chopped
2 garlic cloves, sliced
2.5cm (1in) piece of fresh root ginger,
    peeled and finely chopped
2 tbsp garam masala
1 tbsp tomato purée
450g (1lb) broccoli or cauliflower
    cut into small florets
450ml (15fl oz) vegetable stock
55g (2oz) red lentils, rinsed
6 eggs
225g (8oz) frozen peas
3 tbsp chopped fresh coriander
coarsely grated zest of 1 lime (optional)
salt and pepper
TO GARNISH
lime wedges
sprigs of fresh coriander

1 Heat the oil in a saucepan and fry the onion, garlic and ginger for 3 minutes. Stir in the garam masala and tomato purée. Cook for 1 minute, then add the broccoli or cauliflower and seasoning to taste. Pour in the stock. Bring to the boil, then add the lentils. Cover the pan, reduce the heat and simmer for 15 minutes, stirring occasionally.

2 Meanwhile, put the eggs in a pan of cold water, bring just to the boil and boil gently for 6 minutes. Drain and rinse them under cold water, gently cracking the shells. Peel off the shells, taking care as the eggs will not be completely hard.

3 Add the eggs, whole, and the peas to the lentil mixture and stir gently. Bring back to simmering point, then cover the pan again and cook for about 5 minutes. By this time the peas should be cooked and the spicy sauce thickened with the softened lentils.

4 Remove the eggs with a spoon and cut them in half. Divide the spicy vegetable mixture among 4 plates. Mix the chopped coriander with the grated lime zest, if using, and sprinkle over the vegetables. Top each plate with 3 egg halves. Garnish with lime wedges and sprigs of coriander, and serve immediately.

NUTRITION PER SERVING:
kcal 310, **protein** 24g, **fat** 15g (of which saturated fat 3g), carbohydrate 20g (of which sugars 6g), **fibre** 6g

Moroccan-style pumpkin and butter beans

Middle Eastern spices flavour this casserole, which is full of vegetables and other fibre-rich ingredients

Serves 4

600ml (1 pint) boiling water
1 vegetable stock cube, crumbled, or 2 tsp vegetable
     bouillon powder or paste
½ tsp turmeric
½ tsp ground coriander
pinch of ground cumin
200g (7oz) leeks, halved lengthways and sliced
225g (8oz) parsnips, cut into 1cm (½in) cubes
600g (1lb 5oz) piece of pumpkin, peeled, seeded and
     cut into 1cm (½in) cubes
400g (14oz) yellow or green courgettes, sliced
1 red pepper, seeded and chopped
100g (3½oz) ready-to-eat dried apricots, chopped
1 can butter beans, about 400g, drained
pinch of crushed dried chillies, or to taste (optional)
salt and pepper
TO GARNISH
30g (1oz) pine nuts
chopped parsley or fresh coriander

1 Pour the boiling water into a flameproof casserole. Stir in the stock cube, powder or paste, the turmeric, ground coriander and cumin. Add the leeks and parsnips and bring to the boil. Reduce the heat to moderate, cover the pan and simmer the vegetables for 5 minutes.

2 Add the pumpkin, courgettes and red pepper to the pan, then bring the stock back to the boil. Stir in the apricots, butter beans and chillis, if using, adding more to taste for a spicier result. Season with salt and pepper. Reduce the heat, cover the pan and simmer for 10 minutes or until all the vegetables are tender.

3 Meanwhile, toast the pine nuts in a non-stick frying pan over a moderate heat, stirring constantly, until just beginning to brown and giving off their nutty aroma. Tip the pine nuts onto a board and chop them coarsely.

4 Taste the casserole and adjust the seasoning, if necessary, then ladle it into 4 deep bowls. Sprinkle with the chopped pine nuts and parsley or fresh coriander and serve.

NUTRITION PER SERVING:
kcal 250, **protein** 12g, **fat** 7g (of which saturated fat 1g), carbohydrate 35g (of which sugars 21g), **fibre** 11g

Chakchouka

This dish is popular all over the Mediterranean and there are many variations. Basically it is a tomato-based vegetable stew, like a ratatouille, with eggs poached right in the mixture.

Serves 2

1 tbsp extra virgin olive oil
1 small onion, roughly chopped
2 garlic cloves, crushed
1 red pepper, seeded and thinly sliced
1 green pepper, seeded and thinly sliced
400g (14oz) large ripe tomatoes, roughly chopped
2 tbsp tomato purée
¼ tsp crushed dried chillies (optional)
1 tsp ground cumin
pinch of sugar
4 eggs
salt
sprigs of fresh flat-leaf parsley to garnish

1 Heat the oil in a deep, heavy-based frying pan. Add the onion, garlic, and red and green peppers, and cook gently for 5 minutes or until softened.

2 Stir in the tomatoes, tomato purée, chillies, if using, cumin, sugar, and salt to taste. Cover and cook gently for about 5 minutes or until the mixture is thick and well combined.

3 Make 4 hollows in the vegetable mixture using the back of a wooden spoon, then break an egg into each hollow. Cover the pan again and cook gently for 6–8 minutes or until the eggs are just set.

4 Serve immediately, straight from the pan, garnishing each plate with sprigs of parsley.

NUTRITION PER SERVING:
kcal 321, **protein** 19g, **fat** 20g (of which saturated fat 5g), carbohydrate 18g (of which sugars 17g), **fibre** 6g

PASTA, BEANS & GRAINS

Pasta with fresh sage, rocket and feta cheese

The pasta is topped with salty tasting feta cheese, which goes well with the pancetta, the Italian bacon, chickpeas and tomato in the sauce.

Serves 4

400g (14oz) tubular pasta shapes, such as casarecce (slim rolls), penne or macaroni
50g (1¾oz) pancetta, finely chopped
2 garlic cloves, finely chopped (optional)
2 shallots, finely chopped
8 fresh sage leaves, shredded
1 can chickpeas, about 400g, drained
1 can chopped tomatoes, about 400g
pinch of sugar
50g (1¾oz) rocket, stalks removed if preferred
100g (3½oz) feta cheese, crumbled
pepper

1 Cook the pasta in boiling water for 10–12 minutes, or according to the packet instructions, until al dente. Drain well.

2 While the pasta is cooking, heat a teaspoon of oil in a large frying pan over a moderately high heat. Add the pancetta, garlic, shallots and sage, and cook, stirring frequently, for 6–8 minutes or until the pancetta is golden brown and the shallots are soft.

3 Add the chickpeas, tomatoes with their juice and the sugar, and bring to the boil. Reduce the heat and simmer for 10 minutes or until the sauce has thickened slightly. Season with pepper (there is no need for salt as feta cheese is quite salty).

4 Stir in the pasta until it is well coated with the sauce ingredients. Add the rocket and stir in lightly, then sprinkle with the feta cheese and serve.

NUTRITION PER SERVING:
kcal 600, **protein** 26g, **fat** 15g (of which saturated fat 6g), **carbohydrate** 96g (of which sugars 6.5g), **fibre** 8g

Stir-fried beef with fine noodles

Tangy tamarind and lemongrass infuse a Thai-inspired sauce for tender strips of beef and fine rice noodles. Chilli brings a little heat.

Serves 2

1 tsp tamarind paste
3 tbsp boiling water
2 tbsp soy sauce
2 tsp toasted sesame oil
1 tbsp rice wine (sake or mirin) or sherry
100g (3½oz) fine rice noodles, such as vermicelli
1 tbsp sunflower oil
225g (8oz) lean rump steak, cut into strips
85g (3oz) onion, cut into wedges
2 tsp chopped lemongrass
1 fresh red chilli, seeded and chopped
2 large garlic cloves, crushed
85g (3oz) mange-tout, halved diagonally
6 baby sweetcorn, sliced
100g (3½oz) fresh shiitake or chestnut mushrooms, sliced
SERVE WITH SOY SAUCE

1 In a small bowl, combine the tamarind paste and boiling water and leave to soak for 10 minutes, stirring frequently to break down the paste. Mix the resulting tamarind liquid with the soy sauce, sesame oil and rice wine or sherry.

2 While the tamarind is soaking, soak the rice noodles in boiling water for 4 minutes, or according to the packet instructions. Then drain, rinse under cold running water and set aside to drain thoroughly.

3 Heat the sunflower oil in a wok or very large frying pan and stir-fry the beef over a high heat for about 3 minutes or until cooked. Use a draining spoon to remove the beef from the wok and set it aside.

4 Add the onion, lemongrass, chilli and garlic to the wok and stir-fry over a high heat for 1 minute. Add the mange-tout, sweetcorn and mushrooms, and continue stir-frying for 2 minutes.

5 Return the beef to the wok. Add the tamarind liquid and the noodles and stir for about 1 minute to heat through. Serve immediately, offering soy sauce for extra seasoning as required.

NUTRITION PER SERVING:
kcal 460, **protein** 30g, **fat** 15g (of which saturated fat 3g), **carbohydrate** 49g (of which sugars 6.5g), **fibre** 3g

Pasta with potato, beans and pesto

This is a traditional Ligurian dish that is usually made with potatoes, green beans and baby broad beans. Here, broccoli and courgettes boost the green vegetable content.

Serves 4

600g (1lb 5oz) small new potatoes, halved
 or quartered
225g (8oz) broccoli, cut into small florets
75g (2½oz) shelled broad beans, skinned if
 preferred, 340–400g (12–14oz) in pods
170g (6oz) fine green beans, topped and tailed
2 courgettes, cut into bite-sized chunks
300g (10½oz) tubular or hollow pasta shapes, such as
 casarecce (slim rolled lengths), gemelli
 (narrow spirals), orecchiette (little ears) or
 gnocchi (fluted shells)
sprigs of fresh basil to garnish

TOMATO PESTO SAUCE
4–5 garlic cloves, coarsely chopped
2 tbsp pine nuts
100g (3½oz) fresh basil leaves
55g (2oz) Parmesan cheese, freshly grated
4 tbsp extra virgin olive oil
2 ripe tomatoes, diced
salt

1 Cook the potatoes in boiling water for about 15 minutes or until they are tender, but not soft. Add the broccoli, broad beans, green beans and courgettes, and simmer all together for a further 5 minutes.

2 Meanwhile, cook the pasta in boiling water for 10–12 minutes, or according to the packet instructions, until al dente.

3 Make the pesto sauce while the vegetables and pasta are cooking. Pound the garlic with a pinch of salt and the pine nuts in a mortar using a pestle. Add the basil and continue pounding until the ingredients form a green paste, then work in the Parmesan cheese and oil. Finally, work in the tomatoes. Alternatively, the pesto can be made in a food processor or blender: put all the ingredients, except the oil, in the container and whiz to a paste, then gradually add the oil through the feed tube with the motor running.

4 Drain the pasta and vegetables and toss both together. Top with the pesto, garnish with sprigs of basil, scattering them over the top, and serve immediately.

NUTRITION PER SERVING:
kcal 660, **protein** 25g, **fat** 24g (of which saturated fat 5.5g), **carbohydrate** 90g (of which sugars 7g), **fibre** 9g

Sun-dried tomato and bean risotto

Moist risotto served with a simple side salad makes a satisfying meal, and the risotto can be endlessly varied – all sorts of vegetables (fresh, frozen, canned or dried) can be used.

Serves 4

1 tbsp extra virgin olive oil
1 large onion, chopped
2 garlic cloves, crushed
300g (10½oz) risotto rice
85g (3oz) sun-dried tomatoes (dry-packed),
    coarsely chopped
240ml (8fl oz) dry white wine
1.2 litres (2 pints) hot vegetable stock,
    preferably home-made
225g (8oz) frozen broad beans
55g (2oz) Parmesan cheese, freshly grated
30g (1oz) pine nuts
salt and pepper
12 large fresh basil leaves, freshly shredded,
    to garnish

1 Heat the oil in a large saucepan. Add the onion and garlic and fry over a moderate heat for 5 minutes, stirring frequently, until the onion softens and begins to colour.

2 Stir in the rice and sun-dried tomatoes, making sure the grains are coated in the oil, then pour in the wine. Bring to the boil, stirring occasionally.

3 Pour in half the hot stock and bring back to the boil, then reduce the heat and simmer, stirring frequently, for 10 minutes. Add the broad beans and half the remaining hot stock. Bring back to the boil again, then continue to simmer for about 10 minutes, adding the remaining stock in one or two stages as the rice absorbs the liquid.

4 The risotto is ready when the rice is tender but the grains are still whole, and the broad beans are cooked. It should be moist and creamy.

5 Add the Parmesan cheese and pine nuts with seasoning to taste and stir to mix. Serve at once, sprinkled with shredded basil.

NUTRITION PER SERVING:
kcal 610, **protein** 17g, **fat** 25g (of which saturated fat 5g), **carbohydrate** 67g (of which sugars 5g), **fibre** 4g

Couscous and flageolet niçoise

Couscous is mixed with pale green flageolet beans, then tossed with fresh green beans, tomatoes and cucumber in a piquant dressing made with sun-dried tomatoes.

Serves 4

250g (8½ oz) couscous
400ml (14fl oz) boiling water
1 tbsp extra virgin olive oil
1 tsp dried herbes de Provence
140g (5oz) green beans
½ cucumber
2 cans flageolet beans, about 410g each,
    drained and rinsed
1 small red onion, finely chopped
200g (7oz) cherry tomatoes, cut in half
2 hard-boiled eggs, cut into quarters
8 anchovy fillets, drained and halved lengthways
75g (2½ oz) black olives
SUN-DRIED TOMATO DRESSING
juice of 1 large lemon
2 tbsp extra virgin olive oil
1 tbsp finely chopped sun-dried tomatoes
    packed in oil
salt and pepper

1 First make the dressing. Combine the lemon juice, oil, sun-dried tomatoes and pepper to taste in a screwtop jar, cover and shake well to mix.

2 Put the couscous into a large mixing bowl and pour over the boiling water. Stir in the olive oil and dried herbs, then cover and leave for 5 minutes or until the couscous has absorbed all the water. Uncover, stir to separate the grains. Leave to cool.

3 Meanwhile, steam the green beans for 3–4 minutes or until tender but still crisp. Drain, then refresh under cold running water. Cut in half.

4 Cut the cucumber into thick slices, then cut each slice into 4 wedges. Stir the cucumber into the couscous, together with the flageolet beans, green beans, onion and tomatoes. Add the dressing and toss gently until well mixed. Taste and add salt and pepper, if necessary (remember that the anchovies and olives will be salty).

5 Transfer the salad to a serving bowl. Garnish with the hard-boiled egg quarters, anchovies and black olives, and serve.

NUTRITION PER SERVING:
kcal 424, **protein** 16g, **fat** 18g (of which saturated fat 3g), **carbohydrate** 51g (of which sugars 7g), **fibre** 7g

DESSERTS

Cherry brandy clafoutis

Clafoutis is a classic French dessert in which fruit is baked in a sweetened batter.

Serves 4

2 cans stoned cherries in syrup, about 425g each
2 tbsp brandy
75g (2½oz) plain flour
55g (2oz) light muscovado sugar
250ml (8½fl oz) semi-skimmed milk
3 eggs
1 tsp pure vanilla extract
icing sugar to dust (optional)

1 Preheat the oven to 200°C (400°F, gas mark 6). Drain the cherries, then tip them onto kitchen paper and pat dry.

2 Divide the cherries equally among four 300ml (10fl oz) individual flan dishes, or other ovenproof dishes, spreading them in an even layer. Drizzle the brandy over the cherries. Set aside.

3 Sift the flour into a bowl and add the sugar. In a jug, beat the milk and eggs with the vanilla extract, then whisk into the flour mixture to make a smooth batter. Alternatively, combine the ingredients in a food processor and process until smooth.

4 Pour the batter slowly over the fruit. Bake for 20 minutes or until lightly set and pale golden. Dust with icing sugar, if you like, and serve warm.

NUTRITION PER SERVING:
kcal 380, **protein** 11g, **fat** 6g (of which saturated fat 2g), **carbohydrate** 74g (of which sugars 59g), **fibre** 2g

Summer fruit fool

A quick pudding to rustle up at a moment's notice, this can be made with almost any fruit in season.

Serves 4

300g (10½oz) mixed soft fruit, such as raspberries, blackberries, blueberries or currants
55g (2oz) caster sugar
150ml (5fl oz) whipping cream
grated zest of ½ orange
150g (5½oz) plain low-fat bio yoghurt
finely shredded orange zest to decorate (optional)

1 Reserve about 55g (2oz) of the mixed fruit for decoration. Put the remaining mixed fruit in a saucepan with 2 tablespoons water. Bring just to the boil, then reduce the heat and cook gently for 5 minutes or until soft and very juicy. Stir in the sugar.

2 Remove from the heat and leave to cool slightly. Pour into a food processor or blender and purée. Press the purée through a sieve to remove all the pips. Alternatively, just press the fruit through a sieve to purée it. Set aside to cool completely.

3 Whip the cream with the grated orange zest until thick. Add the yoghurt and lightly whip into the cream, then mix in the cooled fruit purée.

4 Spoon into 4 dessert dishes or goblets. Chill well before serving, decorated with the reserved berries and orange zest, if using.

NUTRITION PER SERVING:
kcal 230, **protein** 3g, **fat** 15g (of which saturated fat 9g), **carbohydrate** 22g (of which sugars 22g), **fibre** 2g

Strawberry shortcake

Based on a quick, light scone mixture and filled with Greek-style yoghurt, whipped cream and juicy fresh strawberries, this shortcake is irresistable.

Serves 8

250g (8½oz) self-raising flour
1 tsp baking powder
75g (2½oz) unsalted butter, cut into small pieces
3 tbsp caster sugar
1 egg, beaten
4 tbsp semi-skimmed milk
½ tsp pure vanilla extract
1 tsp icing sugar

STRAWBERRY FILLING
340g (12oz) strawberries
90ml (3fl oz) whipping cream
85g (3oz) Greek-style yoghurt

1 Preheat the oven to 220°C (425°F, gas mark 7). Sift the flour and baking powder into a bowl. Rub in the butter with your fingertips until the mixture resembles fine breadcrumbs. Stir in the caster sugar and make a well for the centre.

2 Mix together the egg, milk and vanilla extract, and pour into the dry ingredients. Gradually stir the dry ingredients into the liquid, then bring the mixture together with your hand to form a soft dough. Gently pat the dough into a smooth ball and turn it out onto a floured surface.

3 Roll out the dough into a 19cm (7½in) round. Transfer it to a greased baking sheet and bake for 10–15 minutes or until well risen, firm and browned on top. Slide the shortcake onto a wire rack and leave to cool.

Serves 8

45g (1½oz) sultanas
3 tbsp brandy
3 tbsp semolina
340g (12oz) ricotta cheese
3 large egg yolks
85g (3oz) caster sugar
3 tbsp lemon juice
1½ tsp pure vanilla extract
finely grated zest of 2 large lemons

TOPPING: 2 oranges, 2 satsumas, 1 lemon
4 tbsp lemon jelly marmalade

1 Place the sulatanas in a small bowl, add the brandy and leave to soak for at least 30 minutes or until most of the brandy has been absorbed.

2 Preheat the oven to 180°C (350°F, gas mark 4). Line the bottom of a non-stick, 20cm (8in) loose-bottomed sandwich tin with buttered baking parchment. Lightly butter the side of the tin. Sprinkle 1 tablespoon of the semolina into the tin, turn and tilt the tin to coat the bottom and sides, then tap out any excess semolina. Set the tin aside.

3 Put the ricotta cheese into a fine sieve and press it through into a mixing bowl. Beat in the egg yolks, sugar, lemon juice, vanilla extract and remaining semolina. Stir in the lemon zest and the sultanas with any remaining brandy.

4 Spoon the mixture into the prepared tin and smooth the surface. Bake for 35–40 minutes or until the top is browned and the sides are shrinking from the tin. Leave to cool in the switched off oven for 2–3 hours with the door ajar.

5 For topping, peel the oranges, satsumas and lemon, removing all the white pith, then cut out the segments from between the membranes. Warm the marmalade very gently in a small saucepan until it has melted.

6 Carefully remove the cooled cheesecake from the tin and set on a serving platter. Brush with a layer of the melted marmalade. Arrange the citrus segments on top and glaze with the rest of the marmalade. Leave to set before serving.

NUTRITION PER SERVING:
kcal 220, **protein** 7g, **fat** 7g (of which saturated fat 4g),
carbohydrate 32g (of which sugars 26g), **fibre** 1g

4 Using a large serrated knife, slice the shortcake horizontally in half. With a large fish slice, lift the top layer off and place it on a board. Cut into 8 equal wedges, leaving them in place. Place the bottom layer on a serving plate.

5 For the filling, reserve 8 whole strawberries, then hull and thickly slice the remainder. Whip the cream until it forms soft peaks. Stir the yoghurt until smooth, then gently fold into the cream until evenly blended.

6 Spread the cream mixture thickly over the bottom shortcake layer and cover with the sliced strawberries, pressing them into the cream.

7 Sift the icing sugar over the top of the shortcake wedges. Carefully put the wedges into place on top of the shortcake. Slice each reserved strawberry lengthways, leaving the slices attached at the stalk end, then open the slices slightly to fan them out. Place a strawberry fan on each wedge of shortcake. Eat within a few hours of assembling.

NUTRITION PER SERVING:
kcal 275, **protein** 5g, **fat** 14g (of which saturated fat 8g),
carbohydrate 34g (of which sugars 10g), **fibre** 1g

Sultana lemon cheesecake

Cheesecakes are usually high in fat, but this recipe isn't baked with a butter-rich crust, and it uses lower-fat ricotta cheese rather than rich cream cheese so the fat content is much reduced.

A

abdominal fat 44-45

abdominal injections 117, 155, 157

acarbose 77, 144-5, 146, 147

ACE inhibitors 172, 177, 242

acupuncture 206-7

advances in diabetes management

    future 233–5

    for preventing complications 241–44

    recent 10–11, 232

    for restoring pancreatic function 244–47

aerobic exercise 21, 121-5, 130

age

    diabetes risk factor 12

    onset of diabetes 12, 44

AGEs (advanced glycosylation end products) 243

albumin 45, 81, 83-84, 176, 177

alcohol 76, 100, 107, 109-10, 214

alpha-glucosidase inhibitors 146-7

alpha-lipoic acid (ALA) 197

alternative therapies 188-207

amylin 235-6

anger 214-15

antibodies 236, 238

antioxidants 174, 200

anxiety 215-16

appetite control 241-3

apples: apple and blackberry brioches 249

    apple and fennel with blue cheese dressing 253

arterial disease 168-9

aspirin 21, 171-2, 178, 180, 184, 201

atherosclerosis 168-9

attitudes to diabetes 221-2

autonomic neuropathy 182-3

B

bacon and broad bean salad 254-5

banana and mango shake 250

beef: hoisin beef stir-fry 258

    stir-fried beef with fine noodles 274-5

beta-blockers 168

beta cells 37, 38, 39

    amylin production 236

    genetically modified substitutes 238

    islet cell transplants 244-5, 247

    sulphonylureas and 141

    Type 1 diabetes 41

    Type 2 diabetes, 42

bicycling 127

bilberry 196, 200-1

biofeedback 205-6

biotin 203-4

bitter melon 195

blindness 178, 241-2

blood, pricking fingers *see* lancets

blood-glucose meters 19, 52, 66-73, 74-75

blood pressure *see* high blood pressure

blood-sugar levels 10-11

    additional tests 23, 51-2, 80-81

    alcohol and 109

    in children 22

    drugs and 139, 145

    effects of high levels 17-18, 33-34, 166-7

    exercise and 77-79, 80, 114-15, 116-21

    fasting levels 16-17

    fluctuations 34, 39

    food and 75-77, 91, 92

    frequency of tests 63-64

    gestational diabetes 46-48

    Glycaemic Index and 101-2

    goals 62-63

    herbal remedies 193-7

    hyperosmolar syndrome 55, 225

hypoglycaemia 55

illness and 79, 224-5

impaired glucose tolerance 120

insulin and 16-17, 35, 78-79

monitoring 14, 19, 48-52, 58-81

timing injections 151

blueberry and cranberry granola 250

Body Mass Index 46

breakfast 93, 103, 249-50

'burnout' 219-20

C

calcium 99

calories 104-5

carbohydrates 89, 90-93, 101-2, 106, 107

cardiovascular disease: alternative therapies 201-3

exercise and 115

future developments 242-3

heart attack 18, 21, 168, 171, 173, 194, 242

lipid tests 82-83

reducing risks 167-74

salt and 97

cauliflower cheese soup 257

chakchouka 273

cheesecake, sultana lemon 279

cherry brandy clafoutis 277-78

chicken: chicken and sweet potato hash 262

chicken Caesar salad 255-6

chicken with apricots and cumin 262-3

chicken livers sautéed with sage 263-4

children 22, 38-39, 43, 47

chilli, speedy two-bean 271

chiropodists 27

cholesterol 45, 82-83, 92-93, 95, 115, 168, 173

chromium 200, 204

ciabatta with garlic mushrooms 251-2

coma 54-55, 225

combinations: drugs 146-7

insulin 150-3

complications, preventing 164-87

counselling 28-29

couscous and flageolet niçoise 276-7

D

dairy foods 99

dehydration 79, 109, 225-6

dentists 27

depression 212-14, 221

diabetes *see* gestational diabetes; Type 1 diabetes;
Type 2 diabetes

diabetes nurses 24-25

'diabetic' foods 107

diabetologists 24

diagnosis 13-15, 48-52

diet, 20-21, 86-111

alcohol 109-10

carbohydrates 90-93

children's 47

controlling blood-sugar levels 75-77

fats 93-95

fruit and vegetables 96-98

Glycaemic Index 91, 97, 101-2

milk and dairy foods 99

and nerve damage 183-4

nutritional supplements 203-4

portion sizes 105-6

preventing cardiovascular disease 173-4

protein 95-96

and Type 2 diabetes 44

vitamins and minerals 99-100

weight loss 102-5, 107

dieticians 25, 88-89

doctors 23-24, 26, 28

Dolcelatte and pear toasts 252-3

drugs 11, 136-59, 191

ACE inhibitors 172, 177

alpha-glucosidase inhibitors 144-5, 146-7

aspirin 171-2, 178, 180

causing kidney problems 178

combinations 146-7

dosages 147

exercise and 77, 118-19

future developments 232, 236-7, 238

interactions 145, 168

for nerve damage 184

over-the-counter remedies 226

pharmacists 27-28

prandial glucose regulators 145-6, 147

side effects 119, 140

statins 173

thiazolidinediones 143-4, 146, 147, 236-7, 242-3

Type 1 diabetes and 138

Type 2 diabetes 138-9

weight-loss drugs 172

when travelling 227

see also **insulin; metformin; sulphonylureas**

duck braised with crunchy Oriental salad 265

dumbbells 128, 132-3

E

eggs: eggs with spicy peas and lentils 272

scrambled eggs with smoked salmon and dill 249

emergencies 54-55, 173

see also **hyperglycaemia; hypoglycaemia**

emotions, living with diabetes 210-16

environmental triggers 237

epinephrine 35

ethnic groups, risk factors 12, 42, 45-46, 169

exercise 21, 112-35

aerobic exercise 21, 121-5, 130

and blood-sugar levels 77-79, 80, 114-15, 116-21

FIT formula 121-33

full-body workout 132-3

hypoglycaemia 117, 118, 120-1

and impaired glucose tolerance 119-20

personal trainers 28

resistance training 125-9, 130, 131

Type 1 diabetes 117-18

Type 2 diabetes 44, 118-19

when travelling 229

eyes 170, 178-81

alternative therapies 199-201

damage 178-9

blurry vision 36

diabetic retinopathy 160

future developments 241-2

ophthalmologists 180

preventing damage 180-1

symptoms 179-80

tests 26, 180

F

family history, risk factors 12, 40

fasting blood-glucose levels 16-17

fasting plasma glucose (FPG) test 49, 51, 53, 139

fats, in diet 89-90, 93-95, 106

feet 170, 184-7

checking 185-6, 187

chiropodists and podiatrists 27

injuries 185

preventing damage 185-7

tingling 37

ulcers 245-6

fenugreek 194-5

fibre 92-93, 106

fingers, pricking *see* **lancets**

fish and fish oils 95, 174, 200, 266-70

FIT formula, exercise 121-33

fluids 79, 93, 107-9, 119, 225-6

focal neuropathy 182

folic acid 101, 174

food *see* diet

foot problems *see* feet

free radicals 41

fructosamine test 81

fruit 89-90, 96-98, 106-7, 108

future breakthroughs 230-47

G

gamma-linolenic acid (GLA) 198-9, 202-3

garlic 100, 201-2

genetics: future developments 237-38, 239

    and obesity 45-46, 239

    and retinopathy 242

    Type 1 diabetes 40

    Type 2 diabetes 43

gestational diabetes 38, 46-48, 65

ginseng 195-6, 197

glucagon 35, 228, 236

glucose 19, 33, 35, 53-54, 114

    see also blood-sugar levels

Glycaemic Index (GI) 91, 97, 101-2

glycosylated haemoglobin test

    see haemoglobin A1c test

growth hormone 35, 243

gymnema 194, 200

H

haemoglobin A1c (HbA1c) test 52, 80-81, 139

hands, tingling 37

HDL (high-density lipoprotein) 82-83, 95, 115, 143

heart disease *see* cardiovascular disease

heart rate, exercise 122-4

herbal remedies 190, 193-9

high blood pressure: and diabetic complications 169, 177, 180

drugs 168, 172, 177

    reducing 21, 23

    salt and 97, 100, 171

    tests 83

holidays 226-9

hormones 35, 243

    see also insulin

hydrocortisone 35

hyperglycaemia 78, 119, 120

hyperosmolar syndrome 55, 225

hypertension *see* high blood pressure

hypoglycaemia 35

    alcohol and 110

    drugs and 140

    exercise and 117, 118, 120-1

    intensive therapy and 154

    preventing 78-79

    symptoms 55

    treating 55, 76

I

illness, controlling blood-sugar levels 79, 224-6

immune system 36-37, 41, 160-1, 236

impaired glucose tolerance (IGT) 53-54, 119-20, 143, 167

implants, monitoring blood-sugar levels 75

infections 36-37, 223

inhalers 234

injections 38, 117, 151-4, 155-9

insulin 15-17, 78-79, 148-59

    artificial pancreas 246

    combining 150-3

    discovery of 39

    and exercise 77, 117, 118

    functions 35

    future developments 232, 233, 234-5

    gestational diabetes 46-48

    and illness 79

injections 38, 117, 151-4, 155-9

Type 1 diabetes 38, 148, 236

Type 2 diabetes 42, 140, 148, 154-5

types of 148-50

when travelling 227, 228

insulin pens 159

insulin pumps 154, 157-9, 163, 246

insulin resistance 19, 35, 42, 43, 114, 237

intensive therapy 61, 107, 153-4, 155

intermediate-acting insulin 150, 151-4

islet cells, transplants 37, 244-5, 247

J

jet injectors 159

jogging 127

K

ketoacidosis 54-55, 82, 225, 226

ketones 54, 82, 120, 225

kidneys 170, 175-8

alternative therapies 201-3

damage 176-7

future developments 243

preventing complications 177-8

transplants 161

urine tests 83-84

L

lamb: aromatic spiced lamb cutlets 260

lamb steaks with rosemary 259-60

lancets 19, 66, 67-68, 73-74, 160, 232

lancing devices 67-68, 72, 74

laser lancets 73-74, 232

laser surgery, eyes 180-1

L-carnitine 199, 202

LDL (low-density lipoprotein) 82-83, 115, 143

leptin 239-40

lipids, blood tests 82-83

long-acting insulin 149, 150, 151, 153, 154

lutein 100

magnesium 99, 200, 204

magnet therapies 207

Malay-style braised fish 268-9

meals, eating more frequently 106

meat 94, 96, 258-62

menstrual cycle 49, 222-3

metabolic syndrome 45

meters *see* **blood-glucose meters**

metformin 54, 118, 142-3

dosage 147

drug combinations 146-7

side effects 140, 143, 144

microalbuminuria 45, 83-84, 176, 177

milk 41, 99, 239

minerals 99-100, 200, 204

mixed split dose programmes 152

monitoring diabetes 58-85, 232, 233

monounsaturated fats 95, 106

N

naan bread with lentil caviar 251

nanoshell injections 235

needles 155, 156-7, 160

nerve damage 170, 181-4

alternative therapies 197-9

autonomic neuropathy 182-3

feet 185

focal neuropathy 182

polyneuropathy 181-2, 184

signs of 37, 183

tests 181

nervous system, biofeedback 205-6

neuropathy *see* nerve damage

nurses 24-25

nutrition *see* diet

O

oatmeal 100

obesity *see* overweight and obesity

oils 95

omega-3 fatty acids 95, 174

omelette, Chinese-style 265-6

OPCs (oligomeric proanthocyanidin complexes) 201

ophthalmologists 26, 180

oral glucose tolerance test (OGTT) 50-51, 53

oral insulin 234-5

overweight and obesity: appetite control 239-41

Body Mass Index 46

in children 47

exercise and 115

genetic factors 45-46, 239

risk factors 12, 19-20

and Type 2 diabetes 44-46

weight-loss surgery 161-2

P, Q

pain: injections 156

polyneuropathy 184

pancreas 35

artificial pancreas 246

functions 37

transplants 160-1, 244-5, 247

Type 1 diabetes 38, 39-40, 41

Type 2 diabetes 42, 154

see also beta cells; insulin

pasta with fresh sage, rocket and feta cheese 274

pasta with potato, beans and pesto 275

penne primavera 271-2

peptides 238

pharmacists 27-28

pizzas, quick bap 252

plaice rolls, Chinese-style steamed 268

podiatrists 27

polyneuropathy 181-2, 184

polyunsaturated fats 95

pork: pork chops in barbecue sauce 261

seared pork with kumquats 261-2

portion sizes 105-6

potato and bacon chowder 256-7

prandial glucose regulators 145-6, 147

pregnancy 38, 46-48, 65, 223

pricking fingers *see* lancets

prickly pear 197

protein 89-90, 95-96

Pterocarpus marsupium 197

pumpkin and butter beans, Moroccan-style 273

pumps, insulin 154, 157-9, 163, 246

quality of life 210-29

R

random plasma glucose test 49-50, 51

rapid-acting insulin 149, 150, 151, 232

resistance training 125-9, 130, 131

retina *see* eyes

retinopathy *see* eyes

risk factors, diabetes 12

risotto, sun-dried tomato and bean 276

rowing 127

S

safety, disposal of sharps 160

salads 253-6

salmon with mango salsa 266-7

salt 97, 100, 107, 171

saturated fats 94, 106

scallops and prawns, stir-fried 269-70

sex life 222-4

sharps bins 160

shoes 185, 186, 187

short-acting insulin 149, 150, 151-3

side effects, drugs 140

  see also individual drugs

skin, biological substitutes 243-4

smoking 21-23, 41, 171

snacks 79, 108, 118, 120

sodium 100

sole, classic grilled Dover sole 270

sorbitol 242

soups 256-7

soya 100

split dose programmes 152

starches *see* carbohydrates

statins 173

stem cells 245

strawberry shortcake 278-9

stress 217-18

strokes 167, 168, 171, 173, 242

sugar 89-90, 92, 107

sulphonylureas 138, 141-2, 143

  dosage 147

  drug combinations 146, 147

  side effects 141-2

  used with insulin 154

summer fruit fool 278

surgery 160-2, 180-1

sweating 120

sweeteners 91, 92

swimming 127

symptoms 12, 36-37, 42-43

syndrome X 45

syringes 160, 227, 228

  see also injections

T

tabbouleh with goat's cheese 254

taurine 200

tea 173-4

teeth, dental care 27

teriyaki-style noodles with tofu 256

tests: diagnosing diabetes 13, 14-15, 48-52

  eye tests 26, 180

  for kidney damage 177

  monitoring diabetes 58-85

  nerve damage 181

  urine 52, 82, 120

test strips 52, 66-67, 70, 72, 74

thiazolidinediones 143-4, 146, 147, 236-7, 242-3

thirst 36

thyroid disease 14

tingling hands and feet 37

tiredness 36

trans fatty acids 95

transplants: islet cells 244-5, 247

  kidney 161

  pancreas 160-1, 244

travel 226-9

triggers, environmental 237

triglycerides 83, 115, 143, 168

tuna, anchovy and sesame-topped 267

turkey escalopes with chestnut mushrooms
    and Madeira 264

Type 1 diabetes 38-39, 236

    causes 39-41

    complications 167

    and drugs 138

    exercise 117-18

    insulin 15, 148

    ketoacidosis 54-55

    risk factors 12

Type 2 diabetes 38

    causes 43-46

    in children 43, 47

    complications 167

    drugs 138-9

    exercise 118-19

    hyperosmolar syndrome 55

    insulin 15-17, 140, 148, 154-5

    and obesity 44-46

    risk factors 12

    symptoms 42-43

U

ulcers, foot 243-4

undiagnosed diabetes 11-12, 48

urinary tract infections (UTIs) 177-8

urine 175

    albumin in 45, 83-84, 176, 177

    frequent urination 36

    glucose tests 52

    ketone tests 82, 120

V

vagina, dryness 223

vegetables 89-90, 92, 93, 96-98, 106-7, 271-3

very long-acting insulin 149, 150, 151, 153, 154

viruses 40-41

vitamins 96, 99-100, 174, 184, 200, 203-4

W

walking 126

water, drinking 79, 93, 107-9, 119, 225-6

weight: control mechanisms 238-41

    exercise and 115

    intensive therapy and 155

    risk factors 12, 19-20

    surgery 161-2

    weight loss 102-5, 107, 172

weight lifting 125-9, 130, 131

wine 100

Z

zinc 200

PHOTOS

16 TOP TO BOTTOM PhotoDisc, Siede Preis/Getty Images, PhotoDisc, PhotoDisc, **19** PhotoDisc, **22** PhotoDisc, **24** Romilly Lockyer/Brand X Pictures/PictureQuest, **27** Comstock, **40** PhotoDisc, **44** Photodisc, **47** PhotoDisc, **48** C Squared Studios/PhotoDisc/PictureQuest, **50** PhotoDisc, **56** Open Door Images/PictureQuest, **68** LifeScan, Inc., **71** PhotoDisc/ PictureQuest, **74** Abbott Laboratories, MediSense Products, **75** Cygnus, Inc., **79** Photodisc, **89** British Nutrition Foundation, **93** DigitalStock, **95** ALL PhotoDisc, **99** TOP TO BOTTOM PhotoDisc, Comstock, PhotoDisc, Comstock, **103** TOP Comstock, BOTTOM DigitalStock, RIGHT PhotoDisc, **109** Comstock, **117** PhotoDisc, **126** PhotoDisc, **127** TOP TO BOTTOM PhotoDisc, C Squared Studios/Getty Images, PhotoDisc, Rim Light/PhotoLink/Getty Images, **132-133** ALL Reader's Digest Assoc. Inc., ©Beth Bischoff, **159** BOTH Disetronic, **160** Mike Wyndham Medical Picture Collection, **171** Reader's Digest Assoc./GID/Colin Cooke, **181** Getty Images/Eyewire, **187** Corbis/PhotoQuest, **195** Reader's Digest Assoc./GID/Lisa Koenig, **199** Corbis Images, **202** Reader's Digest Assoc./GID/Alan Richardson, **206** Corbis Images, **214** PhotoDisc, **216** Image 100, **220** Open Door Images/Picturequest, **229** Reader's Digest Assoc./GID/ Steven Mays, **237** Getty Images, **240** PhotoDisc, **243** Novartis, **245** Photo Researchers, **246** BOTH Medtronic **248-279** Reader's Digest Assoc.

ILLUSTRATIONS

Medical illustrations: Duckwall Productions

All other illustrations: ©Tracy Walker/www.i2iart.com

Taking Charge of Diabetes was published by The Reader's Digest Association Limited, London
First edition copyright 2003
Reprinted 2007

The Reader's Digest Association Limited,
11 Westferry Circus, Canary Wharf, London E14 4HE

Adapted from Stopping Diabetes in its Tracks © 2002 originated by the editorial team of The Reader's Digest Association Inc., USA

We are commited to both the quality of our products and the service we provide to our customers. We value your comments, so please feel free to contact us on **08705 113366** or via our web site at **www.readersdigest.co.uk**
If you have any comments or suggestions about the content of our pbooks, email us at: **gbeditorial@readersdigest.co.uk**

Book code:	400-246 UP0000-2
ISBN (10) :	0 276 44042 0
ISBN (13)	978 0 276 44042 7
Oracle code:	2500092595H.00.24